A MODERN
DON JUAN

A MODERN DON JUAN

Cantos for These Times by Divers Hands

*Edited by Andy Croft
and N.S. Thompson*

Five Leaves Publications

A Modern Don Juan:
Cantos for These Times by Divers Hands

Edited by Andy Croft and N.S. Thompson
Published by Five Leaves Publications
14a Long Row, Nottingham NG1 2DH
www.fiveleaves.co.uk
www.fiveleavesbookshop.co.uk

ISBN: 978-1910170045

Cover design: Martin Rowson

Typeset and design: Four Sheets Design and Print
Printed by Imprint Digital in Exeter

'Tis hard to venture where our betters fail,
Or lend fresh interest to a twice-told tale;
And yet, perchance, 'tis wiser to prefer
A hackney'd plot, than choose a new, and err;
Yet copy not too closely, but record,
More justly, thought for thought than word for word;
Nor trace your prototype through narrow ways,
But only follow where he merits praise.

Lord Byron, *Hints from Horace*, lines 183–190

DEDICATION

I

Lord Byron! You're a poet, so to speak;
    Unrepresentative of all the race
By virtue of your wit, the sheer technique
    With which you cocked two fingers at disgrace;
If only poets now had half your cheek,
    Perhaps the world would be a better place;
Instead of which (we know you will not thank us
For telling you) it's run by merchant bankers.

II

To dedicate these Cantos to a toff
    Is hard for us, therefore, who must endure
The sight of well-fed porkers in the trough
    And public school-boys stealing from the Poor
Their Benefits. The rich can all fuck off
    And die as far as we're concerned. Since you're
Already dead, this lets you off the hook;
So here it is in verse: a votive book.

III

Although you were a bigwig and a nob,
    (There's some no doubt would spell that with a 'k')
Who liked to make your gentle readers throb
    Regarding Juan's antics in the hay,
Your politics were with the Luddite mob,
    St Peter's dead, and not with Castlereagh;
We sense that your anarchic shade's still there
Among the protests in Syntagma Square.

IV

In other words, we frankly disagree
　With Auden's lazy Fuhrer-Prinzip joke;
We do not see you in the BNP
　Or cadging drinks like some old UKIP soak,
The EDL are not your cup of tea,
　The Cameroons not quite your kind of folk.
Your lordship knew what scholarship must show –
They're *all* mad, bad and dangerous to know.

V

The world has changed since 1824,
　Though not as much as might have been expected,
Our government still wages endless war
　For reasons that must never be inspected,
And poetry these days would make you snore.
　That's why, you see, your Don's been resurrected:
His character's a glass in which we find
The follies of your Age and ours combined.

VI

We think it's safe to say you'd recognise
　The swine who're now high-rolling in the swill,
Incredulous that they can privatise
　The public while the public foots the bill;
And though, as you by now must realise,
　The world has slaves and kings and armies still,
Our violent leaders always find it handy
To know by heart a quote or two by Gandhi.

VII

You may have been a peer, but you were peerless
　At laughing in the face of those in power;
Our cultural life would not be quite so cheerless,
　Our writers locked inside the Leaning Tower,
Our politicians wouldn't be so fearless
　If only you were living at this hour.
The Age of Wilders, Vona, Gove and Grayling's
In urgent need of poets to scourge its failings.

VIII

Since we, who hang out with pedestrian Muses,
  Could never hope to catch the winged steed
Of your iambic metre as it cruises
  (At eighty thousand feet!) we knew we'd need
Some help to rouse your hero from his snoozes
  And bring him up to date and up to speed.
You see, despite the catch that we've just landed,
We still can't match what you caught single-handed.

IX

That we're one Canto short of your *DJ*
  Is very much a matter of regret
(Which fish escaped the net we cannot say);
  If only you'd been here to share the sweat
We would have been in print before today;
  It took fifteen of us (a quindectet?)
To extricate from Hell your pretty fellow
Without the help, this time, of Leporello.

X

Perhaps you think this project a mistake,
  Or what some might call leading with the chin,
An open goal for critics who will take
  The chance to throw it unread in the bin;
Exhuming Donny was a piece of cake
  Compared to trying to give this book a spin;
In short, it's bound to suffer by comparison
Because we are not you (or Tony Harrison).

XI

But though your lordship's wit's beyond compare,
  Your Hudibrastic rhyming quite sublime,
It doesn't mean that we are unaware
  How often you employed a dodgy rhyme;
No man and woman make a common pair
  As tuneless to our ears as in your time,
But if your rhymes are sudden and/or wooden,
As far as you're concerned – the job's a good 'un.

XII

So if our use of metre's sometimes bumpy,
  And if at times the rhymes fall somewhat short,
We don't expect to hear you've gone all grumpy,
  Instead we'd like to think we've your support
(Especially as there's lots of rumpy-pumpy
  Which always was your favourite kind of sport),
We learned our songs from you, at second-hand,
This fifteen-piece Lord Byron tribute band.

AC

***

XIII

And so let us commend ourselves to you
  Lord B, this set of divers hands of ours
And all the hours spent – many or too few –
  And hope we do not get too many glowers
From you above. At least you cannot sue
  Us, even should you wish to, with no powers
Now over what we might make of your hero,
But hope you could mark us above a zero.

XIV

And here he is, a twentieth-century
  Version of your magnificent creation
And if you think we have been rather free
  In our perhaps too-wide interpretation
Of heroism and catastrophe,
  We say times change: a people and its nation
Move fluidly towards the dark abyss,
Miraculously giving it a miss.

XV

But, as you know, this is not thanks to those
  Dear men and women now in politics:
You in your time could don your lordly hose,
  Cloak and garters to rail about the tricks
Of those in office – all men, then – but chose
  A different way to kick against the pricks
That injured and abused the Public Weal
From House of Commons to the Privy Seal.

XVI

Today we poets are a Common Crowd,
   Uncommon, true, in what we try to do,
Especially here, where we are not too proud
   To don the same poetic dress as you
Did in *ottava rima*... Or a shroud
   It may well seem to those who take the view
That poetry today should wear no shackles...
But we feel it would raise our hero's hackles

XVII

If we refused to deck him in the best
   Of raiment, kitted out in what still serves
A narrative and holds the interest
   Of readers keen to see we have strong nerves
And wit enough to pass the driving test
   Along the winding roads and narrow curves
That surely face the English language rhymer
From novice to inveterate old timer.

XVIII

So here we hope that you will find a team
   As dedicated as a rugby squad
To scoring tries and points and if the dream
   Proves way beyond our reach, the gentle prod
Of critics and reviewers with the gleam
   Of mischief in their eyes will wield the rod
And no doubt show no mercy to this new 'un,
Our bold brash modern version of Don Juan...

XIX

Here you will find a Don sent into Space,
   Another off for sex in Amsterdam,
One – EU attaché with a handsome face –
   Gets his in Greece, while one in Nottingham
Opens a restaurant, but the hottest place
   For one Don Juan with the *chic*est glam
Finds his infernal story set in Hell!
But of the others there is much to tell:

XX

One Don, Antipodean, takes a trip
   Into the clublands of Australia,
Another trips all pastoral and hip,
   One in the North talks of his marriage failure
While one Celebrity DJ all lip
   Confronts Campanian Mafia *inter alia*...
His alter ego likes to shoot the breeze
And takes us to the Seedy Land of Sleaze...

XXI

And one Don teaches writing on a course
   Where men reside at HRM's behest,
One enterprising Don seeks out the source
   Of Latin Myth and one to Budapest
Confronts the Velvet Revolution's force,
   Albeit rudely *sans* his pants and vest.
And, last but one, a British squaddy finds
How Sterne a sex-life is behind closed blinds.

XXII

This leaves a final narrative in Greece
   Where our Don finds the offspring of a fling
Brings back fond memories that only cease
   When one more revolution's on the wing:
For our Dons – just like yours – there is no peace,
   Lord B. But of his travails here we sing
And unashamedly report the facts
Of how a *Modern Don Juan* really acts.

XXIII

These truths about him come in many splendours
   And several decades of the recent past:
One notes his numberless and ceaseless benders,
   The number of his women, *chic* and fast,
Or sluts who could be portrayed in *Eastenders*
   And many other walk-ons in the cast.
In short, we have all jumped upon the cart
To turn High Poetry into Popular Art.

XXIV

Adieu, dear Lord, then, we will let you be
   A tranquil denizen of who knows where...
Your soul's address: Sea of Tranquillity
   Set on our Earth's Romantic Moon? Or pair
Of Stars with you in high degree
   At last with one whose love you really share?
Then look with some compassion on our Don
As he flows to his revels off and on.

NST

CONTENTS

BEN BOREK

I

When Donny woke he wasn't sure he'd woken.
  The firmament was black as night, and starless.
He wrenched his eyelids wide apart. A token
  To feed the meter nestled in a parlous
Spaghetti mound of wire (unearthed and broken)
  Beside his throbbing head. He groaned. With far less
Dexterity than space cadets are trained in
He found it, fed the slot, and neon rained in.

II

The clock read 35 past 98.
  His pupils widened into grumpy spheres.
The cabin glowered in its surrogate
  Of earthly light. His brain creaked through its gears.
It's blurred 'to do' list read: unpack the crate
  Of vacuum-sealed repasts (shrunk steaks, dried beers),
Recalibrate the Narcofuel supply,
Call Earth and check his course was not awry.

III

The shelving chore could wait. His cerebellum
  Required an hour of coming into being.
His limbs (dumb shanks encased in wrinkled vellum)
  Now air-walked to the screen. He bent to key in
His password (*Love'sImplacableFlagellum*),
  Bright pixels whorled up tight then scattered, freeing
A face: burnt salmon forehead, Botox-flattened,
Plump nose, wet labia likewise over-fattened.

IV

'Oh Jonny, you look awful! You've just risen?'
  'Mum, sorry. It's the dark here. Soporific.'
'You have *important* work,' she oozed derision.
  Her features formed a sordid hieroglyphic.
'I hope you still feel proud of your decision,
  This sudden lust for frontiers scientific?'
He wanted to respond in self-defence.
Experience said silence made more sense.

V

He sighed, shut off the light, pulled up the blind.
    The Milky Way, a massive starling's wing
Of fairy light, wrapped round his craft. 'Be kind,
    Dear mother, or just don't say anything.'
'I'll choose the latter course, if you don't mind:
    Your pal is here, the Jonk who would be king
Of outer space.' 'Mum, he's my friend. Respect him.
And if you can't do that, at least connect him.'

VI

At this point, Gentle Readers (as it says
    In every bardic handbook I should call you),
I'll pause the scene we joined *in medias res.*
    Apologies should this procedure gall you
But I'll just clarify: we're now in space
    And streaming Mars-wards like a metal ball you
Kicked through the tropo, meso, thermo spheres
And which now sweats with frozen cosmic tears.

VII

But why's our DJ bound for the Red Planet?
    'To blaze a trail for science and electro.'
His mundane life, gone cold as alpine granite,
    Now shrinks behind the fireballs of his jet-flow.
The flames lend Earth the hue of pomegranate,
    His memory lends it little else, as retro-
Spection never suited him, not now,
Nor when he rode 'pon Byron's lustful prow.

VIII

He's lost count of his conquests, males and females.
    Total recall's just for special features:
A lido full of concupiscent she-males,
    A pair of Miss Irans, six nuns, five preachers
(With emphasis on 'Lay'), one Queen whose emails
    Were lovelorn deathbed odes, a dwarf in breeches...
And several more he wished he *could* erase
From Mnemosyne's procession of disgrace.

IX

He's also in the dark as to the measure
  And bright variety of cures he's taken
To ease the blunt *ennui* of sober leisure.
  From sappy forest Sensi (Thai, Jamaican)
And Turkish blocks of doom he's puffed some pleasure;
  From sawn-off plastic bottles, stirred not shaken,
He's gleaned some dulling respite; from brocaded
Nargillas he's sucked joy, but it all faded.

X

For many years indulgence was the norm:
  He started young – a disused Peckham garage.
A teenage Don puffed skunk and played a storm
  Of jungle, house and techno. Soon his carriage
To stronger stuff and bigger things took form:
  He hit the Balearics. There his marriage
Of sub-atomic bass and methamphetamine
Was pepped with oily floor-shows, foam and ketamine.

XI

His life as feted vinyl-spinner span him
  From club to super-club to sold-out stadia.
A host of vampish models overran him
  In multifariously drunk arcadia.
But slowly, a dark seed grew to unman him.
  A diffidence to gamine, hunk or lady, a
Pronounced immunity to pharmacology:
A maudlin rift tore through his frayed psychology.

XII

Waves of depression, dolour, disillusion,
  (A gruesome troika, an *unheimlich* three)
Swept over him. He fought this dissolution
  With yoga, Prozac, talking cures (i.e.
Appearances on chat-shows) – no solution.
  Things reached their zenith (or their apogee)
Six months ago. He stood up Manumission
And fled to Greece to sweat off his condition.

XIII

On Mykonos, his mother's sun-bleached Villa:
　　He found some short-lived respite from the world.
She wrapped him in her matriarch's mantilla
　　Of herbal teas and pep talks. Calmness curled
Its soothing fingers round him like vanilla...
　　Each night above his gaze the stars unfurled
As pointillist schematics of the future.
To Jonny's wounded soul they formed a suture.

XIV

Mum, sceptical, bought several telescopes
　　To mark his thirty-seventh passing summer.
He rigged a hammock up with nets and ropes
　　And nightly, when cicada choirs would strum a
Fierce nocturne from dry Hellenic slopes,
　　He'd watch the stellar frontispiece become a
Suggestion of such depth beneath its shimmer.
His eyes acquired an otherworldly glimmer.

XV

The galaxies were musical to him.
　　A 4/4 beat pulsed from the Hydra cluster;
A bass-line hummed through Libra's milky scrim;
　　Orion was a whirl of Ragga bluster;
Cepheus droned a chilled-out ambient hymn;
　　He lay and listened. Synaesthetic lustre
Washed over him. This sonic-astral climate
Bespoke salvation, came to seem his *heimat*.

XVI

His mother grew concerned. Her ministration
　　Diminished in effect with every week.
Her son, nocturnal, slept all day as Thracian
　　Winds blew through the villa's tiles and teak.
She shook him lucid with this imprecation:
　　'Dear Donny, ξυπνῄστε! ('Wake up!' in Greek,
Her tone as macho as Bellerophon)
'Stay star-struck any longer and I'm gone'.

XVII

He lay inert as if he hadn't heard her. She
  Soon booked herself onto a private flight
To Val d'Isere for *après ski* and surgery
  (Her tummy tuck was not ideally tight
And though to leave him was an act of perjury
  In strict maternal law, she had a right,
She felt, to fight one battle she could win:
She might neglect her son, but not her skin).

XVIII

On Mykonos the party season came
  Just as she left. A flood of burnished money
Invaded every villa. Wealth and fame
  Prize beaches private just as much as sunny
And tan beneath a rarefied dull flame
  On whitewashed sand the hue of antimony.
But with the Gucci-wrapped and Blahnik-heeled
There came an expert in the cosmic field:

XIX

Professor Daedalus Von Jonk (half mad,
  Half Balinese, half Dutch) was with his wife
(three decades junior, Versace-clad)
  To 'decompress'. He'd spent his adult life
Observing Leonids from Volgograd,
  Red shift from Rome, wormholes from Split to Fife,
But recently his science had 'progressed'
To take in *Jazz on Mars*... you guess the rest.

XX

His theories hadn't left his peers divided.
  They'd ostracised him. ('Has the chap been smoking
The coffee shops' best fudge?'). So now, derided,
  His science pals all lost ('He's cracked, or joking'),
Bernice (Miss Orange County) had decided
  A season *à la plage* and thoughtful soaking
In clear Hellenic waters would relieve him
Of stress ('Why would these idiots not believe him!')

XXI

One night too overcast to watch the stars
    Our Donny found himself upon the strand.
The beachfront thrummed with bustle from the bars
    Stuffed full of bling and oligarchs. A band
Played languid, synthy covers. *Life on Mars*
    And *Rocket Man* wafted across the sand.
In Sputnik (cheaper drinks, thus empty) Jonk
Sat nursing half a pint of tree-bark plonk.

XXII

The two ennui-bedraggled souls converged.
    A transit DJ later thought as fated
Propelled him into Sputnik. He had purged
    His liver for a season but deflated
For lack of stellar action he'd emerged
    Beneath the clouds in need of something sated.
He lugged his quart of Mythos to a corner
And thumbed his astral blueprints like a mourner.

XXIII

Jonk saw the maps. His bristled brows inclined.
    Before long cosmic curiosity
Led him across the bar. He left behind
    His sociophobia: a colloquy
Ensued. They bonded in the mutual bind
    Of *weltschmerz* over ouzo till the sea
Glowed rosy in the dawn and salted frills
Lapped up around their drunken espadrilles.

XXIV

(They'd taken to the beach and swerved past barques
    And lobster pots all wrapped in seaweed-lace).
Professor Jonk extemporized on quarks –
    From woe, the conversation turned to space –
He hymned of nebulae, impassioned sparks
    Exploded from his eyes and lit his face.
His fingers prodded heaven-wards in glee
And Donny saw them point his destiny:

XXV

As Jonk's quick, borborygmic baritone
  Drew galaxies and orbits, painted belts
Of asteroids and sculpted worlds unknown
  On planets wrapped in potent mineral pelts,
In Donny's febrile brain testosterone,
  Adrenalin, endorphins surged. Bright veldts,
Ecstatic shapes, lost highways stretched. His pores
Dilated to their synaesthetic scores.

XXVI

He had to tell Jonk how he felt. 'I see,'
  Said Jonk, now nodding ardently. 'You make
Extremely perfect natural sense to me.'
  'I do?' 'You do. The galaxies all shake
With music! There's no relativity...
  There's John Coltrane; that "first" bombastic quake,
You think it was a ball of pent-up mass?
Nope. That was Sun Ra turning up the gas.'

XXVII

To Donny this all came as confirmation.
  (He felt that he had hit on something true,
But doubts lurked, as they do sans affirmation).
  He breathed in deep content. Aegean blue
Swelled up around the pair. Jonk: 'There's a station
  South of Olympus Mons... that's not quite true.
There will be. It's all planned. Just need resources.'
'Like what?' 'A pilot.' 'Oh?' 'And funding sources.'

XXVIII

Things fell into a shape you may have guessed,
  My dear perceptive readers: Donny's bank
Was laden – a Helvetian battle chest
  Of tax-free spoils. It transferred, franc by franc,
To various Jonk soubriquets – 'Gone West',
  'Karl-Heinz Heinz', 'Ursa Minor', 'Sherman Tank'.
A tranche was used to renovate a barn
(Or Cosmic Training School) in Kazakhstan.

XXIX

For three months in the steppe outside Astana
   Jonk coached his astronaut. Their days began
At dawn with yoga (Bikram and Ashthanga),
   A *Spaceboy dry-up* (dehydrated bran)
Then Donny read his manual, all in manga
   (Jonk felt cartoons helped clarify the plan),
He studied thrust, propulsion, zero gravity,
And parking in an awkward Martian cavity.

XXX

For lunch, a cube of lyophilised soup
   Then three hours in Jonk's pod – an ironbound
Adapted sunbed. Inside, on a loop,
   Donny was fed a drip of 'training sound':
A slice of Kazakh library funk, a scoop
   Of Holst, a smattering of Ezra Pound
Repeating through his froth-bespeckled lip
We set up mast and sail on that swart ship.

XXXI

Jonk added, just for Donny, Drum 'n' Bass
   And 90s Happy Hardcore to the mix –
The Prodigy's anthemic *Out of Space*
   And Photek's *UFO*. He'd had to fix
The pod to earth with lengths of Kazakh lace,
   Such was the force of all the snare drum kicks
And manic saw-tooth chords. Once resurrected
Our hero had his balance re-corrected.

XXXII

The routine replicated every weekday
   For twelve weeks (as I wrote three stanzas prior)
With nights reserved for Jonny's deck technique: 'Play
   As if you're in the biggest club!' 'Like Fire
In Vauxhall?' 'How full's Fire at its peak?' 'Say,
   A thousand? Maybe two...' 'Well, aim much higher!
Your audience will number seven billion...
And that's just Earth!' Jonk's face was now vermilion.

XXXIII

'Just think of every sentient observer –
　　Or listener – on planets not yet heard of!'
Here Donny paused. Looked pained. Jonk's purple fervour
　　Had not wholly transferred. 'Prof, every word of
Your spiel sounds great. But will it work?' 'My server
　　Is foolproof, Donny! Do not fret. A third of
Your day is sleep. Not mine. At nights I'm steady
At work – my wormhole fileshare's almost ready.'

XXXIV

'With every beat you play a fey vibration
　　Will stream into the earthbound internet
Then bounce back out from points in every nation
　　(Except for North Korea) like a jet
Of astral code. The sky's insemination
　　Will hum like Artie Shaw on clarinet!
Relax your mind. Dear Donny, spend the night
On spinning tunes. Your set list must be tight!'

XXXV

More reassured, our DJ winked. 'You're right.
　　I really should just focus on the tunes.'
Jonk passed across a foot-long spliff. 'A light?'
　　'No, it's still live.' Above, the Kazakh moon's
Beneficently curdled eye blinked white.
　　Beyond, the rubicund south Martian dunes
Swelled up, the pair now fancied, in a glow
Of warm anticipation for a show.

XXXVI

We're nearly up to speed, back in the *res*
　　The *medias* of which we left a while back.
But first let's watch how Donny got to space:
　　He grasped the cockpit chair and forced a smile back
Across the Launchpad sand at Jonk's bright face.
　　Smoke plumed beneath him. Earth was soon a mile back.
He couldn't look down. Never one for heights,
Temazepam had saved his mundane flights...

XXXVII

...But Jonk had time-locked all the Narcofuel
   (Ingeniously multipurpose juice):
'Until the ship has helter-skeltered through all
   The layers of Earth's atmospheric sluice
The pilot should be sober and accrue all
   The sense-vibrations lucidly.' A noose
(His own gloved hands) ringed Donny's quaking head.
For half an hour he thought he might be dead.

XXXVIII

Things settled down in time. He grew to live with
   The altitude and weightlessness. The food
Still lacked all taste but this he could forgive with
   A drop of Narcofuel. He'd sometimes brood
And watch the universe ('It's just a sieve with
   An infinite amount of holes when viewed
From my tin can's perspective.') but these thoughts
Are natural for all lone astronauts.

XXXIX

His Skype chats with Professor Jonk and Mum
   Soon focused Donny on more human matters.
Jonk pressed him to de-scale the Narco drum,
   Mum criticised – 'My boy, you're getting fat as
Uranus!' (True – his yoga had become
   Irregular. His stomach, once as flat as
East Anglia, was now a bloated paunch...
He'd comfort-fed to help forget the launch.)

XL

The hours stretched into days, the days to weeks.
   He kept himself amused with *Grand Theft Auto*
And working on his set. He gave it tweaks,
   Re-ordering, new fades. The Dubstep quarto
Was sacrificed for Grime, euphoric peaks
   Of German Trance were spaced out and kept short, though,
So Donny felt, appropriate. For Jonk
He added Mingus, Adderly and Monk.

XLI

Weeks stretched to months. A routine formed: rise late
  (For all that meant in non-stop constant blackness),
Steal cars in Venice Beach, uncork a crate
  Of Narco to relieve his sense of slackness,
Spin tunes, eat powder, doze, procrastinate,
  Check dials and cabin readings, Skype them back, dress
(This optional, and only if he chose
To use his webcam and locate his clothes).

XLII

So here we are, we've caught up with our tail,
  Or has our tale caught up with where we started?
Jonk's face seeps from the screen. His features, pale
  And pixelated, form. Mum has departed
To do a think-piece for the *Daily Mail*
  On gastric bands as feministic art. 'Did
You check,' asks Jonk, 'the Narco balance data?'
'Erm, not yet,' Donny says. 'I'll do it later'.

XLIII

'But it's imperative I have the read-out,
  Dear Donny. Every day. The ship could slow
If there's a knot or glitch. We need to weed out
  All gremlins regularly.' 'Jonk, I know.
I'll do it soon.' Jonk's whining seems to bleed out
  From Donny's speakers in a painful flow
Of sibilants and fricatives and fuzz.
Then nothing. Just a shrill metallic buzz.

XLIV

He shrugs. Knocks back some Narco. Shuts the screen.
  Outside the porthole, whirling galaxies
Look beautiful but somehow fake. Their sheen
  Has something of the ersatz plastic trees
He'd heard a song about once. The poteen
  Within his Narco glass runs dry. He frees
Another canister, pours out a double
And downs it. 'Other people, too much trouble...

XLV

...They're always hassle in the end. "Do that.
   Do this." I just don't need it.' He turns down
The lights and swims towards the Narco vat.
   Outside the stars, an oceanic crown
Around his wayward shuttle's drowning sprat,
   Seems suddenly to glower. With a frown
To match the universe's, Donny cracks
The final Narco can. Good night. Relax.

ANDY CROFT

... He's as far
From the enjoyment of the earth and air
Who watches o'er the chain, as they who wear.

for Insy and Jacquesy

I

I do not want a hero may not sound
    The most dramatic way to start this Canto,
But since this is a song (the word is found
    In Latin, Spanish, French and Esperanto)
I want to strike a note that's less profound,
    More suitable to circus ring or panto;
It's hard to play Mariah Carey's *Hero,*
Or *Rocky III* – then introduce a Pierrot.

II

I can't, you see, join in the world's obsession
    With caped crusaders, X-Men and the like
Whose deeds are used to justify aggression
    (Like fearless Siegfried in the old Third Reich),
And since we're in a Double-dip Recession
    I'd rather trust a Chaplin or a Svejk
To understand the world of economics
Than someone in a mask from Marvel Comics.

III

A hero's job's to keep us entertained,
    Or failing that, to keep the masses quiet,
A spectacle of violence unrestrained
    Reminding us it doesn't pay to riot;
So Law and Order's properly maintained,
    They force-feed us a bread-and-circus diet
Which we must chew for hour after hour
(Just like a box-set featuring Jack Bauer).

IV

Meanwhile real life's a bitch, an old Rottweiler
    Which disapproves of thinking in the ranks –
A Samson found in Gaza with Delilah
    Would be run over by Israeli tanks,
A street-wise Hercules (*viz* Bonnie Tyler)
    Would be defeated by the Augean banks,
And Chagos Islanders now realise
Exactly where and why real power lies.

V

But though this is an unheroic Age,
   Our ancient want of heroes is still fed
By paladins of pitch and screen and stage,
   Whose epic labours in the bar and bed
Are bared upon the naked tabloid page
   So we can worship them *before* they're dead.
(Mortality being better left to plebs,
Elysium's now exclusive to celebs.)

VI

Their virtues on a greater scale than ours,
   Our pin-ups strive to be Simply the Best,
Endowed by us with all the super-powers
   We used to think that only gods possessed –
Until, alas, the faithless world devours
   Mistakes that even tabloids can't digest.
We've barely hung the icons on the wall
Before we have to watch our heroes fall.

VII

Rolf Harris, Andy Coulson, Liam Fox!
   How soon it seems the heroes of today
Are swept on fickle tides towards the rocks.
   Rebekah Brooks, James Murdoch, DSK!
Each in their turn paraded in the stocks
   That all the world can see their feet of clay.
How quickly reputations all unravel,
From Cameron and Clegg to Jimmy Savile.

VIII

So brief and thankless is a hero's span!
   You only need a small illegal war
To flush a Bush or Straw straight down the pan,
   Their reputations washed away before
Diogenes could find an honest man.
   It seems the world prefers the kind of flaw
Or *hamartia* (q.v. Aristotle)
That strips a hero down to cock and bottle.

IX

Undone by careless tweet and casual text
  The old heroic lay is tuneless now;
John Terry! Ashley Cole! Whoever next?
  Ah, Signor Berlusconi – take a bow!
Although the rich may think they're over-sexed
  It only takes a wig and botox-brow
To give the rest of us a little chortle
And let us know our heroes are still mortal.

X

From Ronan Keating, Sven and Gen. Petraeus,
  To Ryan Giggs, Chris Huhne and Cyril Smith –
Our idols seem determined to betray us
  (Straight after they've betrayed their kin and kith);
We slowly peel the weeping onion layers
  Until there's nothing left but tears and pith.
To make an ageing Alpha-male look younger
Requires more than a bit of *bunga bunga*.

XI

I'm sure that being a hero isn't easy,
  And fame can be mistaken for success;
A winning smile can soon become too cheesy,
  A pious frown can also look like stress,
And clever clogs make everyone feel queasy,
  Especially when they fall for their own press.
Of course I know it's all been said before –
But there are no Shakespearoes anymore.

XII

One day we hail them as the new Messiah,
  The next, their names are trampled in the dust;
Ingratitude and jealousy conspire
  Until the god-like Tony Blair seems just
An orange-faced, transparent, venal liar
  Whom nobody with any brains would trust.
But then we like our heroes on their arses,
Especially when they're from the *apper clarsses*.

XIII

To every fallen hero it must seem
   The fawning world's turned suddenly ungrateful –
One minute they're a TV chat-show dream
   The next their Twitter feeds are simply *hateful*.
One night they get to lick – ahem – the cream
   Then wake to find they've had a tabloid plateful.
Each in their turn like Banquo's monarchs stalk;
They talked the talk, and now they have to walk.

XIV

A Byron trying to swim the Hellespont,
   A Hero waiting for her own Leander,
A posh cunt in a punt without a quant,
   The chances of a fuck if you're a panda –
Confusing what you need with what you want
   Is typical Romantic propaganda,
A schoolboy error. Yet it doth appear
To be the reason why we're all in here.

XV

In here? You mean to say you haven't guessed?
   My fault. I thought you'd recognise the smells
Of polish, fags and chips and all the rest,
   The hollow halls, with sparry roofs and cells.
In other words, like me, you're now a guest
   Of Her Britannic Majesty's hotels:
Which one is not important for our tale,
The point is that this Canto's set in gaol.

XVI

I'd like to give you all a guided tour,
   (You must hand in your mobiles at the Gate);
Alas, this is quite contrary to the Law
   That says a man must be prepared to wait
For twenty hours a day behind his door,
   Reduced unto a space twelve foot by eight.
And if this gives our tale a narrowed view,
I hope such limits make it ring more true.

XVII

Because I'm not allowed to show you round
  You'll have to let me tell you what I know,
And since I'm buried six feet under ground
  I'm going to have to tell instead of show;
I know this is a heresy that's frowned
  Upon by critics everywhere you go,
But I would rather trust in my own eyes
To perfect knowledge of the boundless skies.

XVIII

If you want heroes, gaol's the place to be.
  They're at the windows, Bang-up to Unlock;
There's plastic gangsters down on Houseblock 3,
  And YPs swinging batteries in a sock,
There's blokes from EDL and BNP,
  And would-be Charlie Bronsons down the Block,
And Muslim lads who think they look Jihadist.
And each, of course, believes that they're the *baddest*.

XIX

They're not bad lads though, most of them in here,
  A few not right inside their heads, perhaps;
Too many have been too long on the gear
  And ricochet from rehab to relapse;
Too many raised in poverty and fear,
  Too few have ever tasted more than scraps.
A warehouse full of damaged minds and bodies –
And that's before we talk about the squaddies.

XX

We send them out to Helmand and Iraq
  Just like when half the globe was coloured red,
Then guiltily we fly the bodies back;
  Not quite a hero's welcome, but instead
A coffin wrapped inside a Union Jack.
  We call them heroes when they're safely dead,
But there's now twice as many in the can
As there are serving in Afghanistan.

XXI

The screws, meanwhile, are from the self-same mould,
   Same class, same towns, same football teams, same wars;
But something in the way the dice were rolled
   Means they go home when we're behind our doors;
They warm themselves at night; our nights are cold;
   And while penologists debate the cause,
We keep them in employment; our mistakes
Are just the flip-side of their lucky breaks.

XXII

A thousand men banged-up from dusk to dawn
   Is not, by anybody's definition,
A happy place to be; there's no man born
   Could flourish in this sunless, dull condition
Illumined only by the grey of morn
   (As if the penny-pinching Coalition
Condemned the day before it had begun,
To pacify the readers of the *Sun*).

XXIII

The lowest of the low, you see, that's us.
   The outcasts, outlaws, losers out and in,
Our punishment gives other folk a buzz,
   We have to lose so other folk can win;
And yet we know – if anybody does –
   That we're all brothers underneath the skin.
The day you get to walk out through the Gate,
Your pad's filled by some lad from your estate.

XXIV

It's not a *choice* to sit here, years on end,
   There's not a man inside who doesn't miss
The warmth of lover, parent, child and friend,
   There's no-one *wants* to spend their time like this;
And just because there's some lads who pretend
   Incarceration is a piece of piss,
It doesn't mean that prison makes you tougher;
The more you say you don't, the more you suffer.

XXV

Which doesn't mean that everybody's blameless,
    Or prison is a bad idea *per se*;
We may look like we're from the cast of *Shameless,*
    Unlucky, stupid, hopeless, you might say,
But most are here because our lives are aimless,
    And not because we planned to live this way.
No matter if you think you don't deserve it,
Be wary, watch the time, and always serve it.

XXVI

We're prisoners here of more than our own Fate,
    Combatants in an economic war
In which the forces of the modern State
    Are used to discipline the jobless poor
By offering us a choice of Going Straight
    Or years spent learning How to Mop a Floor.
I know, I know, you probably think I'm shitting,
But that's the way it looks from where I'm sitting.

XXVII

A cheap supply of labour – that's our job,
    To undercut the pay of those outside.
No unions here, of course. The bastards rob
    You blind then sell you back your one good eye;
Between the dole queue and the tabloid mob,
    The Market and the Law in gaol collide.
We've seen the future and it doesn't pay.
A prisoner works for 80p a day.

XXVIII

For anyone who's stuck inside the whale
    When you wake up you know your head's in shreds;
Like Charon's bark of spectres, dull and pale,
    We shuffle down the Wing to get our meds,
To help us through another day in gaol,
    Another lonely day inside our heads.
Society in here's one polish'd horde
Formed of two tribes, the Boring and the Bored.

XXIX

From friends, and home, and freedom far estranged,
   A crowd of shivering slaves of every nation.
Poor bastards! Youth's good looks are sadly changed
   By years of ultraviolet deprivation;
One half denied, the other half deranged,
   All save the Yardies, jaded with vexation;
The poorest, more philosophy display,
They're used to this, as bankers to their pay.

XXX

One morning I was cleaning on the 2s,
   When in walks this young lad with all his kit
Escorted by the usual pair of Screws.
   A new arrival usually looks like shit,
But this one was a cross between Tom Cruise
   Jake Gyllenhaal, Tom Hardy and Brad Pitt;
A lot more Charlie Brown than Charlie Bronson.
Apparently his name was Donald Johnson.

XXXI

The lads on B Wing liked him straight away,
   He had what you might call a moonshine smile;
What was he in for? Donny wouldn't say.
   'A crime,' he'd shrug (remorse was not his style).
Somebody thought to call the boy DJ
   Because he'd worked the decks on some Greek isle;
The club – run by a very special lady –
Before it was shut down, was called *The Haidée.*

XXXII

He was a proper ladeez man, was Don;
   He had them writing letters from all over;
He stuck their photos up, a real Don Juan
   Our Donny was, a right old Casanova,
His talent was to turn the lasses on
   (Then turn 'em off) from Aberdeen to Dover;
In short, the kind of bloke who thinks his duty's
To pleasure all of Albion's female beauties.

XXXIII

Although regarding other people's wives
   He could have been a little more discreet,
I doubt he was the sort of bloke who thrives
   On playing games of marital deceit;
But randy cats like that have several lives
   And Donny always landed on his feet.
In short, it seemed that this cat wasn't fussy
As long as he was never short of pussy.

XXXIV

Which brings me to the next part of our drama.
   A few weeks later we were down the Gym;
While Donny's biceps bulged like body armour
   At my age I was running to stay slim,
While he moved with the grace of an Obama
   I felt the years in every weary limb.
You do your time, but time keeps marching on.
One day your life's before you. Then it's gone.

XXXV

Time marches on, and yet all prisoners know
   How slow the grains of sand fall through the glass,
Some days it seems the minutes go so slow
   You almost hear the ticking decades pass.
Perhaps that's why I said that I would go
   With Don to the Creative Writing Class
With *cups of tea* (the usual prison bribery)
Beginning Wednesday morning in the library.

XXXVI

O ye, who make your fortunes writing books!
   Remember those who tend the temple flame
In prison libraries. *O fiat lux!*
   They get so little thanks and so much blame
For trying to help a bunch of cons and crooks
   Find out about the world from which we came,
Or failing that, to find upon these shelves
The words with which to speak about ourselves.

XXXVII

As somebody once said, 'All poets steal'
    And every prison's full of thieves turned writers;
Confinement makes the need to write more real,
    And lads who in their normal lives are fighters
In prison want to write down how they feel.
    Though some may think this kind of art detritus,
It's infinitely preferable to
The shit they print in *Poetry Review*.

XXXVIII

So many prizes and so little art!
    For those whose lives are cabin'd, cribb'd, confined,
Nobody ever needs to set apart
    The dancer from the dance; art's not designed
To elevate the lucky and the smart
    But to remind us what we share in kind,
And that this lonely world's not always friendless.
Though Art is brief, in prison Life is endless.

XXXIX

I don't know what we thought we might achieve,
    But by next week twelve lads had put in apps –
Two rappers and a Byron-fan called Steve,
    Four nature poets, a vampire buff, two saps
Who though it was calligraphy (believe!)
    Plus me and Don – a dozen wary chaps
And one of our Creative Writing tutors,
Sat like Penelope among her suitors.

XL

A poet – Spoken Word Performer *please*!
    (She saw herself as one who broke the mould) –
She'd slammed at raves and rapped with grime MCs,
    Her Glasto set last year was download gold,
Her blog about the plight of Burmese bees
    Went viral overnight (the rights were sold
To Channel 4), meanwhile her pamphlet *Voice*
Was this month's Poetry Book Society Choice.

XLI

Her debut album with The Useless Fucks
    Had earned her much acclaim and several prizes –
It said so on the back of both her books
    (As slim as Donna was) – but my surmise is
The judges were acquainted with her looks;
    Though talent comes in many shapes and sizes,
Success is rarely given to the plain,
And woman's face was never form'd in vain.

XLII

She told us that she was a great believer
    In writers who interrogate taboo,
Waxed lyrical of Wilde and Eldridge Cleaver,
    Un Prophète, Dostoevsky and Camus,
And worked herself into a right old fever
    While reading from a book by you know who.
God knows why she was telling us this stuff,
But when she talked we couldn't get enough.

XLIII

This woman was (but how should I describe
    Her virtues?) of the overpowering kind;
Unless some beauty with a kiss should bribe,
    I'd say most men grow old and never find
So rare a model of the tender tribe,
    So perfect for the onanistic mind.
O Love! How perfect is thy mystic art!
And how deceitful is the sagest heart!

XLIV

Of course once news of Donna got about
    The apps came pouring in. The following week
The place was packed. So many years without
    A lovely female face makes strong men weak.
And Donna had a face, without a doubt;
    It seemed her conscious heart glowed in her cheek,
And we began to feel, in every lecture,
More *Cool Hand Luke* than Norman Stanley Fletcher.

XLV

Each week we bared our souls for her to read
    (And in return we'd mentally undress her);
We poured our bleeding hearts out by the screed,
    If we were sinners, she was our confessor,
And yet we somehow knew we'd not succeed –
    Our sentences seemed only to depress her –
She said she wanted something darker, *raw*,
Transgressive nature red in tooth and claw.

XLVI

Her answer was to hold a Poetry Slam,
    That *Vade Mecum* of the true sublime,
Where vanity competes with bad Am Dram
    And every joke's delivered with a rhyme.
Some started cramming as for an exam
    While others started rhyming all the time,
Perhaps believing there's some urban glamour
To be obtained while slamming in the Slammer.

XLVII

The day arrived at last. The place was heaving.
    The mood was tense. The poets, though rehearsed,
Were nervous as before a night of thieving;
    Each meant to do their best (or do their worst),
Each dry-mouthed author hoping and believing
    That they might win the prize and come in first.
While, wise and cunning as Minerva's Owl,
Sat Donna in the role of Simon Cowell.

XLVIII

The thin white rappers rapped and slapped their bitches,
    The Nature poets sang their Nonny Nonny,
The vampire moaned about some Gothic witches,
    The Stand-ups stood up and sat down, while Donny
Had everybody in the room in stitches
    With something borrowed straight from *Purple Ronnie*;
When my turn came I stared into my coffee,
For as you know, I cannot write for toffee.

XLIX

Last up was Steve the Byron fan, first seen
  In Stanza 39, with some new lay
About the current economic scene –
  Which prospect filled the audience with dismay
(I should explain, Steve is a cross between
  Andreas Baader, Malcolm X and Che).
But if not Orpheus quite, when Greece was young,
He sang, or would, or could, or should have sung:

***

The trials of Greece, the trials of Greece!
  Where noble Byron loved and sung,
Now suicidal rates increase
  Among the jobless Attic young;
Eternal summer gilds them yet,
But all, except their sun, is debt.

Dictatorship and civil war,
  A US-bankrolled Fascist coup,
Could not achieve what EU law
  And international banks now do;
For Greeks a blush, for Greece a tear.
For tourists, dearer *Mythos* beer.

The harp's unstrung, the lute is mute.
  The dream that Greece might still be free
Is lost on those in hot pursuit
  Of sun and sex and sand and sea,
Who only want to dance till morn
And chill out in the Golden Dawn.

As likely send a prayer to Isis
  As hope that we might fight the greed
Of those who caused the Euro Crisis;
  Europa bullied does not need
Another despot of this kind;
Such chains as these are sure to bind.

What, silent still? And silent all?
  The isles of Greece are held in thrall
Because we did not heed the call
  Inscribed upon the Doric wall,
Ευρώπη ξεσηκώσου!
Ευρώπη ξεσηκώσου!

***

L

He stopped abruptly, blushing as our Muse,
   The blessed Donna, opened her critique
By saying it was very hard to choose
   Between so many talents – even Greek!
(Steve blushed again.) Though poets should enthuse,
   She said they should be *sassy, dark, oblique.*
Steve blushed again with pleasure, whereupon
She said the champion Slammer was – our Don.

LI

And that was when the trouble started brewing.
   While Donny did his best to hide a smirk,
The Goth went pale, the Stand-ups started booing,
   The rappers flapped and yapped about their work,
It sounded like the Georgian poets were mooing,
   And Steve appeared about to go berserk;
At which point Donna, seeing what she'd started,
Decided it was time that she departed.

LII

Next thing we knew, they'd closed the Writing Group
   And Steve was nicked (which seemed a tad unjust),
While Donna, who was clearly in the soup,
   Had promptly vanished in a cloud of dust,
Thus leaving us, who cannot fly the coop
   As easily as that, somewhat nonplussed.
Next thing we knew, they gave Don his Cat D,
And with one bound the cat was – almost – free.

LIII

What happened next is anybody's guess.
   Time spent inside an open prison's not
The holiday imagined by the press;
   Put one foot wrong, you're back in like a shot.
Some fail because they just can't stand the stress,
   At least in here you're left alone to rot,
But in an open-nick you're easy sport.
In short, the odds on Don's return were short.

46

LIV

A few months later, sitting in my pad,
   I'm writing letters with my telly on
(No word from Donald Johnson, I might add,
   Though many men fall silent once they've gone).
First *News at Ten*, some ads, then *Mad 'n' Bad*
   A late-night arts show featuring – our Don
And drop-dead Donna, looking like a dream.
Both purring like the cats that got the cream.

LV

He sat there like a very naughty kitten
   While Donna talked about *The Awesome Fleece*,
A hip-hop opera which they'd just co-written
   For this year's Byron festival in Greece;
While Tony Parsons was 'completely smitten'
   And Jay-Z called the work 'a masterpiece',
Mark Lawson said he thought this new libretto
Was W.H. Auden meets the Ghetto.

LVI

It seemed that Don – our Don! – had struck it rich
   Since he got out; the boy was now rebranded
As Don-Catraz, a new persona which,
   As ludicrous as it was less than candid,
No doubt would prove to be a useful pitch
   For *Guardian* critics. Looked like Don had landed
With both feet on the ground, 'a modern Rimbaud'
Dressed up to look like Tupac and/or Rambo.

LVII

Of course the boy was always rather dapper,
   He had the Jack the Lad good looks in spades,
But now they'd dressed him up just like a rapper
   In baggy trousers, hoodie, trainers, shades,
An outsize trucker-cap upon his nappa,
   His hair in geometric cornrow braids;
As innocent as Rousseau's *Bon Sauvage,*
The handsome Caliban who made it large:

The aisles of Greece, the aisles of Greece!
   It's time to party with the Don
And celebrate the boy's release,
   So hit the dance-floor, get it on,
'Cos when you're really off your tree,
This deejay makes a cool emcee.

I'll get you dancing in the aisles
   On Kavos, Kos and Ayia Napa,
A crowd of blissed-out aceed smiles
   Because I is a well sick Rapper,
A toke, a drink, a pill, a line,
Fill high the cup with Samian wine!

From midnight till the sun comes up
   The virgins dance beneath the shade,
While awkward heroes stand and sup
   And gaze upon each glowing maid
Competing in the Pyrrhic dances,
And try to calculate their chances.

The Scian and the Teian muse
   Are in the toilets, selling dope;
Heroic bosoms, soaked in booze,
   Are caught in poses which they hope
Will decorate their Facebook page,
To prove that they have come of age.

Behold his lordship on the decks!
   The dance-floor packed with kids on eez
Who come to Greece for Club Med sex
   And pick up nasty STDs
To sounds which echo further west,
Then back to uni for a rest...

LVIII

To tell the truth, the boy had never seemed
   To be the brightest monkey in the lab,
But judging by the way they whooped and screamed
   When Donny did his krumping street-dance jab,
He'd clearly morphed himself (or was he memed?)
   To something which the world now thought was fab;
For just one moment even I was jealous;
Old Donny was the luckiest of fellers.

LIX

Soon Don and Donna were a tabloid item
   To rival Brad and Jen or Pete and Katie;
Their tweets were shared as fast as they could write 'em,
   Their plans to build an orphanage on Haiti
Were splashed in *Bitch* and *Knobz*, *ad infinitum*.
   In short, the world was so pleased they were matey
That, after cloying the gazettes with cant,
Don hinted that his Donna was *enceinte*.

LX

Alas, their happy tale had just begun
   When next we heard she'd hit him for a six
(Perhaps you saw the photos in the *Sun*);
   It seemed she'd caught him up to his old tricks
And when she found out what the boy had done,
   Poor Donna dropped him like a ton of bricks.
But then good scandals make the press a blessing,
Especially if you're photographed undressing.

LXI

Soon after that Don disappeared from view.
   The tabloid trail went cold. They'd better phones
To hack, and more vendettas to pursue.
   No doubt he's off exploring other zones
Erogenous and warm, in pastures new;
   The world out there is full of Donna clones
Who in a tender, moonlight situation
Will disregard a hero's reputation.

LXII

Meanwhile, the lads on B Wing are still here
    And every day's as pointless as the last.
The passing of another useless year
    Reminds us that we're going nowhere fast –
Except the pockets of the privateer
    Who's bought all the dead souls in this *oblast*.
The surest way to profit from austerity
Is passing on the invoice to posterity.

LXIII

O Time! Why must thou pause? Take up thy sickle!
    How long before we wake to see the light?
For any length of days in such a pickle
    A man must soon become an eremite;
The sand inside the glass slows to a trickle
    When you're locked in a toilet day and night.
In order to placate the tabloid editors,
They feed us to the privatising predators.

LXIV

Hark! Through the silence of the cold, dull night,
    The hum of prisons gather rank on rank
To keep us out of mind and out of sight:
    Ten million human beings in the tank
On this poor planet. Sold without a fight.
    Trust not for freedom to the merchant bank.
Or look for justice from the BBC.
The truth is that the truth won't set you free.

LXV

So if I've bent the truth, or botched my rhymes,
    It clearly wasn't done for bloody payment.
These days I'm sure that there are greater crimes
    (An extra bedroom when you're still a claimant
Will get you on the front-page of *The Times*).
    And since there are no angels in bright raiment
We need (and please don't think I'm being satirical)
A revolution – or a fucking miracle.

LXVI

Though governments in our time like to claim
    That every year the crime statistics fall,
The public still needs somebody to blame,
    As though behind each breezeblock prison wall
The public tries to hide their private shame
    At how our liberties were sold, how all
The nations are in prison, behind bars
That circumscribe your world as much as ours.

LXVII

Inside or out, we haven't got a hope.
    Between CCTV and IPP
Our freedom's on a short and slippery slope;
    And though they like to tell you that you're free
This goes for you as well; your longer rope
    Allows you just the freedom to agree
The liberties they take are justified.
And if you don't, there's room for you inside.

CLAUDIA DAVENTRY

I

The year is 1992, and Don
  is squinting in the mirror at his teeth.
Two caps, a right occlusal molar gone;
  the bridgework hides receding gums beneath.
That chic 'holistic' dentist was a con
  he thinks. *So much for Hampstead Heath.*
His train of thought is broken by the tone
of digi-waltz – his Nokia Mobile Phone –

II

He grabs the chunky handset. *'Don? It's Sam.'*
  Coincidence or serendipity?
Sam's the dodgy, wheeler-dealing, cham-
  pagne-swilling bastard whose mate Zebedee
had sent him to that bloody dentist. *'Am*
  I misinformed, or are you feeling fidgety?'
Now Don's a little rattled. Does Sam know
that he was pushed before he meant to go?

III

I'm going to have to take you back a bit:
  it's been a while since Don has been the man
he used to be. If he'd forecasted it
  he could've got himself a BUPA plan;
he's getting on. He wakes: he looks like shit,
  his breath smells like a souk in Rajasthan.
He's got a certain slackness in the jowls.
He's short of breath. He's gassy in the bowels,

IV

And with all this, he finds his pulling power's
  lost some of its pull. It used to be
he'd toss his curls, or tuck a little flower
  in the corner of his mouth, and she
– that's any she he wanted, any hour,
  any Haidée, Zoe, Kate or Rose-Marie –
would look as though she'd been hit on the head
by Cassius Clay, and drag him straight to bed.

V

But things have changed, and not just in the sack.
　　His whole career seems blighted by the Fates:
there was a day when he'd serve up a rack
　　of minted lamb on Conran 'Bistro' plates,
or have chicks groovin' down to Fleetwood Mac
　　at gigs (lieutenanted by Simon Bates)
but enterprise can be shortlived. His died.
He took a dead-end job, and now he's fried.

VI

Not only fried, but fired; harsh anagram
　　that brings us back to DJ on his phone.
He's not best pleased to hear from Slippy Sam
　　and offers up a small, involuntary moan.
'*Are you OK, old chap?*' says Sam. '*I am,*'
　　says Don. '*It's just – I've just been on my own
too long. I'm fine. Now tell me – what's your pitch?*'
Sam goes: '*We're going to make you rich.*'

VII

'*When you say "we",*' says Don, '*who do you mean?*
　　Don't think I missed what happened to your shares
in Lloyds last month: they're calling it obscene
　　that any reinsurance company that "cares"
could wriggle out of asbestosis. I'm not keen
　　to have a Name start running my affairs.'
'*Ah, your affairs,*' said Sam, '*that takes me back...*
How long's it been, Don? Have we lost the knack?'

VIII

You could have heard a Grecian maiden drop
　　her knickers in the silence that ensued.
Here Sam had hit the bullseye. And, on top
　　of that – and at the risk of being crude –
Don was still smarting from his recent *flop*
　　while servicing a girl called Ermintrude
he'd picked up in a bar on Muswell Hill
(more later. But she handed him the bill).

IX

'OK, OK. You'd better spit it out,'
   says Don, *'but make it quick. I haven't got*
all day to listen to some spiv go on about
   his get-rich schemes again. You know that rot-
ten dentist that you sent me to? That Kraut
   with his Holistic crap? He should be shot.
If **this** *plan isn't good, you know where you*
can stick it, don't you, mate?' Sam goes *'I do.'*

X

So Sam explains his half-hatched plot to Don,
   who listens, to begin with, unimpressed
though, bit by bit, he starts to cotton on
   and by the end he's thinking it's the best
aimed volley shot since Evonne Goolagong
   was made an honorary white. *'Invest*
in Tommy Nutter now,' concluded Sam,
'and get a one-way ride to Amsterdam.'

XI

Don went to Nutters: got a Jagger suit
   and headed out to Amsterdam. The plot
is this: though getting on a tad, Don's cute,
   or cutish, still; at least, more cute than not
– the peppered curls. His back's not too hirsute.
   He's good at holding in his belly-pot...
the truth is, when you get to forty-six,
it's wallet, more than looks, attracts the chicks.

XII

And that's all understood: there's loadsa wedge
   in it for him if he can up his game.
Sam's right-hand mucker, Zebedee, a hedge-
   fund manager (myopic, bald and slightly lame)
is putting up the funds to start-up 'Edge':
   a brand-new sports apparel brand. A shame
that Reebok, adidas and Nike (said-
-as-goddess; 'Nikey') are so far from dead –

XIII

Though healthy competition is the root
　　of booming business; so said Kenneth Clarke
that year, from somewhere in his rumpled suit,
　　his shoelace trailing, and a grubby mark
on his lapel, but nonetheless astute
　　on matters of Exchequer. So a shark,
– who might perhaps be lazy, maybe; greedy,
disinclined to work too hard, but needy –

XIV

takes to skulking round the hunting-grounds
　　of bigger predators whose *net success*
is proven in the field. The crunching sounds
　　you hear in offices like these, the mess
you find on fire escapes, the mounds
　　of bones and skulls, the scent of raw distress
are just the human by-products of this:
surviving it's a little hit-or-miss.

XV

But Donny is a narcissist, which means
　　genetically he's tingling and wired
to make the most of all these nasty scenes.
　　He laps it up. The fact that he was sired
by Satan may have helped a bit – his genes
　　are pure Beelzebub. He's rarely tired.
Like Mrs T, he barely sleeps at all,
occasionally walks sulphur down the hall

XVI

And leaves his pitchfork smoking by the stairs,
　　with trails of slime, at times, around the sink,
and verdigris. And sometimes, on the chairs,
　　you see a smear of pitch. A fetid stink
that drifts up, like a smell of singeing hair,
　　from somewhere in the basement... through a chink
between the yellow nets, you catch a glimpse
of DJ – and a silhouette that limps.

XVII

Who's Zebedee? And why's he in the story?
   Let me see... I'll do the potted version:
Zebedee met Sam in early glory
   days; say nineteen sixty-three. Immersion
in a druggy kind of culture, whorey
   nights and LSD, or smoking Persian
black, was only just the start. The rest –
'we drink therefore we am', they more than once profeshed –

XVIII

And that's Descartes, but à la Carte des Vins.
   They talked philosophy until the Taos came home
au *Deux Magots* with Sartre on Saint Germain,
   and existentialised, and asked Simone
to get the tea, *poupée*, while we read Antonin
   Artaud. She seemed *fâchée*, the *jolie môme*
– they weren't sure why. She had a pretty *derrière*:
'de Beauvoir' means 'nice view' so – harsh, but fair.

XIX

They neatly sidestepped nineteen sixty-eight
   in Paris, once they'd made a bomb by selling
boxes of half-bricks to students. Fate
   took them via Czechoslovakia – a stalling
detour, where they bought some silver plate
   dead cheap from Škvorecký, who was sailing
off to Canada to save his neck (as Prague
had lost its Spring) and start a Nouvelle Vague –

XX

Short-circuiting the Poles, they bought a club
   and put on jazz, and rock'n'roll, and blues
and made another mint. An English pub
   was next, a line of trendy boots and shoes
called 'Czech it Out': a guy called M. Holub
   wrote straplines and – give him his dues –
was pathological about the task.
Don't know how much they paid. I didn't ask.

XXI

So how do these two reprobates meet Don?
  (the problem with digression – it digresses;
too easy to bang on and on, and on,
  forgetting it's conciseness that impresses,
not rambling detours, like a Marathon
  run slowly, stopping off to try on dresses.)
They meet him when he's only twenty-five
and working as a DJ in some dive

XXII

In Leatherhead. Yes, Leatherhead in Surrey,
  a county just establishing its name
as Divorce City, Place to Have a Curry
  Out with Someone Else's Squeeze, a Game
of Glass Ashtrays and Carkeys (hurry
  for the DB5 or you might shame
yourself by driving home the Anglia), gin
and Jaguars and stockbrokers and sin.

XXIII

Zebedee and Sam saw Don was fit
  enough to run the scam they had in mind;
if he could put on records, talk and hit
  on Surrey women *à la fois*, he could wind
a pretty yarn while *selling people shit*
  and still *rake in the cash*. Don signed
along the dotted line. Mnemosyne
was there as witness; Sam, and Zebedee.

XXIV

So nineteen seventy sees Don as *dueño*
  of his own *Alhambra* bar, a dancing-cabaret
of grim repute in London's sleazy Soho
  that reeked of cigarettes and flat champagne by day.
At the French House, Don eats *carré d'agneau*
  with Paul Raymond, Jeff Bernard, a Kray
(but not the twins, who were banged up by then),
a couple of *contessas* who'd been men

XXV

– Who came with April Ashley, Pete O'Toole,
  and Francis Bacon (taciturn. He swore
at anyone who took his glass). Don's rule
  is simple: drink all day, but nothing more
than apple juice – or you'll be anybody's fool –
  by night. He hires girls from Singapore,
from Bangkok; Kazakhs, Uzbeks, French girls, Swedes,
and has them dancing, naked, but for beads;

XXVI

No touching. Any House of Disrepute
  is not a place one should be seen to run
(that's touching things, and squeezing things to boot)
  or undercover 'writers' from *The Sun*
shrug on their dirty macs and file the brutal
  exposés – once they've 'researched' the fun –
to get you cuffed and slung in Pentonville
smiling at Reg and Ronnie through your swill.

XXVII

So none of that. No; Donny's place is clean.
  He's close to Ronnie Scott's, and in his lobby
he has pictures of his clientèle. The Queen
  may be a drag artist, but – Norma and Bobby
Charlton are for real, and Barry Sheene.
  Keith Richard's out of focus, but that's Nobby
Stiles without his teeth after The Game.
Like or hate it, that's one Hall of Fame.

XXVIII

Ah, Fame is but shortlived, and *vanitas*
  brings small reminders of mortality
as plans go bust. You want to watch that glass
  of Cristal you sneaked through as a banality,
for when the taxman hears, he'll tan your ass
  (I have to spell it that way or brutality
could break out in the ranks, I'm afraid,
between the 'long-A'/'shorter-A' brigade).

XXIX

Don was fond of women and champagne
  – how can that be deemed a mortal sin? –
but sadly there are powers that be, whose reign
  does *not* allow such peccadilloes in.
They struck: like Castillon in Aquitaine
  when France consigned the English to *le bin.*
They took away his licence, and his cellar,
nicked the dancers – and our hapless fella.

XXX

Funny how some people, at the whiff
  of trouble melt into the background. Sam
was onesuch. Zebedee was, too. And if
  you think they came to bail out Don, I am
the Pope. I think that's why they found it stiff
  convincing Don to go to Amsterdam
two decades later: they'd abused his trust.
And once abused, let's face it, trust is dust.

XXXI

It wasn't just the spell in Wormwood Scrubs
  – to which he turned his handiworkings, as
the prisoners were bored, what with no pubs.
  Don's spliffing jinxed their air with voodoo jazz
and little riffs of discontent; first grubs
  of disenchantment with their Alcatraz,
which, barely fledged, would grow past pupa stage
until they stormed the roof in fullblown rage:

XXXII

It's called Bad Apple syndrome. Don was bad.
  Not *Bad* like Michael Jackson (who was still
a black kid with big hair, a pushy Dad
  and recent hit about a rat called Bill
or Ben; his only friend, which made us sad).
  No. Don was handsome, always dressed to kill,
at first, he'd make you trust him with your life
then, Iago-like, he'd sweetly slip the knife

XXXIII

Between your ribs, and all this with a smirk –
   metaphorically, he'd have your side
slit open, watch your nervous system jerk
   your innards from their tethers, see them slide
like glistening butchers' offal from their murk
   and plop into his hand – and call it suicide,
then find a girl, and weep, upon her breast,
assorted woes until she got undressed.

XXXIV

His wake was strewn with corpses foul and fair
   – *this* had been the talent Sam had spotted
from the dancefloor as Don pumped out *Stair-*
   way to Heaven – and got pelted with besotted
womens' underclothes. He didn't care
   about their qualities: he just garotted
females with the smoulder in his eye,
then buried them alive with lie on lie.

XXXV

He'd caused the prison riot, then managed bail
   by chatting up a Wardress with a tush
like Barbara Windsor, so he couldn't fail.
   She gave her sister's husband's mate a push
(he was the Governor of Reading Gaol)
   and Don was soon back on the street, hush-hush,
albeit affianced to the Wardress (Pam,
by then expecting), so he had to scram.

XXXVI

He went to Birmingham, grew a moustache
   and with some banknotes hidden in his car
(say what you like: he'd had a hunch the stash
   could see him through the sudden or bizarre
– a craving for a monster lump of hash,
   that rainy day, a rocket to a star)
he bought a little Bistro, in a fever
giving it the name *The Eager Belvoir*

XXXVII

Which, he felt, had something Anglo-Gallic:
    a sense of the unknown, excitement, charm,
(nothing like a nightclub, nothing phallic,
    nothing that could raise a false alarm).
The wines he served were decent; non-metallic.
    Then *andouillette* with offal off the farm.
Fromage de tête, or jellied pig's head. Grated
frogs with *mâche* and gravy, nicely plated.

XXXVIII

He sat and studied films with Peter Sellers
    in them, learning pouts and Gallic shrugs
while wearing jaunty hats and raincoats. Dwellers
    in his Complex thought it must be drugs
but DJ didn't care: his aim – like Mellors
    in the Chatterleys' garden, finding slugs –
was *ignorez les detracteurs*, the while
just concentrating on his clients' smile.

XXXIX

We aim to please, *aimons à pleaser*. Don's
    French was coming on a treat. In Brum
they had a sprinkling of Frenchmen, *sans
    culottes* and *avec*. As it happened, some
were Huguenots who still banged Calvin's *fons
    vitae*-as-blessed-Holy-Spirit drum,
but mostly did it quietly (and *sans* unction:
usually around Spaghetti Junction).

XL

Don's bent was Catholic, or so he'd say.
    His rosary was somewhat underused –
his Aunt Dolores brought it back, one day
    from Lourdes/slash/Salamanca. He refused
to learn his Catechism but liked to pray:
    he mumbled softly by the beds of bruised
damsels in a shaft of gothic light
(a combo of stained glass/slash/moonlit night).

XLI

This waitress was his latest *coup de grace*,
　　she'd started in the kitchen; said she'd rather
swap to Front of House, he thought she'd pass
　　– she had the gab, the Blarney and the blether
and by coincidence a most beguiling ask-
　　no-questions-tell-no-lies. She said her father
always came to pick her up at two
when he'd finished all his missions; '*Who*

XLII

In fuck's name is your Daddy? Roger Moore?'
　　Don goes – she'd pulled a flick-knife from her bra
and backed towards the Aston's throaty roar
　　as it pulled up, at five to two. '*Ha ha,*'
she said, '*you're funny. Yeah. But be in awe*
　　of him, cos he's a gangster, and his car
ain't the only thing that makes a noise...'
she leaned in: '*Daddy tortures little boys.*'

XLIII

He blenched, but he was looking down her *embonpoint*
　　and didn't see the driver of the beast,
who chanced to shoot a glance at Don, *en plein*
　　ogle of his daughter's candy-feast.
Moustache notwithstanding, *dans un coin*
　　de sa mémoire there stirred at very least
a *soupçon* of – *that nose... that face again...*
which filtered in, insistent as a *madeleine.*

XLIV

And then the penny dropped. Oh, *temps perdu*
　　such wasted days we realise are spent
wiping the memory-slate; forgetting you!
　　The lazy afternoon, the balmy scent
of honeysuckle under the aching blue
　　of an August sky. The time you almost went
to Glastonbury but broke down in the rain;
the smell of diesel... that recurring *madeleine...*

XLV

Sam pulled himself together (it was he).
   He'd come to get his daughter, not to muse
on literature or Proust's longevity,
   but, judging from Don's curling lip, *his* ruse
was still to get his mitts on Emily
   and no prospective Dad-in-law would choose
a son-in-law like Don, however debonair
the chap's allure or lush his facial hair.

XLVI

'Bonjour, monsieur,' he said, *'et garde-à-vous!*
What the hell d'you think you're looking at,
hein, sivooplay? Your slimy eyes me rendent fou
   for that's ma fille, you salaud. Grubby rat.'
Startled, Don looks up and, peering through
   the darkness, seems to recognise that hat,
those Foster-Grant Reactolites – but then
it could be that repeating *madeleine*.

XLVII

'Why, Sir,' he says, with Clouseautastic twang,
   'ah waz jus' makingue sure zis leetle lady
waz eau-K.' 'Eau-K?' goes Sam. *'Yes, dang*
   you, Sir, eau-K,' says Don, *'zere are some shady*
types round 'ere, you kneau. You 'ear a bang
   and you are toast.' He shrugged. *'I call a spady*
spady.' *'A **spade**,'* said Sam. *'As well you know.*
Get in the car,' he said to Emily. *'Let's go.'*

XLVIII

Had he been discovered, though? On tenterhooks
   Don carried on; his masquerading Other
presiding over napiery, the banter cooks
   will bandy round the kitchen, someone's brother
looking for a job, the pointy hooks
   for hanging up the hams, until his mother
called and bent his ear. He had to change
his accent back to normal, which felt strange:

IL

'Hi, Mum. I know. I know. It's been a while.
  I know. It's been – I know. I'm sorry. Yes.
Oh, that's not fair. You know it's not my style.
  Not really. Well – not always. Mum. But yes,
I got it. No, I didn't. That's right. Pile
  it on, why don't you...nothing! Joking. Yes.
I will. More often. Yes. You know, I try.
I love you too. Yes. Mwuh-mwuh. Yes, Mum. Bye.'

L

The thing is, now we've inched past stanza forty
  we need to segue to the padded eighties:
Don watched Raymond Blanc (between the naughty
  VHSes); learned to steam potaties,
julienne carrots, chargrill chard and sporty
  surfy-turfy combos, wondering if a skate is
better blackened on a skillet or the grill, or
if his guests would die of salmonella –

LI

– Which they did, in spasms. Not just one
  but twenty-seven diners, after *bouillabaisse*
were rushed to hospital with vomiting, went numb –
  and all were DOA. I heard that lesser
French-food damage happened at Verdun
  when Falkenhayn had just blown up the Mess.
Oh, cieux! Malheur! Don's salad days are fading.
The *Belvoir*, not so *Eager* now, ceased trading.

LII

This is the bit we call the middle eight,
  the bridge, or maybe *entr'acte*, where our hero
takes a small step back to contemplate
  the nature of the mess he's in: his sorrow.
Young Werther ain't got nothin' on Don's fate.
  Remember all those miners' strikes, near Jarrow:
Easington and Orgreave, hard at war
with Maggie? Yes – it's 1984

LIII

The year that Orwell said we'd have dystopia
   and mind control, the Ministry of Truth
and propaganda, doublethink, myopia
   as *Minipax*, a disenfranchised youth...
So Don's another Winston Smith, but gropier.
   His Julias are laissez-faire, uncouth
or elegant and svelte; all on the shelf.
All say *'You only care about yourself,'*

LIV

– They're right – he does. So, girl by girl
   he makes his way from Birmingham to Leeds,
he lervs his way through Tyne and Wear to Hull
   – bestowing roses, interested in breeds
of dog while helping owners to unfurl
   umbrellas in the wind – then, sensing needs,
a grain of loneliness; he brushes fingers,
plants the little yearning look that lingers...

LV

Sometimes they slap him. Mostly, they do not
   and, anyway, his skin is thick as rhino hide:
he doesn't give a fig or care a jot
   (as people say, when taken for a ride).
Neither does he need them to be 'hot'
   (to use Page Three-speak: 'Turn to more inside!!!').
But if they've half a brain it ups the chance
they'll spot his tactics, spoiling his advance.

LVI

This bird-seducing Panzer tank grinds on,
   crushing maidens with its treads, snagging
strappy tops and grinning: *'Hi, I'm Don,*
   babe, what's your sign?' – relentless, brute, unflagging.
He's got a boyish charm (like that LeBon
   who did his bit for Band Aid; smiling, dragging
starving children in to boost the sales).
He's smooth, out-aftershaving other males.

LVII

The years before Sam tracks him down again
    are pretty tough, but Don falls on his feet.
His life is, yogically, a shambles — which is when
    the stars align and one's destined to meet
The One. She had a business, *Now and Zen*,
    a bit of cash, a flat in Southwark Street:
they were in love! He zips in like a rabbit;
marries her. Now she can fund his habit.

LVIII

The new wife's name is Zara. She reads tarot,
    is Buddho-zoroastrian, wears *dhoti*
has a trust fund (Daddy went to Harrow
    and has a copper bangle and a goatee).
She imports silk and sells it on a barrow
    along Brick Lane when she's not doing floaty
dances out in Covent Garden Piazza
draped in seven veils. Quite a *ragazza*.

LIX

Don is so in love he cannot bear
    to be alone without her when she goes
to Buddho-zoroastrianish prayer
    or putting on the floaty-dancey shows.
He feels a little churlish not to share
    her lovely pad with somebody who'd care
for it and him: a little *señorita*
who'd do odd jobs and make the kitchen neater.

LX

He finds a yellow postcard in a phonebox
    by his stamping-ground, Old Compton Street.
Tucked amongst the tits and overgrown cocks
    graffitoed there, the card – fluorescent, neat
and advertising slyly 'to the Lone Fox'
    is direct mail to Don, who wants to meet
the *'Discipline and Polishing with Expertease
Exclusive In You're Home'* girl – on his knees.

LXI

She polished in the kitchen and the hall.
   She wore a fetching uniform and heels.
She polished quite a lot of mirrored wall.
   Don felt as though his keks were full of eels;
he didn't want her polishing at all.
   He followed her and polished her: her squeals
were audible in Southwark Street, where poor
old Zara was just stepping through the door.

LXII

So Don's divorce came through a month or two
   before the incident in Muswell Hill.
This Ermintrude – I mentioned her to you
   because she'd been his nemesis – was ill-
equipped from Donny's point of view
   (in spite of looking *fit* and *dressed to kill*)
as, fumbling in the dark, he found his Venus
came with hairy bollocks and a penis.

LXIII

And how she'd laughed, and charged him for the *craic*.
   Mortified, he'd stumbled to his feet,
and staggered out without once glancing back.
   Safe in his rented flat, he hit *delete*
inside his head, but couldn't get that six-pack
   from his mind, the silken shaft, that sweet –
NO – what was he thinking? Don is straight.
He always has been, always will be. Mate.

LXIV

'Oh hairy, ballsy masculinity!
   Come grapple with my biceps. Let's swill beer.
I beat my chest at all your – girly vanity.
   Oi. Wotchoo looking at? Oi. Come out 'ere
and say that an' I'll knock you to infinity.'
   Don, snarling at the mirror, gives a leer
and this is when he spots his teeth. *'They're bone,*
I'm mortal. Shit.' And then we hear his phone.

LXV

Rewind; fast forward. So – he reconnects
    with Sam and Zebedee, agrees to go
to Amsterdam in search of better sex
    which will be plenty plentiful (and hetero),
with pillow-talk in Dutch and divers dialects
    or other funny languages. Although
he's telling Sam his focus will be work,
and Sam believes him (being your average jerk).

LXVI

Schiphol, August 1992.
    Don hands his Louis Vuitton to the driver,
steps into the waiting Merc. *Il* shoe
    is Gucci, sock *è* silk. Even his saliva
is designer (yes. He got a chewy
    toffee from the lady at Godiva).
He's staring at the taxi-driver's boots,
    not thinking of the flight attendant's glutes.

LXVII

Not thinking of the flight-attendant's arms
    in that white shirt. Not thinking of that neck
or any of the flight-attendant's other charms.
    Not thinking of the fact he had to check
his fantasies of flight-attendant farms,
    or imagining the plane crash-landed, and the wreck
had only spared him, Don, and one survivor:
that heterosexual flight-attendant, Ivor.

LXVIII

NO – what's he thinking? Straight as a *die*.
    He pays the taxi; heads to his *apartement*
on KNSM Island, has to try
    negotiating office space. '*Een leuk tent
op de grachten,*' says the *makelaar.* 'I
    don't speak Dutch. And I'm not bent.'
She sighs and Don forgets to watch her breasts,
being, er, hung up on flight attendants' chests.

LXIX

So he's installed on Prinsengracht; a well-
    appointed office on the *bel-étage*,
once visited and sung in by Jacques Brel.
    The ceilings are still high, the windows large,
the mayor of Amsterdam insists the smell
    has more to do with tourists than the barge
traffic and *Rondvaart* boats on the canal.
Don yawns. It's overwhelmingly banal.

LXX

He pays the *makelaar* her x percent.
    And now it's his, all his. The launch of *Edge*.
Tomorrow's interviewing secretaries, sent
    by the agency. An employee called Rodge
who's going to come and do accounts, and rent,
    and guff like that. The man from Zap-o-Midge
who's putting up the *klamboes*, or mosquito nets.
Those bloodsuckers you wouldn't want as pets.

LXXI

Bloodsuckers you wouldn't want as pets...
    it's funny; Don's heard that before somewhere,
someplace; in his childhood, at the vet's?
    He can't remember, doesn't really care;
his focus is the link-up to the Mets
    game in Reception, on the big screen, where
they're showing baseball; sport – that stuff
he doesn't like. He's sold his soul so – tough.

LXXII

A tortured soul's a rag of smoke, a wraith,
    a scrap of shadow, maybe worth a pound,
a dollar, half a nine-bob note. With death
    the soul goes travelling – without a sound,
or flinching, it dissolves. It floats. It's faith
    that's anchored: faith stays on the ground.
Keep the faith and let your soul go begging.
Without faith, might as well start digging.

LXXIII

Oh, FINE, I get it: this is propaganda,
  you may cry. *They're going to do the God*
thing. Well. I'm off to call my friend Amanda
  /get Nigella's recipe for cod
with salsa verde/kip on the verandah
  /go on Google (look: an 'arthropod'
just means a spider or invertebrate
without a shell that doesn't ruminate).

LXXIV

I wasn't going to mention gods at all.
  The faith our Donny needs is older than
the hills, the book, the Dead Sea scrolls, the scrawl
  on troglodytic tide-smoothed boulders, than
the quarks, or whether supernovas fall
  into black holes. It's on our narrow shoulders
from the moment we're conceived: the 'me':
if Don can't love, he might as well not be.

LXXV

I appreciate you haven't mashed your way
  through sixty stanzas for a West Coast homily,
some spirit mumbo-jumbo from LA
  the yinyangism of the Global Family
a quasi-yogic chant from beachfront bay
  /hotels where wealthy girls (like Emily)
sit in lotus, slick with sunblock, waiting
for the sun to rise – and then, still, waiting,

LXXVI

Not understanding why they come back home
  with glowing skin and muscle tone but, underneath,
unsatisfied, and sad-while-tanned, poorer
  in more than purse; not knowing to think – as they tossed
back alcohol-free skinny Mojitos on the jetty,
  waiting for the boat-man to take them into the blue –
how, in the spritz of lime zest and crushed mint
the stab of salt on the rim of the glass is lost.

LXXVII

There's a reason why the moon is bright,
    but it's not the one we dream when we see it shine.
The moon is dead and cold, dependent for light
    and heat from a fiery star. See, we define
ourselves by the shadow we make: any might
    we think we have's no more than this. What's mine
is borrowed, on borrowed time. We say we must
make sense of the given chaos before we're dust.

LXXVIII

And here is why the metre, and the rhyme.
    It's been accused of binding the fluid word
with the plastic washing-line of time
    and subjugating feelings, to be heard
only as the manufactured chime
    of a municipal clock in a mad third
world dictatorship. Bong-bong bonanza
and press on to the next bonging stanza

LXXIX

And all the words, their heads in drawstring bags
    sobbing for mercy, or fallen silent, too sad
to make a sound. Forgotten, that before hashtags,
    world-wide web, type and print, the Iliad
was spoken word. The voice – as glossy mags
    or TV of its day, when the latest fad
was troubadours – took full responsibility
in rhyme and metre for the mind's agility

LXXX

And rhyme and metre, far from mummifying words
    preserve them in the memory, mark each beat
with music, raise them, in augmented thirds
    or major sixths, dactylic or iambic feet
and closer to a universal song – like birds,
    no sound an island, pure, liquid, complete:
a language superseding Babel. Order
in the dark's the final goal, not murder.

74

LXXXI

While we digress, our Don is causing trouble.
  The order in his chaos being seduction
he's headed to the redlight on the double
  to browse the windows, see what sort of action
he can score in office hours, the bubble
  created by our nine-to-five 'work' fiction.
Materially there's not much need to *be* there
when you can hang your jacket on your chair

LXXXII

So this – the jacket trick – is what he does.
  In shirtsleeves, then, he strolls along the Dam
towards De Wallen, soaking up the buzz
  of the Rosse Buurt by day, waving at a *femme
fatale* or two *en route*. Stops by Ms
  Mariska Majoor's place. *'Douleur de l'âme
is why men come and why they've always come'*,
she says; *'it's just a rule of thumb'*.

LXXXIII

Don wasn't really looking for excuses
  but now he's vindicated: goes to stroll
among the shifty husbands on the sluices,
  (watched by pairs of eyes in heavy kohl)
marriage round their wretched necks like nooses;
  discovery would really pain the soul.
Girls knock with rings on windows, flaunt a basque,
'Sir's wildest dream!... Sir only have to ask.'

LXXXIV

A foreign supermarket's always fun,
  no doubt about it – this, more fun than most.
Don browses with his trolley. That's the one.
  No, maybe that – a spot of Ivory Coast –
Hello, love: coming in, then, honeybun?
  that one's too thin; eyes of a ghost.
In ultra-violet light her scrap of loin-
cloth glows above the track-marks in her groin.

LXXXV

Now something's up: Don doesn't feel like lunch
    so much. *Airconditioned sadomasochism?*
Douleur de l'âme has hit him with a crunch
    and suddenly he thinks about his Catechism,
out of the blue. He has a sudden hunch
    he's needed at the office, a yawning chasm
in his gut... A *bakkerij*: again.
Vanilla whiff. That pesky *madeleine.*

LXXXVI

Back in the office, Rodge is up a ladder
    fixing some air-con, or a bit of stucco.
Don walks in, beholds him and feels sadder
    still: his Man Friday has hints of Puck,
Ophelia and Othello... if Don were badder,
    he could swing both ways, *beter gezegt* fuck
both ways, or, come to that, in many ways
but he cannot, will not, is not, is not gay.

LXXXVII

'I LOVE WOMEN AND AM NOT GAY.'
    Don speaks out loud to the urinal
in the gents, where he has come to say
    just that – no NO, *not* that: to have a final
blokey piss then get back to his day.
    'But what if you're both?' 'But what if that got anal?'
the quarrel's raging in his head. *'DJ,'*
comes Rodge's voice, *'I couldn't help but hear,*
and have to say, I think you're smashing, dear.'

LXXXVIII

Rodge stands close behind him, at the stalls.
    DJ zips up in haste. *'Oh, shucks,'* he mumbles;
'that earworm again. It always galls
    me how I can't remember lyrics... jumble
so much up, it's ludicrous...appalls
    me. But you're just a kid: I guess you've rumbled
me. I'm old.' 'I've rumbled you, alright,
says Rodge, unflinching. *'Stay with me tonight.'*

LXXXIX

Don's womanising flits before his eyes.
  Not only does he have a reputation
to uphold, but this is, uh, surprising.
  Rodge has now reversed the situation
of boss and underling. Is this how guys
  snare other guys? And is the culmination
of his gigolo's career to come to this:
to find Othello's arms, and *die upon a kiss*?

XC

'I see at least you're thinking it over.' Rodge
  runs a finger down Don's spine and leaves.
Don's troubled, now. This image isn't *Edge*.
  Edge is the sports brand with Achiever
stamped all over it; *'The Edge in Legend'*
  goes the line. Dammit, he signed Steve
Ovett just last week: all this could spoil it.
Can't have male staff flirting in the toilet.

XCI

Don cycles home and dons his brand-new lycra
  then goes running in the Vondelpark, does weights
at Splash (a lot of sweaty men in micro
  shorts, but also lots of birds, yeah, mate),
cycles more, straps on some nifty velcro
  cycling shoes and finds a girl called Kate
to cycle with. She bores the pants off him,
quite literally. He goes back to the gym.

XCII

Time goes by like this until the day
  that Sam and Zebedee come visiting the Dam
with bad news up their sleeves. *'We have to say
  there's no point being a VC if the scam
your money's backing isn't going to pay.
  What's going on, here? Nike's huge. I am
frustrated,'* stated Zebedee. *'And adidas
is doing nothing less than kicking ass.'*

XCIII

'We should've known,' said Sam, *'that everything*
  this halfbaked loser touches turns to shit.
I'm pulling out. And sorry, but we'll sting
  him for the office bills and the whole bit.
From now on, we don't fund another thing –'
  (a nasty smile) *'– so, lucky, now, you're fit.'*
They stalk out with the liquidation folder.
Don breaks down and cries – on Rodge's shoulder.

XCIV

Later on, Don's staring at the ceiling
  of Rodge's houseboat, heavy-limbed with wine
and sweet with love. It's love, this thing he's feeling;
  different from the nine hundred and nine
lovers he's known before, he thinks, stealing
  another look at Rodge's set of fine
leather-bound volumes of the classics. Look:
Don's changed. Tomorrow, he might read a book.

IAN DUHIG

It's a terrible deception of love that it begins by engaging us in play not with a woman of the external world but with a doll fashioned in our brain – the only woman moreover that we have always at our disposal, the only one we shall ever possess.
Marcel Proust

I

If *canto*'s rooted in the Latin word for song,
    it harmonises here with English 'cant',
so often wriggling on Lord Byron's prong
    and target of that *Tristram Shandy* rant
where he deems critics most display this wrong –
    forgive me if I play too much descant:
digressive faults, like Byron's, caught from Sterne,
so to our tale directly do we turn:

II

I – straight away some critic's handbag flies:
    we're in a fight about identities,
my narrative presumptions, lyric *I*s...
    Considering the practicalities,
I opt for '*I*' here to ventriloquize
    my prejudices, whims or views.
'*Je' est un autre!* Rimbaud said (I keep
such quotes to hand to make myself sound deep).

III

But we're not here to wrangle reasons why
    or age-old problems of philosophy
which Sterne sent up: '*as sure as I am I –*
    and you are you – and who are you? said he.
Don't puzzle me; said I.' You think I lie?
    See *Tristram Shandy*, VII, xxxiii!
For – though I should be – I am not the hero:
so we move from number one to zero,

IV

DJ, crushed again in love and war
    through falling for a soldier on home leave –
so short of time, she knew what time was for,
    and played love-games the tame would not believe –
he, shuttlecock to his love's battledore...
    to cut this Tristramsquely short, he'd grieve
when duty called on whom he'd such a crush
(for all his hard-ons, DJ's soul was mush) –

81

V

I love – you'd guessed – it hardly need be said –
   a shortened dash of Sterne for punctuation –
first persons lying on this page's bed,
   as breathless as DJ for copulation.
My inserts might be sometimes bracketed;
   odd bits of colons offer variation –
ellipses, too, like breadcrumbs of the lost...
lead back to DJ on love's tempest tossed.

VI

Camilla was the name in DJ's heart;
   Camilla, Virgil's Volscian Amazon;
Camilla, who felled DJ with love's dart,
   who was our Charley's Queen, and then was gone;
who for him (he felt) didn't give a fart,
   who'd loved and left him (as once he'd've done)
exactly when she told him she would go
to fight whom politicians made her foe.

VII

The myth it's men made Brits a warrior race
   not Boudicca nor Thatcher could destroy;
romanticizing writers liked to trace
   our ancestry as from the Fall of Troy,
when Brutus fled here, claimed and named this place,
   which gave a certain – what? – *je ne sais quoi*
to stories our French conquerors liked to hear,
small comfort for our weather, food and beer.

VIII

Apollo shipped with Brutus to this shore,
   that god who's always tugging at my sleeves
to get this show back on the road once more;
   I'd plump, if gods must wait on me like Jeeves,
for Hermes – he'd be far less of a bore:
   for Greeks and Romans both, their god of thieves
(a certain interchangeability's
the mark of classical divinities).

IX

Hermes was Trismegistus's first name,
   whose surname Walter meant for Tristram's first –
a misdelivered message being to blame
   for 'Tristram', which poor Walter felt was cursed
since *nomen est omen* – but all the same,
   he thought, as crushings go, not the worst...
more irony, like Toby's love of war
which we can hate, yet love the warrior.

X

James Joyce opined, as apter for their work,
   that Swift and Sterne should have each other's name
and though Joyce sometimes came on like a berk –
   the racist insult version sounds the same
as this but differs in its spelling: *burke*...
   See? I can play the anti-racist game –
I'm not sure 'berk' and 'burke' would count as rhyme
before the letters game of our own time.

XI

Sterne's name suggests both arse (or 'ass') and star,
   while 'Shandy' then meant 'crazy', later 'wank':
I realise the traps that such words are,
   so gloss them for the Canuck, Mick or Yank –
and 'trap' means mouth, and mine's run on too far,
   which makes me feel like I'm in that film *Crank*
because I feel a digging in my ribs
from my great supernatural His Nibs.

XII

The way to most men's hearts, a woman knows,
   runs straighter than the M1 through his penis –
this only could sound cynical to those
   who've looked at us but haven't really seen us;
straight or gay, we're pricks upon love's rose –
   junk science makes out women come from Venus,
most men aren't remote from *Life on Mars:*
such amatoria's now all my ars.

XIII

'What kind of poet speaks such treachery?
   The lad's a cad or mad or sad or bad;
throughout his art's star-studded history,
   love's all some of our greatest poets had
to write their very greatest poetry,
   not like this doggerel Gonadiad
who's author's even dimmer than he looks
and needs to buy himself some decent books!'

XIV

Is *any* romance not 'self-love *à deux*'?
   No selfish gene's imperative,
society or family norm, but 'the
   best reason human beings have to live'?
I ask rhetorically: DJ grunts 'Huh?'
   To care requires a toss he can't now give
since every answer's anyway debatable –
which proves to him, at least, that love's inflatable.

XV

There's something in a huge balloon... please note
   this empty joke from Wordsworth's 'Peter Bell'
for DJ doomed on emptiness to dote,
   who was now of his old self just a shell...
Judge not! Whatever floats your Prologue's boat:
   his saviour Mae West is no Jezebel
but guardian angel waiting in the wings,
as light as all the airs a poet sings.

XVI

My love is song and what is song but air?
   Pygmalionism of the afflatus
blows us bards away – it's only fair,
   since muses use us for their apparatus
Bellmer-like to spread seed everywhere.
   So I tell moralists: have a heart! Us
male artists are narcissists, it's true,
but love's still love, though I love I or you.

XVII

When Alma booted Oskar into touch,
   he tried to get his own back with a doll
commissioned from great Fräulein Such-and-such
   the spit of Alma for some fol-de-rol,
with working crotch (which, aptly, Brits call *crutch).*
   But OK realised he'd stooped to foll-
y finally: after he'd mated it
one last time, he decapitated it.

XVIII

Our DJ sought a love-life off the rack,
   so bought a blow-up doll one afternoon
from 'Guys & Dolls', whose owner loves the *craic*
   and said he'd 'Muslim Dolls' arriving soon –
'They blow themselves up!' DJ volleyed back:
   'What's the difference between a balloon
and the PBI? A balloon won't scream
when you blow it up...' Pain letting off steam.

XIX

'Poor Bloody Infantry', that PBI,
   whose job in war's as dirty as you'd wish,
to kill the foe they're looking in the eye,
   to 'Fight In Someone's House' as they say – FISH,
in army jargon. Squaddies do and die
   and while DJ's Camilla was a dish,
she loved her FISH and CHIPS for Afghan treats –
CHIPS being 'Causing Havoc In People's Streets'...

XX

Not what they'd call last century PC –
   foreshortened wisdom of the acronym!
DJ and I show NPD and ADD,
   so telescoping all of me and him
to NHS file terminology.
   We're men of letters, yet you're still as dim
about the way our characters were set.
Does poetry transcend its alphabet?

XXI

(One acronym that chills some to the bone,
   the interweb being paranoid as Hell,
not needing much excuse to have a moan
   now whine about the NSA as well,
no longer needing bug or microphone
   or much excuse to stick you in a cell,
are damned for having spied on the EU,
in much the same way as GCHQ.)

XXII

Not quite your DSK, our hero-slob,
   DJ is all that we need call him by
for name, being name too of his so-called job –
   he borrows music, which is not what I
do: being a poet, music's what I rob
   as we the lands our forces occupy
till, like the Irish, at some future date
the Umma'll see the UK as its mate.

XXIII

A poem's tone, as Auden wrote a friend,
   should be like that of an intimate letter.
Poetry's a crossword in the end
   in which the reader sometimes is the setter,
a Scotch bard said, which might sound round the bend
   to some, but still, I like it rather better
than this art as therapy, education –
worse, aristocratic recreation:

XXIV

Lords and Ladies B,C,D,F,G
   with vowels on home leave from Baudelaire –
no: *Rimbaud* – through to Z (or US *Z*)
   the Scotch Gaels thought a whoreson one and spare,
so cut it, e.g. K, X, Q, since C
   with S does their jobs, noo required nae mair –
(the best thing about Gaelic in my eye?
It undoes Donne by making 'Island', *I*.)

XXV

Sic – sorry: *such* is only for wee chancers
   dootless – excuse me – without a doubt.
Today, among my paper's crossword's answers
   (clue: *'Liars Cameron is right about'*)
turns out to be, as you'll have guessed, *'Romancers'* –
   sincerity from verse is put to rout,
fun too, bar Paulyurethane Muldoon's,
who dances while he's playing his own tunes.

XXVI

'Writer enters composition' – that's *'Sterne'*,
   who enters my Byronic composition
just about at every other turn,
   since thievery's the poet's disposition –
carpe diem? *'Carpe'* isn't 'earn';
   entre nous, on the QT, sport's my mission:
anag, acronym and synonym
help hobbyhorse outstrip the Houyhnhnm.

XXVII

One acronym we all bought's RBS –
   excuse me while I give a little cough –
the *Royal* Bank of Scotland, and no less.
   Your banker's popular as Bobby Waugh,
for F&M but our bank did say yes,
   and would – to handouts from the public trough
to help them with their crushing onuses,
guaranteeing staff their bonuses.

XXVIII

Another acronym that once broke free
   (as Scots might in our archipelago)
to leave its meaning in a silver sea
   with consequences all of us would know,
the acronym in question being BP,
   which ebonized the Gulf of Mexico –
'But BP's *B* no longer stands for *British*,
pleaded Brits when Yanks were getting skittish.

XXIX

'Beyond Petroleum'! You have to laugh
   at strokes that BP campaign tried to pull:
I take my hat off to its PR staff –
   a 'green' oil company is beautiful.
The Gulf of Mexico would blow the gaff
   on that, but these are masters of the bull
whose mazy ways would lose a Daedalus –
but now Apollo would back-pedal us.

XXX

Hummerika, my not-so-new-found land,
   home of few braves now, although mostly free;
we thought you'd want a lot more oil to hand
   instead of fighting wars in Araby
against its ingrates on their endless sand –
   but still, we give you our apology,
though anything that Brits give can be bubble –
sorry: rhyming slang for Greek – still trouble!

XXXI

One example an historian picks on:
   *Clansmen: An Historical Romance
of the Ku Klux Klan* by Reverend Dixon;
   Cameron, its hero's called (by chance)
has Scots ancestry, a point he sticks on.
   Griffiths filmed this, then 'Intolerance',
accused of whitewashing the KKK –
but my attention's wandering far away:

XXXII

DJ's inflatable he called Camilla,
   lending his intent a certain frisson;
it might not be a cooer and a biller –
   nor yet hear duty calling and be gone,
in looks, though, this doll truly was a killer;
   (which obviously's a *sine qua non*
among the Romeos of PVC)
he'd lost Camilla's living company

XXXIII

Who'd soon found DJ the wrong kind of bore;
    she liked things cool and mathematical,
(you might feel here she's settling some old score...)
    his love was rather more fanatical,
Camilla'd met such drama kings before –
    emotionally autocratical,
Moody Judies, selfish, solipsistic –
she only liked real shells to go ballistic.

XXXIV

His doll stayed put when standards were unfurled,
    unstirred to hear the distant bugle's sound,
pneumatic as that girl in *Brave New World*:
    ideal for DJ on a quick rebound.
He dived on her, sank in – to be then hurled
    A over T and dick-first to the ground,
where, like the Fisher King, he nursed his rod,
and wept, and fell again to cursing God –

XXXV

And that reminds my god to moan again
    who has this wham-bam view of poetry
as intercourse between the gods and men
    and coitus uninterruptedly
getting to the point. I say: what then?
    Break out the cigarettes? Put on the tea?
Avoiding premature ejaculation
's half a writer's tactics in narration.

XXXVI

A while back, Rove (then Presidential aide)
    explained our brave new world's strange ways to me –
his point was Kafkaesque, yet still well made:
    the 'reality-based community'
was out of touch with it, he was afraid,
    being blinded by its need for clarity,
for facts and rational analysis –
hence its political paralysis...

XXXVII

'When Bishop Berkeley said there was no matter'
   (*esse est* something – once I'd have it pat),
at first it sounded so much insane chatter:
   this aide I thought was talking through his hat,
at first – but our world's madder than the hatter
   at his own tea party (fancy that!)
My muses don't include the muse of fiction,
writing untaxed by any such restriction.

XXXVIII

Desire to be a poet once seemed mad,
   yet nowadays such itches seem much madder;
insanity in poets might seem sad,
   but sanity among them's even sadder;
the times for poetry are worse than bad,
   with baby boomers pulling up the ladder,
public schoolkids running all that's left:
like Satan's hoof, the UK is now cleft

XXXIX

Again by class as nationality,
   by gender, region, colour – even taste
in our benighted lousy poetry;
   the jewels in its crown are so much paste,
its naked emperors too quick to see
   the land around their quads as so much waste:
if Byron sniffed a bit at rhyming cobblers,
nowadays the lords of verse throw wobblers.

XL

Landfill poets' low *esprit de corps*
   I try to lift and fill our souls with iron
(pity you can't see my thrust-out jaw,
   pugnacious as that portrait of Lord Byron);
I shout our kind of *tiocfaidh ár lá* –
   the bard as polarising class war siren,
pole-dancing round my controversial *I*
in high-heeled clogs, with gaiters to my thigh.

XLI

Perhaps my image strikes you as grotesque?
  The hallowed hollows out in time to camp,
while rebels tend to end up at a desk;
  the dialectics' march can give you cramp,
'Turns what was once romantic to burlesque';
  the poet, not the lady, is the tramp –
that's even when, like Byron, she's a snob:
the pose of worldly Marxoid's just the job.

XLII

I'd steal the clothes of scholar, lord or poet,
  (it's good to have a few spare souls to sell)
although the scholar and the poet know it
  earns the fate of thieves in Dante's Hell,
doomed to own no form – but undergo it,
  and you truly know our fleshly shell:
the tapeworm's appetite survives its host,
as love the lover in that crap film 'Ghost'.

XLIII

New Labour's brave old souls have had their day:
  the bubble burst, and they changed seats with those
who've made their piles and wanted to make hay:
  'And wild and high the '*Cameron's gathering*' rose!'
where *Cam* means 'bent', as 'out of true', 'agley' –
  the rest being from the Gaelic word for 'nose' –
I'll join those noses rooting in the trough,
not born for opposition, but to scoff.

XLIV

My weight balloons till coke must roll it back,
  like Byron, who the purgatives made pale;
our yo-yo diets' forward-pause-then-back
  are mirrors of the progress of this tale:
we detour here for some delicious snack,
  now there to get that garlic-buttered snail.
(I'm banking on being handsome when I die
to find my beauty in another's eye).

XLV

Once Ashdown spoke of Clegg as Lochinvar,
    that brave romantic gallant sung by Scott:
'So faithful in love and so dauntless in war'...
    Does that sound like Clegg to you? I'd say not:
old Paddy stretched there chivalry too far
    for Clegg, who played off tartans for his plot –
dispatching wounded Brown, none could be slicker:
he could claim his motto's '*I mak sikker*'.

XLVI

? Was named 'MacSikker' by Geoff Hill,
    among we dwarfish poets, King Magog,
Rapallo-cagefighting top of the bill
    with Prynne, his foil and alter ego Gog.
The outcome of their battle's undecided still,
    being fought in an impenetrable fog
(is Prynne why now your average college nerdsworth
shuns Lord Byron to study bloody Wordsworth?).

XLVII

'Battle!' 'Poetry Wars!' it makes me puke
    till I puke air: what war's like to a kid.
Yeats wrote about the billion fucks some Duke
    won't give for what the hipsters thought or did.
In real wars, you cock rifles, not a snook
    and military language we should rid
ourselves of includes *avant garde* – it's barmy!
None I've heard of fire on their own army.

XLVIII

My madrasa – 'School of Quietude' –
    taught me to churn out home-made, deadly verse,
which might seem passé to your cooler dude,
    but does a job all over foes or worse.
But we must put away this childish feud
    and *irritabile vatum*'s a curse
since now we're in the 'Post-Division Era',
battle-lines are newer and much clearer.

XLIX

Uncreative Writing's my new jam
   and more or less what I am doing here;
again lit crit gets lit by Uncle Sam
   whose Torch of Liberty makes all things clear
and printing off the internet's no scam –
   the NSA must do it twice a year.
I did ask Kenny for a photocopy:
Silence. Maybe he felt I was stroppy...

L

Anyway the whip's cracked by Apollo,
   champing, like his horses, at the bit.
From him this 'god of art' guff's rather hollow,
   given his small godlike view of it.
As far as I'm concerned, he talks pure *bolleaux* –
   reader: I can't serve you as is fit;
he won't accept digression has a function,
never mind ellipsis and disjunction,

LI

Fixing, godlike, on the straight and narrow.
   No road's straighter than DJ's to Hell,
where he must nurse his blunted Cupid's arrow.
   Proudest at the moment that he fell,
for what he's up to next, you need no Tarot,
   just the index. Apollo rings the bell
for one whose bell-end here's been wrung so hard;
who'll live, though hoisted with his own petard –

LII

Unlike another, as a new day broke:
   the real Camilla finds an IED...
no scream (as in poor DJ's bitter joke),
   a shivering of air is all you see,
a mirage mirroring a puff of smoke.
   The letter killeth still, believe you me –
of course you can't. Her death's another lie.
In worlds of letters, only authors die.

RACHEL HADAS

I

Don Juan stretched and yawned. Was he awake?
   Where had he been carousing all night long?
He saw a soft green hill, a distant lake,
   While morning birds tuned up their sleepy song.
Bucolic enclave... while the drowsy rake
   Pauses in mid-career 'twixt right and wrong
To fold his sleeping bag and tie his shoes,
I'll pay quick homage to the pastoral muse.

II

What many of us seek in the green wood
   (I speak for poets; Byron understands)
Is something not too far from solitude:
   Some peace and quiet and congenial friends
Scattered throughout a tranquil neighbourhood
   Of hills and farms and fields. Then summer ends.
It's time to sigh – the country is so pretty –
Then head back to one's day job in the city.

III

School's back in session now. What do I teach?
   A variegated field is poetry,
Its reading and its writing; pleasures each
   Challenging in a distinctive way.
Language – vocabulary, syntax, speech –
   Blend with emotion, slice and dice, sauté...
Why such a spate of culinary tropes
When there are others? I teach them the ropes,

IV

Map various terrains, say tragedy
   And comedy, the epic or the sonnet.
Genres exist on which they can rely.
   A friend gives us an arm, we lean upon it.
Mythic constructions help them feel their way
   From Homer to Shakespeare to Vonnegut.
When students turn to their own poetry,
They blossom into versatility.

V

Possibility and limitation
   Are the themes here: what's new and what is not,
The space afforded by imagination
   In which to soar; which realms are separate
And yet how much we share. Communication,
   Young poets are too liable to forget,
Is one *sine qua non* of versifying.
To teach this isn't easy. I keep trying.

VI

We left his lordship waking in a field
   Criss-crossed by hedges of *ottava rima.*
Lean on some limits and behold! They yield;
   Meander as you please within the schema
Of rime and stanza. Form's a sturdy shield.
   Extravagance and safety are the theme – a
Congenial pair, at once walled in and free,
Offering a fertile site for poetry.

VII

Lines cross the page and bodies move in space.
   Don Juan wakes; this poet shakes her head.
What appetites nudge us from place to place?
   'Don't worry about plot; Byron never did,'
Advised my kindly correspondent. Trac-
   Ing what a character has said or read
Proves easier than pushing on the story.
Let's say we find him in mid-trajectory,

VIII

Drowsy, confused, hungover, hungry – more,
   Uncertain if his past was all a dream.
The list of women – he cannot keep score –
   Is out of keeping with the sleepy green
Field he now strolls through, though his feet are sore,
   In search of eggs, or strawberries and cream.
Finally he spies a sign of humanity –
Hand-made, hand-painted, nailed to a tall tree.

IX

His hopes of breakfast, though, must be deferred.
  This is no rural restaurant he sees;
The sloppy painted letters spell a word
  That seems incongruous among the trees.
He knows the concept, but he hasn't heard
  Discussion of abstractions like these
Since his days (did he dream them?) at the 'varsity,
Studying classics and philosophy.

X

Yet the green theatre of pastoral
  Provides a venue good as any other
For tuneful arguments on matters moral
  Or ethical or logical. Why bother
Pretending that such topics should be for all
  Tastes? Still, this scenic sylvan world of brother
Shepherds' competing ditties is ideal
For the pursuit of what the letters spell.

XI

Musing, Don Juan reads it: MEDITATION.
  As in what lucky Tityrus can do
On his shepherd's pipe? Or cogitation
  Of past and future, choices old and new
He's made or will make – that inward narration
  Which thanks to subjectivity feels true?
He's wondering, when from behind the tree
Appears a damsel with a cup of tea.

XII

'You look tired and thirsty; do sit down,'
  Says this blond angel, handing him the cup.
He takes it gratefully. 'Might one ask your name,
  My dear?' and drains the beverage in one gulp.
'My name is Mandala; this is my home,' –
  She gestures toward a tent whose flowered flap
Had been concealed by the leaves' dappled shadow;
He'd taken it for a patch of flowery meadow.

XIII

Behind her in the woodland row on row
    Of neat green tents he notices, from which
Yawning and smiling people issue now
    With a quiet buzz of cheerful morning speech.
But in a trice the tents are folded (how-
    Ever this is done, it's with dispatch)
And all sit down cross-legged on the ground
Or rug or mat, attentive to the sound

XIV

Of a struck gong. Ommmm! The echoes fade
    Gradually. She hisses; 'Meditate!
I'll explain later.' So in the tree's shade
    Don Juan obediently takes a seat...
Memories file past him in a weird parade.
    The early episodes look clear, the late
Foggy and blurry, all the in-betweens
Chaotic, slivered into smithereens.

XV

He knows his name, for starters: Donny Jon,
    Don Juan, DJ, Donald Johnson – all
These will work. But where he hails from,
    Of what country he's a national,
What language he is written in: strange, none
    Of these questions has a rational
Or easy answer. And he doesn't care.
Decades drift away like puffs of air.

XVI

Seville, an island, a harem, and more
    Flash through his head and float off like balloons.
What driving forces – lust, risk, and desire –
    Turned him and all those women to buffoons?
Fierce appetites, a longing to acquire
    A bit of flesh? Of love? His memory spins
Like a broken compass' dizzy arrow.
The past is wobbly. What about tomorrow?

XVII

Who he was, what he did, when – all unclear.
  But a less murky matter than plot, time,
Place, and the details of his career,
  Is that he led his life in blocks of rhyme,
In eight-line stanzas with an easy flair.
  His life was giddy, but not so the form.
As bows tied round wrapped presents make them smart,
Each final couplet gleams with careful art.

XVIII

All his past lives, however picaresque,
  Libidinous, ditsy, improvisatory
Humorous, satirical, grotesque,
  Are strung together on a chain of story.
Wearing a domino as at a masque,
  The more he hides himself then all the more he
Is unmistakable. The clever poet
Is barely in disguise; he knows we know it.

XIX

This train of thought, if that is what it is,
  Another gong derails, and now all rise
And smile and stretch; again the peaceful buzz
  Of conversation. 'May I ask you, Miss
Mandala, just what is the point of this
  Silent exertion (is that what it is?)?
Behind my eyes my whole life is careening.
What's the idea, intention, or meaning?'

XX

And so they stroll apart a little way
  And softly she expatiates the Dharma,
The path from which mankind is apt to stray,
  As well as the mysterious laws of karma.
What happens is no accident, okay?
  We reap what we have sown. With all the charm a
Girl has who is blooming if ascetic,
Her doctrine is to DJ quite emetic,

XXI

With its stern stress upon renunciation.
    The world, the flesh – but what to do for fun?
Poised for perpetual reincarnation,
    Cutting off pleasures we have just begun –
Is virtue then to be one's sole vocation?
    This thorny path is not for everyone,
Surely, although one piece of it does ring
True for him: change, which runs through everything

XXII

So uncontrollably that yesterday's
    Fond fantasy this morning's dream erases.
Each fresh desire redesigns a maze
    Through which we're drawn by serial pretty faces.
But any pleasure once obtained decays,
    And on we roam toward other, greener places.
The Noble Truths contain this common sense:
Appetite slaked leads to indifference.

XXIII

Still, to this pastoral interlude all hail!
    He thanks her gallantly and packs his gear,
Seeking another turning of the trail
    At some more suspenseful spot than here.
We're each in quest of our peculiar grail
    And quickly sated once it does appear,
But his solution isn't to renounce.
A predator will choose his prey, then pounce.

XXIV

And yet somehow the equanimity,
    Calm, or indifference, or all intertwined
His gentle docent taught beneath that tree
    Linger subliminally in his mind.
The newest conquest, whosoe'er she be –
    Even moving towards her, he's resigned
To disappointment, as a brand new flavour
Is gradually leeched of zest and savour.

XXV

Here let us leave him in this milder mood
   (As narrative can do) and press Rewind.
Whence had he wandered into the dim wood
   Of meditators? Reader, never mind.
I don't know. I'd tell you if I could.
   But let me improvise some intertwined
Plotlines of prior possibility,
Backstories – briefly – numbering at least three,

XXVI

Answering questions like precisely how
   He came to this green juncture midcareer.
We make up stories. I remember now
   An image that for decades has stayed clear,
As childhood reading does for me (and you?):
   The Wood Between the Worlds. That leap from here
To there, the magic pools beneath the trees –
Perhaps DJ fell into one of these,

XXVII

As Polly and Diggory in their various quests
   Fall into Charn and later stumble in-
To Narnia, and we know all the rest.
   I love that Lewis makes the tale begin
From randomness: courageous children, pressed
   By a wicked uncle, in between
Separate realms of being manage to
Discover a place unnamed, pristine, and new.

XXVIII

The Magician's Nephew and *DJ*?
   Apples and oranges, I don't deny.
Yet Lewis had read Byron, certainly.
   More to the point this minute is that I
Know both, and take one strand of fantasy
   And get to splice it into a backstory.
Why is our hero wandering like a fool?
Perhaps he jumped into some magic pool.

XXIX

The possibilities are myriad –
  One of the great joys of confabulation.
Alternative to the pool scenario: had
  Don Juan been subject to rustication?
A university career gone bad –
  Whores, failures, gambling debts, defenestration:
Take any, all; no need to pick and choose.
How generous the non-generic Muse!

XXX

A paradise must argue, after all,
  Expulsion. If he wanders in the wood,
There's been some garden, there has been a fall.
  No need to spell this out; it's understood.
Of all things, I've been reading, in Nepal,
  Paradise Lost, which still is pretty good.
Lost Eden? We assume this, then forget,
But riding an elephant may remember it,

XXXI

In silence, through the grasslands, into dense
  Forest as thick as Milton's virgin scene.
Mahout and *howdah*; slow magnificence
  Of our plodding passage in between
Tall underbrush that forms a kind of fence
  Screening us from the utterly unknown.
That lithe proboscis wreathed, though not in play,
But pulling grasses, snacking through the day.

XXXII

Digression piled upon digression –
  Nor am I done with these meanderings.
The pool into a new world; the young man
  Sent down for any one of many things
From university – to these add one
  Further possibility, which brings
To DJ's picaresque a darker hue.
In this plot, his sanity must go.

XXXIII

In this scenario DJ plays the rake
    Indeed, but not the flash Byronic kind;
Rather the type who pays for his mistake
    By losing past and future – i.e. his mind;
And – gentle, helpless – needs some place to take
    Him in; no mere vacation to unwind,
But some safe haven lunatics will come
To, with luck: a sanitarium.

XXXIV

His wanderings in this version will seem
    Like an amnesiac's fumblings with the tale
Of who he is. Identity, past, name –
    The weakening grasp of memory makes these all
Equally meaningless and all the same.
    One's former life looms large or shrinks down small,
But once that mind has lost its grasp, the life
Floats free. I've learned this firsthand, as the wife

XXXV

Of someone lithe and nimble with his brain
    Who wrote, composed, and played piano, chess,
Until – no telling when – some secret drain
    Commenced; his brilliance grew slowly less,
With his ability to speak, act, plan;
    Aphasia took the place of liveliness.
And now ten years have passed. He's dumb and meek
As a sick baby, lamb, or lunatic.

XXXVI

Dementia makes a genre change its key.
    Satire and lust turn tender, gentle, mild.
Arias of insult and ribaldry
    Give way to someone crooning to a child –
Anne Trulove and Tom Rakewell, Q.E.D.
    Could this be why DJ was no more wild
When we encountered him in the green meadow
Than Tom when he had lost the game with Shadow?

XXXVII

Even absent some mental malady,
   It's possible to judge our hero strayed
Into a different pasture from what he
   Intended, or what we sat down to read.
Hero or poet: both might equally
   Wander from their neatly mapped-out road
Into some world where different rules obtain
And sexy scapegraces are sought in vain.

XXXVIII

If poetry abruptly switches mode,
   Well, so does life. We start with comedy;
Then sunny mornings vanish into cloud,
   Our optimism unexpectedly
Dunking its brilliant prospects deep in mud.
   Or melodrama turns to tragedy,
Or a disaster comes out not too bad,
Etcetera. (See Shakespeare's sonnet: 'Why
Didst thou promise such a beauteous day?')

XXXIX

Perhaps such modal morphing and confusion
   Explain our hero's entrance *medias res*
And my tale's failure to move toward a conclusion.
   The action ambles at a gentle pace,
Mild mystery without any solution,
   Joke with no punch line, nothing we can trace
In the way of logic or suspense;
At most a sense of dreamy immanence.

XL

Dreamy! Of all the reasons we found Don
   Juan wandering in the green glade,
The realm of Morpheus is surely one
   Not to discount: he was asleep in bed
(Or somewhere else – say napping in the sun)
   And dreaming his strange wanderings instead
Of living them. All of us sometimes swim
In such murky waters; life can seem

XLI

Dreamlike. As Keats wrote, 'Do I wake or sleep?'
  (Did Byron know the *Nightingale*? Don't know.)
My own dream fragments on this recent trip
  Have furnished a kaleidoscopic show
Of past and future, shattered and opaque
  But vivid with recoveries, as if no
Least piece were lost, the lived, the still to come
Equal in the aorist of dream.

XLII

Yet sequence, order, story, incident
  Do provide footholds to which memory clings.
We keep a clearer sense of what is meant
  If episodes are strung like beads on strings
In dreams. Just so a tale-teller's intent
  Helps focus our attention, and brings
Pleasure through the sense of forward motion
Which is what we look for in narration.

XLIII

We left DJ in Stanza 25
  And wandered off without him. So rewind:
Put shoulder to the wheel of narrative?
  Try to intuit what he had in mind
(No easy matter)? But he's still alive
  And urged by appetite, like all mankind.
Some things never change, although it's true
Change grows too changeable (Stanza 82)

XLIV

Without being new adds Byron (Canto XI).
  Plus ca change, I take it, is his theme.
I'm 62. The year is 2011.
  We're all still motivated by the dream
Of – satisfaction? Bliss? Some earthly heaven.
  Generic templates follow the same scheme:
Conflict, adventure, wanderlust: we roam,
Rebel, grow old and weary, and come home,

XLV

Living through quest and flight and fantasy
  Or tying hopeful knots of celebration:
Leaving behind whatever culture we
  Have shaped to benefit a generation
Still to come. We will not live to see
  The destiny of this accumulation;
Will (say) this poem prove a proud possession
Or simply one more thing to deaccession?

XLVI

But let me to my story. I must own,
  If I have any fault, it is digression,
Leaving my people to proceed alone
  While I soliloquize beyond expression,
Byron admits – a fault that's also mine,
  So let me share in his urbane confession.
Into a poem's basket one can fling
Digressions about almost anything.

XLVII

Into soliloquy narration slides:
  Musings on history, politics, and art,
Perennial, mutable... thus Byron glides
  From the Whigs to his own weary heart,
With notes on travel and a lot besides.
  Each *ottava* stanza's a fresh start.
I ne'er decide what I shall say, and this I call
(Bowing ironically) *much too poetical.*

XLVIII

Men should know why they write, and for what end
  (He scribbles, shrugs his shoulders). *Note or text,*
(Half boast and half a weakness to defend),
  I never know the word which will come next.
The automatic Muse can be a friend,
  Even if her vagaries leave us perplexed.
Divine afflatus? Bardic inspiration?
Or something else much closer to dictation?

XLIX

So Byron wanders, and so does DJ,
  And so do I, back into the green wood,
In some ways tethered and in others free
  To stray to any pasture that looks good,
Constrained by art or else by destiny
  (However these vague terms are understood) –
Otherwise free to manage our affairs
Just as we please, since no-one really cares.

L

We left Don Juan waiting patiently,
  Preoccupied and dreamy, in a daze,
While I traced the several paths that he
  Might have pursued to that point, various ways
To reach the place we found him, sleepily
  Coming to consciousness *in medias res.*
Some whys and hows were sketched in, more or less,
Though who he is is anybody's guess.

LI

Byron's describes Juan's youthful love affair
  With sympathy and wit, satire and zest,
And strings along the escapades from there –
  Shipwreck, Haidée, harem, and all the rest –
All swallowed up into anterior
  Amnesia. Fleeting memories are the best.
The future waits, a virgin page. And then
The absent-minded Muse picks up her pen.

LII

Enough of sitting! DJ finds his feet
  And strolls down a dirt road. At the first town
He comes to, ambling down its main street
  He spies a small white building and looks in.
Shelves, tables, chairs. A traveller's retreat?
  A caravansary (that is, an inn)?
Since my Don Juan isn't Levantine,
I'll use plain English to say what I mean.

LIII

He found a bed and breakfast three doors down
    And so is in no need of a hotel.
But back to this small structure he is drawn,
    As one attracted by a savoury smell
Or strain of music ventures further on.
    What the attraction is he cannot tell.
I think I can, though. What is it he lacks?
This is a library, and these are books.

LIV

The understated power of such places!
    They let us riffle through humanity,
Its highs and lows, its triumphs and disgraces,
    Absorbing knowledge idiosyncratically,
Guided by taste and chance, at our own paces,
    Half choosing and half groping. And when we
Read, we are both alone and not alone,
A fruitful paradox for poor Don Juan,

LV

Who's travelled, fought, and f*cked; but has he read?
    We aren't told. He's studied, to be sure.
No doubt his bookish mother Inez made
    The life of the intellect seem a dreary bore.
And Donna Julia tutored him in bed
    In other fields than academic lore.
Their story shows how abstract speculation
Mingled with hormones yields up fornication.

LVI

What Juan signally has lacked is leisure,
    Or *otium*, as Horace used to write.
Action, disaster, danger are his pleasure:
    Risk, disguise, escape, seduction, fight
Are the criteria by which to measure
    His young life's quality – which is all right
For thrillers and romances, bodice-rippers
(Is the male equivalent ripped zippers?).

LVII

But that was in his youth, and youth is over.
   Our DJ (though he's ageless, he's not young)
Is less inclined by now to be a lover
   And more to browse and ruminate among
Paths in a wood he has yet to discover.
   He senses life is short and art is long
And many virgin streams from which to drink
Await him, places he can sit and think

LVIII

And read: the pleasure of non-doing, what
   Mandala had preached in the green wood
We found our hero wandering in. But
   Cannot inaction best be understood
At times not only as the path of thought
   But diving into books as the great good,
Where there are untold riches to discover
For one who is no longer a young lover?

LIX

Much have I travelled in the realms of gold
   And many goodly states and kingdoms seen:
Keats's grand tour, truncated, is soon told.
   Round many western islands have I been
Which bards in fealty to Apollo hold.
   He knows we will construe these lines to mean
He tropes his reading as itinerary;
His Grecian cruise is purely allegory.

LX

Contrast DJ's creator, who indeed –
   Self-exiled, restless, not without resources –
Left home definitively, hit the road
   Attended by a retinue: ape, horses,
A whole menagerie, and, yes, books to read,
   But was distracted; love affairs ran their courses,
Messy, tempestuous. Life didn't stop.
Each isle of Greece looked luminous with hope,

LXI

But faded closer up – no steadfast star
   Like Keats's virgin vision of desire
Coveted and studied from afar,
   But smoky, ashy as a dying fire.
Dabbling in love, conspiracy, and war,
   He lived so hard that he began to tire.
You'd think he'd then slow down and rest and read,
But somehow Byron wrote *Don Juan* instead.

LXII

The irony is Byron never could
   Have spun his hero's story out in rhyme
If he himself had not been so well-read.
   His precocious hero, though, lacks time
To sit, peruse – he wants to live instead.
   The poet and his creation are the same
In rarely sitting still to ruminate.
(Hence DJ had to learn to meditate.)

LXIII

So DJ ventures in (it's just one room,
   Not crowded), finds a chair, leans back, and sighs.
Others are there, but no-one looks at him;
   No flirtatious glances, batted eyes.
Not that the place is silent as a tomb.
   Low exchanges, questions, and replies
Are audible, but the attention seems
To be on some interior. Whether dreams

LXIV

Or memories or data, everyone
   Appears abstracted, seeking a solution
Either to some private question
   Or stubborn riddle needing resolution
Or an assignment needing to be done.
   He notes the quiet buzz with some confusion.
And yet how peaceful! No-one seems perplexed
He's here, and no-one cares what he'll do next.

LXV

His chair is comfortable. As I've said,
  He leans back in it, shifts his weight, and sighs,
And dozes off. No wonder. Seeing that bed
  Has been for him these past two centuries
Not a place for sleeping but instead
  Devoted to more active exercise,
The poor man's tired. Let him nap. He wakes
Before too long, collects his wits; stands; takes

LXVI

A step toward the shelf, where books are waiting
  With that patience only books possess
(Not crazed like *homo sapiens* when mating).
  He knows what he is after, more or less:
Not page-turners, but something more sedating,
  Some sort of respite from the headlong pace
At which he used to live. Philosophy?
Close, but no cigar. Ah: poetry!

LXVII

A source of refuge and a looking-glass,
  Reflective haven where we see our own
Image as it is and as it was.
  He can sit still and let the verses run
Before him, like a slow car others pass.
  In their haste to get some journey done,
Pedal to metal they are hurrying – where?
In this room DJ finds he doesn't care.

LXVIII

The poems matter, not the name or date
  Of poets. Here is Shelley, his late friend,
Revising on a visionary note
  Prometheus, who now seems to be unbound;
And here is an obscure New England poet
  With some of the same images in mind.
Both let life or death pass calmly by,
While they observe them. Whether lyrically

113

LXIX

Or wryly written or in a neutral tone,
  Their visions are uncannily alike.
Writes Emily: 'We passed the Setting Sun –
  Or rather – He passed Us –'. And spirits evoke
In Shelley's drama a mystic voyage down
  From *Age's Icy Caves* to *Manhood* back
To *Youth* and *Shadow-Peopled Infancy.*
Both poets trace a path for us to see

LXX

Beyond the private niche of generation
  A grander flow of time construed as space:
Those icy caves, a frozen Arctic ocean,
  That setting sun we watch from a safe place.
Of course our fleeting lives remain in motion,
  Yet as observers we feel motionless.
We're sitting in life's library; years roll
By and we read them as if from a scroll.

LXXI

And so the Don: each line on which he chances
  Opens a vista into his own past,
His escapades and perils and romances,
  As if in two dimensions: first and last
Experiences memory equally enhances.
  Memory? Poetry. Nothing is lost;
All is immediate and vivid, yet
Remote and patterned as a minuet.

LXXII

Some poems seem conceived for him alone.
  Within their structure, one incandescent line
('Because I could not stop for Death' is one)
  Bypasses eyes, goes straight to heart and brain
As if the poet wrote with him in mind –
  His boyhood path, his pleasures, and his pain.
Hasn't he lived his life as if cessation
Or even slowing down meant annihilation?

114

LXXIII

The generosity of poetry
  Is new to our tired hero, as he browses
And naps and ponders his biography
  Strangely mirrored by these friendly muses.
He lingers in the library all day
  Until a mild but pleasant pang arouses
A consciousness that it is time to dine.
Fresh local fare; a single glass of wine;

LXXIV

And then to bed. And then to bed alone.
  Next day he's at the library once more,
Contentedly abstracted until noon.
  And, gentle reader, let us leave him there.
His day, his journey, ours – they all march on
  To destinations scattered everywhere.
Still, we might sketch a clutch of destinies.
DJ and reader, choose whiche'er you please.

LXXV

First, since our tale is set, presumably,
  Squarely in the information age,
DJ might face the new technology,
  The screen instead of a mere printed page,
With implications for psychology –
  New skills to master, new qualms to assuage.
Our Don might well turn cyberman complete.
Does he spend hours on Facebook? Does he tweet?

LXXVI

The net, the web: this gap that yawns between
  Byron's generation and now:
Hiatus hardly vaster than my own
  Willed ignorance of what people get up to
(Both young and not so young) when they're online
  (And when aren't they online?) This much I know:
Byron loved and his hero loves distraction,
All kinds of interaction and attraction.

LXXVII

Leaving that thread, let's turn instead to knowledge.
    Another way our hero's way might wend:
Would be for DJ to enrol in college –
    Sequestered space and time to make a friend
And to assemble a personal *bricolage*,
    An intellectual construct. To what end
Who knows? Still, an amusing episode
(And note those muses) – succour for the road

LXXXVIII

Ahead. Perhaps he'll get an MFA.
    Having emerged from the imagination,
Don Juan does have a feel for poetry.
    If being a *picaro* was his first vocation,
He's grown into a taste for prosody,
    For satire and mock-epic and narration.
A genre many writers now find attractive
Is memoir. When your life has been quite active,

LXXIX

Having first lived it, then sit down and shape
    It into story: love and war, seduction,
Shipwreck and harem, joy, despair, and hope
    Come alive through character and action.
Adultery, cannibalism, rape
    When versified take on a new complexion.
As we live our lives we look ahead,
But writing them makes us look back instead.

LXXX

So he may choose to get an MFA,
    Become a poet or write a memoir.
Another question lingers: whether he
    Will find a person suitable to share
This quite serene new life domestically.
    I see no major difficulties here:
The passage of a century or two
Has not harmed his ability to woo.

LXXXI

Into his lap the women seem to topple
  (Such was Byron's experience, at least),
Supplying both companionship and trouble.
  He wonders if the single life is best,
But what if mating means the joy is double
  And pain's divided, breast by loving breast?
Perhaps this is a formula to try.
Can we expect a wedding by and by?

LXXXII

Nuptials are a satisfactory way
  Of ending plays and novels: celebration
(So long as the mode is comedy)
  In joyful bibulous anticipation
Of a new production, a new day,
  And (bottom line) a brand-new generation.
Our story isn't quite in comic mode,
Though neither is it tragedy. Instead

LXXXIII

DJ's part satire and part picaresque,
  And part the well-known story of a rake,
Versified, yet avoiding the grotesque,
  With plenty of digressions for the sake
Of intellectual hijinks: arabesques,
  Meanders, and in sum a big baroque
Generic hybrid with no proper ending.
My hero, I predict, will keep on wending

LXXXIV

His way through space and time. He'll read and learn,
  For he has reached a contemplative stage.
He will not marry; neither will he burn.
  Two centuries old, he's shy of middle age.
Each episode unfolds, then takes a turn –
  And off he goes before we turn the page
In search of greener grass and pastures new
Where he'll discover something else to do.

117

W.N. HERBERT

... I must be fated
To wander and to change; when the mast creaks
I smell the salt and know my soul unsated
Until it finds the language no man speaks.
Edwin Morgan

Thus the doors of the sea and the keys of the universe, with
anything of a reasonable sort of management, will of course
enable its proprietors to give laws to both oceans...
William Paterson

Look at the map.
Chekhov

J'ai seul la clef de cette parade sauvage.
Rimbaud

I

I met him in Caracas on the Mount,
    a sermoniser from the outset, one
who shouts in mirrors, loud as life: the Count,
    slumped in a darkened cable car, alone,
apart from that quick voice; Milord, that fount
    of filth and fiery judgement – anglophone
but with Hispanic hints, all lisp and spit
dangling above the forest's tropic pit.

II

He had, he told me, taken on a floor
    of that disused hotel, the Humboldt, high
cylinder, symbol of the wealth before
    Chavez, before all Castro's hopeful lies,
Peron's romance of truth. Paused at the door,
    he apologised before I'd half-surmised
his motive, strode to open curtains on
fit Caribbean backdrop to – the Don.

III

Over a cheap *arepa* at the State-
    sponsored cafe, he mentioned how he'd bribed
a pretty tour guide for the key – he'd hate
    to get her into trouble, but described
his *Callipygita* so intimate-
    ly that the sort of trouble was transcribed
into a tender cursive by his mouth –
I asked how long had he adored the South?

IV

'I came here on a Dundee merchant ship
    as junior engineer. I crawled its keel,
the long propeller shaft, and felt the grip
    of tides along its vertebrae of steel.
We docked at Demerara's sugared hips,
    and drank until the Scotsmen couldn't reel.
I challenged one to swim the brown-lipped river –
they rescued me, but he went down to clabber.

V

'I jumped ship then and walked into the jungle,
   took work on cane plantations, hopped planes north.
I hunted capybara, learned to mingle
   with *Llanos* cowboys and *Guajiros* furth
of Orinoco; played harp, got entangled
   with Maracaibo oilmen's daughters worth
more than my life, so, jinking *mal' fortuna*,
sought haven on the islands of the Kuna...'

VI

'Before you tell me what they are,' I asked,
   'I know it's more than drifting drives you on,
or dodging the paternal bullet?' Tasked,
   he ordered rum, sat mum a while, then yawned.
'You want an Atlas of the soul... Alask-
   a links to Russia; Panama's a join;
the Horns are hinges to the Orient's door –
the Earth's a board game we can fold in four.

VII

'The Chinese thought that Heaven rested here
   at four fixed points upon their ancient map;
the Persians that four genies strained to bear
   the upper realms – we know now that's all crap,
but still conceive in joinery, think we're
   linked, that our economic quoins hold up
the whole world's roof, that nation speaks to nation
in Capital's one tongue without translation...

VIII

'Since Mercator unpeeled this fruitful globe
   and set her segments out for all to gauge,
the Earth's four edges' mystique's been disrobed –
   we realise the world is not a page;
but still we hope for pockets we can probe
   for keys to open our omniscient cage,
so to the corners of the continents
we look for ingress to our lost intents.

IX

'I wanted to cost human intimacy –
    the price paid for its lack, not just the ghosts
of lust we're haunted by or hunt, their lacy
    trace of love's spoor across the body's coasts
and hinterlands: the print of intricacies
    mind mints to trade between thought's guests, thoughts' host –
negotiating where we do not know
the stakes, what closenesses are only show?'

X

I watched him strain his arms out wide as though
    they'd reach around the earth and somehow touch;
next he bowed down until he clamped his jaw
    upon his glass – half-crucified, half-crouched,
both charlatan and sacrifice – swallowed
    a slug by snapping back in swift embouch –
and talked, as though I were his last acknowledger;
and talked, as though to amputate an onager.

XI

And what he said is carried over here –
    to versify is cutting through the truth
to find another verity: the sheer
    edge of its grain, the fact as foot, and both
translations of each other, bere to beer
    and beer as liquid bread: he said, 'To Youth!'
Our glasses clashed; I wrote, 'To Youth's departure.'
He lost himself to story, herein captured.

XII

He said, 'I woke up in an iron bed
    ringed by my public, in the attic room
of Love's Museum – rain's ecstatic threads
    belaboured at the Stamboul glass. Entombed
in Orhan's Innocence, I lay unread
    till closing time, then slunk into the gloom
of January, pausing at the shoppie
for a translation – but they had no copy.

XIII

'Climbing the hill past junk-shops, the *hammam*,
    I met two pals who claimed they browsed for busts
of Ataturk, and moaned that I'd become
    pseudo-Kemal, the Lazarus of lust –
that plague that feeds on neediness, shame's sham
    dictator, who spontaneously combusts
the tinder hearts of rutting's sad obsessives,
those who in social grammar are possessives...'

XIV

'I have to be the Porlock to your Khan:
    how did we get to Istanbul from – where
were we, exactly?' 'Broken up in Pan-
    ama, alas – la Kuna on the tear.
We'll see that lachrymose lagoon again
    before we have to leave this liars' lair...
first, after I woke up inside a book,
let's see the turn that Turkish evening took.

XV

'We argued over love as a museum,
    since letters can't preserve the flesh we've felt.
Lips' press on cigarette stubs are the dumb
    flex of time's perineum. Organs melt
like soap, our photos ghost us, mausoleums
    of glass hold raki relics – memory's pelt
hangs on the Sultan's wall to honour him,
and not the lover left without a limb.

XVI

'Another raki off the Rue de Pera –
    Ricardo, rancorous, declared Pamuk's
authorial hubris daunts mere pride – how dare he
    erect a monument to his own book?
Vida took theoretic task: compare a
    concept to a fiction: what's more worth a look?
I said I know where this can be resolved –
the Loser's Club, where reason is devolved.

XVII

'Istiklal's pavements cackled in the rain
   as we resumed our scuttling to Taksim.
(This was before the riots – or between,
   to be more accurate, since rights, it seems,
are always interim.) Now, in my brain
   the route was clear, or rather, in my dreams –
though we searched side-streets, asked in dim hotels,
the Loser's Club was washed away, like smells

XVIII

'Of cooking that would make your uncle cry...
   The irony of losing it began
to make itself clear, as we failures dried
   ourselves off in a tiny restaurant.
I hired an upstairs room – they fed the fire
   with broken furniture, and brought us scran
of Anatolia, ripped us off for whisky –
and we told tales about the lost grown frisky.

XIX

'The Loser's Club's no place that you can find
   and still be called a member – you and Groucho
already knew this – it's that state of mind
   that like a ghost dog tracks you, polter-pooch who
drunks meet in small hour streets and nameless wynds.
   It is that table, knocking when you slouch to
slumber, as though you'd let in reason's monsters.
Revolvers are its chambers, Scotch its minster.

XX

'Vida, mind on the Princes' Islands, ordered
   some grilled sardines and macaronic Greek
for 'Pussy Nisi' – where cats' numbers bordered
   on epidemic. "There Purr Pashas squeak
Turkish," she claimed, "and have all songbirds murdered.
   Should the catch fail, they'd eat us in a week.
Let wakes of feathers catch bread from our ferry:
farewell to felines, insular as worry!"

XXI

'Ricardo, thinking back to how we'd sprawled
    like bream upon Çemerlitaş's slab,
its pepper pot dome overhead, recalled
    how Sinan was caught idling on the job,
or so great Süleyman supposed, appalled
    he'd gone to Hagia Sofia for a nap.
His architect replied, "To best Justinian,
just listen to this silence of dominion."'

XXII

'What story did you tell?' 'Of Soutar Johnny,
    who was, while Tam o' Shanter played his field
of fancies shaped like females, making money –
    far likelier to cause gleg Kate to yield
than Tam's tall tale about his tail-less pony.
    And so he haunted her, till she revealed
that instrument her husband used to play,
and taught him tunes while Tammas was away.'

XXIII

He broke off suddenly, grinned and confessed,
    'All this is an extended metaphor
for something or someone I must repress –
    good faith, bad trade: it's what a symbol's for.
Some lovers find no profit in excess
    while others claim that love itself breeds more:
Having been both, I will not quantify
love's quantum here – I know you want to pry,

XXIV

'But power is atomised into each cell
    in which we meet – behind a bedroom door
or in a judge's chambers: one compels,
    if only the once; another must demur.
Pure continuity's craved by the self
    more than sex, and, if granted, how we whore
ourselves to those who save us from the facts,
permitting us to live in *entr'acte*.

XXV

'We took the ferry back in early morning,
　　the Bosphorus a laminate of moon
scattered with daylight's roe; watched gulls' slow turning,
　　high in the interstitial air, balloons
of mosques still almost rising; stayed out, spurning
　　the cabin's warmth to stir with plastic spoons
the *sahlep*'s hot and cinnamony trance –
and think of sleep, its arrogant advance.

XXVI

'Did I tell you the route to NovoTsargrad?'
　　he asked me suddenly, and I looked up:
his face was frozen over, crackled, haggard.
　　'We only met today.' 'That was some trip:
you might as well have crossed the bridge to Asgard –
　　no railway then, just boredom and the whip;
by tarantass, barouches, ferries, sleds,
a whaleship – to the Empire of the Dead!

XXVII

'You won't find where we went in any atlas,
　　and I should know because I drew the map:
cryptocartography's my field, the subtlest
　　of military arts – we fooled the Japs
for years until *katana* came to cutlass.
　　Atlantis of the Arctic Circle slipped
beneath the pack ice, Dallas Borealis,
the Bering Straits' Byzantium, sunk by malice...'

XXVIII

'You're saying there's a second Istanbul
　　between Siberia and Alaska?' 'Was,
dear boy, for centuries – we couldn't fool
　　the weather or the waking world, alas,
past Revolution, but before that fall
　　into the post-imperial crevasse,
there was a long-legged city straddling ice
where Greek was sung – a polar paradise.

XXIX

'To get there, though, was Purgatory worse
   than Dante had to clamber through – the mud
that jellied into boots; the stupid horse,
   the lame one; skeeters suckling on your blood;
your fellow officers, those maddening bores,
   bellowing re boots, horses, and bad food –
those sausages like dogs' tails dipped in tar;
then fish-faced bourgeois, brains like caviar –

XXX

'And everyone a writer – police inspectors,
   the college registrar – their poems, plays
and novels bursting from their breeches – actors
   sick for applause. One shadowed us for days:
pince-nez, a rusty cough, some Moscow doctor
   who must reform our prisons – people say
what tosh they like out there, no fear of trouble...
a card-game helped relieve him of his roubles

XXXI

'While waiting for the Baikal ferry, bored
   out of our fishless, milkless, breadless brains –
who fetches while there's vodka? We ignored
   the massive mirror of that sea, complained
competitively: best was first aboard,
   and straight into the galley to explain,
"*Cher* chef, my kingdom for a chicken soup!"
Filthy plate, horse-stink – and delicious gloop.

XXXII

'Halfway across you stare straight down a mile
   as though you woke to find yourself mid-cloud.
The whole ship shuddered like a convict while
   the hangman chats, and straightens out his shroud,
as though Leviathan gave us a smile
   and rose to swallow up both meek and proud.
We hit the shore, took horse, and, lathering leather,
escaped the lake, its dreadful placid weather.

XXXIII

'The doctor/writer came with us to catch
   the Amur ferry, though he couldn't stand
our boon companion, Schmidt, who liked to screech
   his arias as we rode. When he complained,
the loud lieutenant said, "Out here, we each
   must be as liberal as we understand."
This was the smartest thing that he'd professed,
and even passing beavers looked impressed.

XXXIV

'I fucked a Japanese professional
   while comets filled the cabin or my head –
fireflies, although they didn't seem that small.
   She did: I barely found her in my bed;
I steered by tits and tittering until
   her fold of cotton wiped up what I'd shed.
As I admired the lacquer of her locks
we turned, and in the doorway sat a fox.

XXXV

'And that was when we started going mad:
   the mountains were too mountainous, too high;
the laughter from next door too shrill, too sad;
   the tea was far too hot, the fox too shy,
and far-off Vladivostok, well, too Vlad.
   Each thing was so itself it seemed a lie:
the Chinaman I shared with smoked his pipe,
freaked out to find himself a holotype.

XXXVI

'From Khabarovsk we followed when the river
   skewed north, as though it fled the failing sun;
and commandeered the boat in that endeavour,
   endearing us to crew, whores, everyone
(Lieutenant Schmidt would cause a bear to shiver).
   So, no love lost, the Amur our bad pun,
we left the hawthorn and the poplar's slopes
for sandbanks and Sakhalin's lack of hope.

XXXVII

'I've drawn the island like a drowned girl's husk,
    her profile stares at Russia, at her back
a roaring, ice-clogged sea, the raw Okhotsk.
    We missed the final lighthouse, caught the smoke
a whaler's stack sent up into the dusk.
    A filthy crossing almost saw us wrecked,
and then, upon the *Kelet*'s prow, an eagle
the captain had chained there: old Empire's signal.

XXXVIII

'We left the women – fair enough exchange:
    convicts need wives, and we required supplies.
Above the vast trench of the deep, estranged
    from anywhere, with fishscales in our eyes,
we passed Kamchatka's charged volcanic range –
    calderas' spume and whale-steam equalised.
The wind appeared to skin us of our names,
but still the stink of blubber clung like shame.

XXXIX

'The captain's name, Atlasov, stuck with me
    because this sea, he claimed, was only charted
on his brain's parchment – and his ancestry
    included that brave Cossack who cavorted
down the peninsula on murderous sprees
    till butchered in his bed. Each morning started
with his releasing of the eagle, who
then promptly caught a salmon both would chew.

XL

'He kept no log, and so we didn't know
    how long it took to reach the whalebone walls
of NovoTsargrad: twenty feet high snow-
    packed ribs they topped with giant greying skulls.
Chukotka warriors manned the checkpoints, so
    we had to wait there for three days until
a *dragoumanos* came from Diomede,
the island where Vyronas has his seat.

130

XLI

'Chukotka like to tell cod tales, Atlasov
　　to mistranslate – we sat below the glow
of baleful bile auroras, rendered passive
　　by vodka and accounts of that freakshow
emperor: his girl-headed flies; his massive
　　sea-worms that cough up frozen ships; the two
gold-tusked guard-walruses that flank his throne
astride the dateline; his own timeless zone.

XLII

'Vyronas was a demigod or despot,
　　though which precisely seemed to be unclear.
The Bering Straits were certainly his piss-pot:
　　each trapper, whaler, fisher owed his share,
and vassal tribes like theirs must live in cesspits
　　while he reclined on pelts of polar bear;
from *Avrio Anaktoron*, in quartz
and ice and ivory, he controlled their ports.

XLIII

'Some said he fled Byzantium at the Fall,
　　while others claimed he'd led the '21 –
all knew him as white-armoured, mute-mouthed, tall
　　beyond all tribesmen, speaking to no-one
except his daughter, and invulnerable
　　to arrow or harpoon – they'd pinned him down
that last rebellion, shattered all their spears –
he'd fed their hearts to his eight-legged bears.

XLIV

'His daughter, Ada, famously would ride
　　to take the census on a mammoth's back;
her quick wits saw her ruling at his side,
　　her saga on his reign was just the facts
in fifteen vols; she swam against the tide
　　two miles to warn him of the Yanks' attack –
I wondered as we finally retired
what further gifts of hers I might admire?

XLV

'They'd lock us in a concrete lookout tower –
  though where we'd go they knew we'd no idea.
The curtains rustled as in Ada's bower –
  except there were no curtains: what we'd hear
were cockroach colloquies and bugs in showers,
  pouring through ceiling cracks to crawl in ears
and sleeves and boots. *Hôtel Splendide* it wasn't –
each morning we awoke bamboozled, dozent.

XLVI

'Remember how the Norse gods, Loki, Thor,
  on reaching Jotunheim, put themselves up
in an abandoned mead-hall hung with fur,
  sharing its bedroom, gurning at this slap
in the face – no-one feasting them – before
  they recognised the hall where they had slept:
a giant's mitt. And so we passed the night,
awaiting Hermes in the dawn's lame light.'

XLVII

And as he finished dawn was rolling in
  to fill the valleys eastward to the sea.
We ordered coffee, watched a dorsal fin
  of mist roll over in the rising heat
through caffeinated steam. Where to begin?
  'Did you and this Vyronas ever meet?
Was he the poet?' 'Who?' 'Is this a ploy?
How did Byzantium become Dalstroy?'

XLVIII

'I met a poet once in Africa...'
  'I have to know: how did that radical
of morals and poetics... please, what flaw
  metamorphoses Byron...' 'What do d'ye call
him?' '... into Berzin?' 'Him I did once know –
  ironically in Philly. I recall
that loveless *bratka* browsing gramophones –
the greedy troll-king played Grieg to his drones.'

XLIX

'But back to Africa, upon the Horn...'
   – And so he'd leap; impossible to steer
away from veering, as befits one born
   to variation; schooled by bitter years
in deft digression, he had come to scorn
   frankness the way a vintner would scorn beer.
Put plainly, good plain English was obtuse:
for any muse but fog he had no use.

L

'I was with Burton down in Berbera
   when Speke was spiked eleven times and lived –
he didn't talk about it much, whereas
   Ricardo would orate in volumes vivid
as that Somali spear that pierced his jaw
   on themes like Harar's emir who perceived
the glint of British greed behind his pose –
which was why Rimbaud liked me, I suppose.'

LI

'Really. Where was this?' 'Aden, probably,
   Perhaps *Le Grand Hôtel de l'Univers* –
the heat is not an aid to memory.'
   'And you ran guns?' 'Well, I was barely there,
too stoned to be particular, while he...
   with him you'd never know, you'd just infer.
He never spoke, or far too much, as though
words were another way of saying no.'

LII

'You must have known your cargo.' 'We'd spend weeks,
   months, in some port that was a dozen shacks,
a score of *akal*s made of rags and sticks,
   awaiting papers, paying *bakshish*, "tax";
our goods stacked in the shade where shady Greeks
   appended theirs. You can't prepare, relax –
"L'air de Djibouti égare les sens..." Time crazes,
And things take *longtemps* in these filthy places.

LIII

'Eventually you leave before the dawn –
  a hundred camels and a hundred men,
a legion entering the burnt place on
  an instinct passing commerce: to depend
on no man's system. Rest each afternoon,
  then march till, kraaled in dark, your last defence
is what the camels sense: they'll chew the cud,
then stop and point, then piss themselves with dread.

LIV

'Somalis milk a camel reaching up
  so juggle with their milk-jug and one knee –
a sort of yoga pose to fill your cup.
  Each supper was a slap of rice and ghee;
his silence by the fireside – up he'd hop,
  and off: don't think I ever saw him sleep.
Each morning there he'd stomp, the most awake,
left shoulder leading, hauling in his wake

LV

'The whole shebang of dromedaries, goods,
  clansmen, armed Abyssinians, unarmed mules,
and even me, poor drochle of the brood
  of Donna Ines, in his shoes, the soles
of which, of Afar make, were heeled and toed
  the same way, suitable, he said, for fools
like us, who don't know if we come or go
avec semelles de vent on sand or snow.

LVI

'Those times that terrify the most – our deaths
  (our own, our others' – those that love must claim) –
burn out time's circuitry: are space, have depth.
  The consciousness imagines it must calm
the panicked animal it's cabined with,
  but then it rescues us, poor surly camel,
and carries us across that frightening place
like nomads. I could see it in his face,

LVII

'How Rimbaud was compelled to seek it out,
    to burn and scatter pages of the self,
rinçures of reason: genius was the lout
    to be precise, desire an empty shelf –
you align the inner and the outer gulf
    by ledger, rifle, *gaflah*; be the scout
of barrenness, the *abban* to the void.
Chew khat, trade coffee, try to stay employed.

LVIII

'Then we Shadrached into the shadeless zone
    and the breath of the furnace baked our faces,
and we Meshached among the mountains, cones
    like robes of Sufis whirling in the graces
of God, until we were Abed-Negone –
    at which point someone shimmered in the blaze's
distance, approaching like a fiery stroller,
his arms draped from the stick across his shoulders.

LIX

'This was some herdsman Rimbaud seemed to know
    and trust enough to halt the caravan –
"A poet, so he says, though they all do,"
    was all he'd say, and then a marathon
of trotting over glitter, squeezing through
    thorn-gulches, following our paragon
of silence into valleys draped with burqas
of evening shade – less hike and more mazurka.

LX

'Until we halted at a giant bell,
    a *Tsarsky Kolokol* of solid rock
to summon Ozymandias from Hell,
    and on the flanks of this huge egg, this cloche,
were paintings, ancient as the stone itself
    or so they seemed out here, before all clocks:
giraffes, an elephant, a lucid fever
of colour, and, *une liberté plus libre*,

LXI

'Banner-large cattle, men with arms flung wide,
    and on the next rock and the next, arms splayed,
ecstatic figures – "The Uncrucified",
    he called them, following this long parade
and laughing for the first time. By their side
    his self-sewn sails of clothing, dust-caked, frayed,
were of a piece. The herdsman tapped his pole,
"No camels, look. Before we need a soul."

LXII

'I caught a fever then for real, from where
    who knew? – just God's small notice He was out.
They rigged a litter up, paid four to bear
    me for a thaler each. (I'm too kaput
to bargain, seeing things, part-child, part-hare,
    that walk beside me, flinching when I shout.)
And thus I crossed the great Rift Valley, climbed
into the highlands, raving, self-beslimed.

LXIII

'We sat in Harar at that journey's end,
    the city's wall enclosing like the hull
of night's high ark, and heard hyenas rend
    meat market scraps. He mentioned how he'd culled
two thousand dogs with strychnine, how his friends –
    the Europeans – laughed, but were appalled.
"I'm Abdo Rinbo now," he deadpan-muttered,
and from those eyes my own stared back, anothered.

LXIV

'Which brings me back by circumjackery
    to Darien, asylum of the Scots...'
I took this for a try at waggery,
    or else as proof that he had lost all plots;
his vanity would stun a Thackeray,
    but this was a Flash Gordian of knots.
'You can't get there from Harar!' I exclaimed.
He eyed me sharply, laughed, and then explained:

LXV

'If Harar was a ship, its captain was
   the Ras, soon father of the emperor,
Tafari, in whose cabin I, because
   of shipwreck, was nicknamed *Naufragio*, or
'The Drowned'; while Rimbaud, rebel for applause,
   played Long John Silver, tucking a twelve-bore
into his oxter, claiming those who'd sailed
on Scottish vessels were aquatic Gaels.

LXVI

'And so, when I, washed-up, was washed up on
   Isla Ballena, crannog to the Kuna,
Darien, gyte colony of slow despond
   for Scotland, lay nearby. The village *junta*,
hearing in their long house of my sick bond
   with hubris and with greed, decreed the *Punta
Escoces* might be visited, so I
could pay respects to Death before I die.

LXVII

'Before that, though, I tried to build up strength
   by pacing round the tiny central square
where, with a large mock turtle for a plinth,
   a good Scots cannon sat, as though to scare
the *waga* jaguars away. At length
   the girls emerged to watch, with cropped black hair
and *mola* blouses, each brocaded with
birds, superheroes, healing plants and myths.

LXVIII

'An elder sold me a machete – showed
   me how, by notching it into bamboo,
you file it fit for Occam; helped me load
   the *cayuco*, then listed terrors to
avoid: tarantulas, palm vipers, toads,
   red fire-ants, sand-flies... As we paddled through
the excremental halo round the island,
his list went on – my heart was in the highlands

LXIX

'Or lowlands, Govan – anywhere but here.
  Again with the translucence: leopard rays
pacing a coral Alhambra's corridor.
  Then, at the inlet's entrance, something raised
a three-foot fin, U-Boating out before
  we scraped our way in over living blades –
And suddenly the jungle was about
our barque: its stink, its silent sullen glut

LXX

'Broken by capuchins' high chittery chat –
  the Elder Tomas, expert in distress,
said, "Monkey like to cack upon your hat."
  I peered up into clammy gloom, impressed
that they could see to aim, and glimpsed fruit-bats
  like foxes hung in sacks. I sniffed the cess
of mangrove, brackish pools, rainforest floor,
and, wobbling wildly, tried to step ashore.

LXXI

'There was, of course, of Nuevo Edinburgh
  no trace. The jungle, like an anaconda,
swallowed it whole. A few spars, like a curragh,
  showed where "The Olive Branch" had sunk, gone under
without a shot – a cooper in a hurry
  for the drink took a candle, and... no wonder,
trapped between bad luck, the flux and Spain,
two thousand Scots should fail to call this "hame".

LXXII

'We found earthworks, belt-buckles, and the well
  the last defenders dug behind their ditch –
no bones: oblivion's boa ate those as well.
  Queen Anne would later recompense the rich;
the Equivalent Society would swell
  into the Royal Bank, or, England's Bitch.
Meanwhile, brown pelicans flop out to sea,
and white-lipped peccaries rush through the trees.

LXIII

'I classified the last, to keep me calm:
   cedro espina, a giant, centuries old;
swamp apple, *bombacopsis*, prickle palm;
   the candle-tree... then Tomas stopped me, told
the story of his Kuna Blanco dream:
   how searching in the mountain streams for gold
he'd found plantations growing peppers, maize,
pineapples, yams, just like in ancient days.

LXXIV

'The people farming there invited him
   to feast with them, and all their tables creaked
like ships at sea with fresh-caught fish, roast game –
   and then he sees that they are white, and speak
in English, but their faces are the same
   as his grandparents in their youth, just bleached
like bones, and grainy like old photographs:
they tell him that he's dreaming, and they laugh,

LXXV

'Which wakes him – then he laughs because it's true.
   We think our dreams are spirits, so we find
they're angry with us, that we can't see through
   their veil into the world. So he's some kind
of glorious unmute Hume who'd have me throw
   my demons out by chewing on some vine –
I puked my visions up with Castaneda,
besides, it's evening, and we can see *nada*.'

LXXVI

And it was evening in Caracas too.
   Somehow we were in some *heladería*,
though how we'd got there, as he'd say – who knew?
   Through barrios and barricades' hysteria,
oblivious or ghosts ourselves by now,
   we'd walked and talked our way to Altamira.
Perhaps wherever he was, was the eye
of some tornado of the psyche – why,

LXXVII

I'd no more time to ponder: years, it seemed,
    had passed since we first met, and I felt tired
beyond whatever weariness could mean.
    I left him sitting there to be admired
anew, still talking, chomping on ice cream –
    turrón, the flavour of his youth's desires.
His words, that proved more intimate than kisses,
already drew the scorn of cool-eyed misses:

LXXVIII

'Darien in darkness is where failure meets
    its own: poor Fergusson in piss-straw hell;
or on Point Look Out's battlements, John Keats,
    his silence a Constantinople's fall.
Unwritten books are like revised defeats;
    burnt libraries reform in small hours' pall.
The bay fills with a legion of such ghosts,
all rotting fiercely as the Scots' house posts.

LXXIX

'With insect hymnals printed on our bones,
    we woke to find our kit of interest
to Don Agouti, and breakfast not our own,
    according to the millipedes. There passed
an hour of turquoise butterflies, who shone
    and shimmered up a canal headed west –
cut through the coral, narrow as a pend –
I tracked for miles, but never found an end...'

GEORGE JOWETT

I

Christ, Seaham, what a god-forsaken spot!
　The wind whips in across the grey North Sea.
It's miserable and cold. It rains a lot.
　It's not a place where I would choose to be.
For only one thing famous. But for what
　You ask? Well, long ago, mad, bad Lord B
Came limping to the Hall to take a bride.
There's little else of interest here beside.

II

Employment? Industry? There's nothing much,
　Not since the pit closed many years ago.
An industrial estate with a clutch
　Of vacant units (apply >>spectrum.co);
A retail park; some local shops and such,
　But all will tell you trade is very slow.
What brings me to this dismal and run-down,
Dilapidated, Northern, coastal town?

III

I've come to meet a fellow in a pub.
　His name? It's Alfred Onso. He lives here.
I've come to interview him. That's the nub,
　I'm hoping if I buy the guy a beer
He'll tell his story to me. I'm a Grub
　Street hack, a journalist with an idea
For a feature. This is research today.
That's why I've driven up the Motorway.

IV

I write for *Knobz*, fortnightly magazine,
　A mix of true-life stories, mainly smut,
And gossip from the minor celeb scene,
　(Which actress is a lush and which a slut.)
We're not exactly *Tatler, Style* or *Queen.*
　Not quite the posh end of the market but
Nonetheless we have our standards, although
It is unfortunate they're quite so low!

143

V

We are the gutter press, but oh we sell.
  Our circulation's soaring. People read
The stuff I write. I don't say I write well
  But I'm well read. It seems that some folk need
To read the sort of stories that we tell.
  Hypocrisy and sordid sex and greed,
They're still the staples. They're our stock in trade.
The same old sins our ancestors displayed.

VI

The piece I'm now researching? You haven't guessed?
  Do you remember Donald Johnson's name?
Yes, Donny Johnny. That's the chap. Incest?
  Something about his sister's secret shame?
You've got it. Fled the country? I'm impressed.
  He did indeed, for once he knew the game
Was up what could he do? Yes, Donny's flown
To Northern Cyprus where I've tracked him down.

VII

But Cyprus isn't where our story starts
  (Though it may stage this drama's final scene),
Nor any of the other foreign parts
  Where Donny in his travels may have been.
No D.J. plied his trade of breaking hearts
  At Seaton sands and Castle Eden Dene
Strange and unlikely, but dismiss your doubts,
  For Donny lived and worked once hereabouts.

VIII

And Alfred Onso? What's his part in this?
  Well, Donald Johnson stole his wife away.
He did. His Ex. Don spoiled their married bliss,
  And tempted her, snake that he is, to stray.
He sowed the seeds of strife. Yah, boo and hiss!
  He played the villain. Type-cast, Alf will say
I'm sure when, through this slanting rain and sleet,
I find the pub where we've arranged to meet.

144

IX

This could be it, up here, just on the right.
  I'll turn into the car park. Wipers off.
My God, that is a miserable sight!
  If Seaham in itself weren't bad enough
The pub we've picked appears as if it might
  Be less than great. A Wetherspoons! That's tough,
But tough or not I'd better get inside
And see what info Onso can provide.

X

That must be him, there, standing at the bar.
  He doesn't seem exactly overjoyed
To be here. 'Mr. Onso? Right you are,
  Alf. Hope you've not been waiting long? I'm Lloyd,
Lloyd Byram. Nice to meet you, Alf. By car.
  I've driven up today. It's what? It's hoyed
It down? Damn near all the way. Another drink?
A pint for you? I'll have the same, I think.

XI

'Let's find a quiet table, sit somewhere
  Where we can talk in private. Here will do.
That? It's my Dictaphone. Pull up a chair,
  Alf. Your good health. All the best. Cheers. Salut.
No, that's it now. I've nothing to prepare,
  Just turn the tape on, than it's down to you
To tell me what you can of Donny Johnny.
No Alf, I wasn't trying to be funny,

XII

'But I need you to help me spill the beans,
  To paint a picture of the harm he's done,
The stuff we've overlooked, those early scenes,
  Forgotten long ago by everyone.
A hatchet job's exactly what it means,
  So when the truth is out people will shun
Him. Exiled, outcast, he'll be a pariah.
Well that's my aim and object, my desire.

XIII

'So tell me how he stole your wife away.
　　You don't know where to start? Well, come on, man.
This is your chance, the chance to have your say.
　　Just start at the beginning if you can
And set the scene for us. Is that okay?
　　Explain exactly how it all began.
How Donnie, the sly sod, seduced your wife,
And what effect it's had upon your life.'

XIV

...I ran a care home here, if you must know,
　　For people with a mental handicap.
That's what we called them twenty years ago.
　　Politically incorrect? Yes, perhaps.
The world's moved on a bit? Well, maybe so,
　　But using euphemisms and claptrap
Isn't what I'd call progress, I'm afraid.
I'd much prefer we call a spade a spade.

XV

But I digress. I ran a care home here
　　And Julie worked for me. One of my staff.
Late twenties, blonde, a shapely derriere
　　And big tits too. You've seen her photograph?
Attractive? God, I'll say, but it was clear
　　That she could do the job as well, not half!
She was outstanding really, quite first class.
A caring carer with a lovely arse.

XVI

I fell for her. Besotted? Well, a bit.
　　Not that surprising, I was forty-five.
My marriage had grown stale. My life seemed shit.
　　I struggled on though, hoping to survive.
A mid-life crisis loomed. This could be it,
　　For when she smiled I seemed to come alive.
At first I didn't dare to say a word.
The thought she might like me seemed too absurd.

146

XVII

Her smile though, offered some encouragement
    And faint heart never won a single thing.
Tongue-tied, I tried to tell her what I meant,
    Not even sure that she was listening.
But then to my complete astonishment
    She said she felt the same. My heart took wing.
Her marriage, it appeared, was far from happy,
And Julie felt her life, like mine, was crappy.

XVIII

Well, that was that. Aware we felt the same,
    What need for further caution or restraint?
Passions ignited, we both burst into flame.
    We jettisoned reserve and all constraint.
Lovers, to put it bluntly, we became
    That very night. I don't intend to paint
A detailed picture of our passion's throes.
I'm sure you've some idea of how it goes.

XIX

It's best kept private, all that steamy sex.
    I'd find it awkward to be more specific.
Not quite as glam, maybe, as Posh and Becks
    But that first night we were just as prolific.
We shagged like rabbits! She may be my ex
    But still I will admit she was terrific,
Adventurous and dirty and delicious.
Alas, next day her husband grew suspicious.

XX

He challenged her about it. She confessed.
    Yes, Julie let the cat out of the bag.
He was upset, (well, naturally) distressed.
    He called her whore and harlot, tart and slag.
She didn't need to say, I sort of guessed
    He'd hit her too. (The guy had lost his rag.)
My Julie to escape him had to flee,
And naturally, poor girl, she came to me.

XXI

She looked to me to rescue and defend her,
  And fair enough, that's what we White Knights do.
We offer any service we can render
  To our Princess to prove our love is true.
I must find somewhere safe where I could send her,
  But couldn't think of anywhere I knew.
A sanctuary? In desperation I
  Thought of my wife. Might she be worth a try?

XXII

As ideas go, a bad one. In hindsight
  I think that love had addled my poor brain.
Did I imagine it would be alright?
  (Had I gone temporarily insane?)
My wife let Julie stay for just one night
  And then insisted she could not remain
One minute longer. No, she had to go
And take me with her too. That was a blow.

XXIII

But actually we really didn't care,
  Although we knew exactly what it meant.
It meant no turning back. We'd have to share
  Our lives from here on in. We were content.
That's what we'd wanted. Bridges burned, just where
  Those rosy, combined futures would be spent
Seemed not to matter. Guest House, rooms, a flat,
Who cared? Our first job was to sort all that.

XXIV

A B&B while we searched out a let,
  But pretty soon we found ourselves a pad.
With few belongings and not one regret
  Between us, we'd moved in. We were just glad
To be together. And it got better yet
  When twelve weeks later Julie said she had
Some news. 'I've fallen pregnant.' Overjoyed,
The happiness we shared was unalloyed.

XXV

A couple now. A baby on the way.
　　Our former plans would have to be redrawn,
But that was fine, just fine. I have to say
　　A golden era was about to dawn.
It promised love and laughter every-day
　　And would begin when our first child was born.
And it turned out like that, or so it seemed,
We'd found the happiness of which we'd dreamed.

XXVI

Soon Julie gave up work, then my divorce
　　Was finalised, and we bought our first home.
The baby came at last. Both thrilled, of course,
　　A family, that's what we had become.
Next, Julie thought she'd do a College course
　　In social work. It must appeal to some.
I know that Julie couldn't wait to do it,
Although she wondered how she would get through it.

XXVII

She studied for it part-time. Three years passed,
　　Till in the end her object was achieved.
A social worker! Qualified, at last!
　　We were so proud and happy and relieved.
Our prospects were improving. They seemed vast
　　For now it should be easy, we believed
For Julie to achieve one more ambition
And land herself a manager's position.

XXVIII

And so she did. She soon secured a post
　　As manager of a home in Hartlepool,
A little less than ten miles down the coast.
　　Perhaps it's not enough to make you drool
(The salary was 20k at most),
　　But for doing what she loved even you'll
Admit my Julie could be satisfied.
Her wishes had been largely gratified.

149

XXIX

What else could we have asked for? Life seemed great.
  In love, in work and in the money too.
The years sped by at an alarming rate.
  Then Julie changed her job, and Baby Two
Appeared. A third soon followed. But why wait?
  We both agreed for us three kids would do,
Our happy family was at last complete.
Another plus upon Life's balance sheet.

XXX

Quite when the rot set in I can't be sure.
  Perhaps the humdrum had replaced romance?
Perhaps for Julie life became a bore?
  Perhaps she just felt trapped by circumstance?
But suddenly I felt, well, less secure,
  There couldn't, could there, be the slightest chance...?
Of course not. Me and Julie, still the perfect match
Were simply going through a sticky patch.

XXXI

There were some pressures on us, I suppose.
  At night our fretful baby liked to cry.
My aged, widowed mother also chose
  To move to sheltered housing quite nearby
Where we could help support her. And if those
  Weren't quite enough (I really don't know why),
My Julie, restless, swapped her job once more
To run a respite home in Spennymoor.

XXXII

Over a decade now we'd been together.
  (Our eldest, Lucy, had that year turned ten.)
Though recently we'd seen some stormy weather
  I still believed the sea would calm, and when
It did we'd sail on happily forever.
  What reason had I to be worried then
When Julie said she thought we ought to move
To somewhere bigger? She must feel our love

XXXIII

Would far outlast our present perturbation.
   Why else would she suggest we start again
With mortgages and all the aggravation
   Of moving? No, it must be pretty plain
To Julie we'd be there for the duration.
   She thought a move might just relieve the strain.
My only reservations were financial.
The mortgage we would need would be substantial,

XXXIV

And I was fifty-seven, too old I thought
   To take on debt and all that it entailed.
Of course I tried to argue with her, sought
   To point out all the pitfalls, but I failed.
I knew I would. Experience had taught
   Me Julie's wishes generally prevailed.
And so they did this time. We upped and moved
To our new house, but nothing else improved.

XXXV

In fact I felt things rapidly declined.
   My wife grew more unloving and remote.
I guessed she had things preying on her mind.
   But what were they and what did they denote?
Small wonder if, neglected, I repined.
   A little love would be the antidote.
But Julie was a stranger to arousal
And said she felt she was premenopausal.

XXXVI

She wouldn't come to bed till very late,
   But sat at her computer half the night.
She'd work to do, she'd say, that couldn't wait.
   I should go up. Yes, she would be alright.
Upstairs I'd lie alone and masturbate.
   Then sleep would briefly bring me some respite.
But suddenly the baby'd wake up crying.
Some nights she took a lot of pacifying.

XXXVII

I wasn't always calm and understanding,
  Nor patient as I should be, I confess.
I could be grumpy, angry and demanding,
  But often I felt under some duress.
And if you could have stood where I was standing
  You'd have some sympathy for me, I'd guess,
Though Julie didn't seem to, I'll allow,
And there were times we'd have a flaming row.

XXXVIII

It wasn't only Julie drove me batty,
  For I'd become a carer if you please,
And Mother, ninety-five and slightly scatty,
  Did little to contribute to my ease.
Not her fault if at times she made me ratty.
  No, age-related, degenerative disease
Meant she was frail, forgetful and dependent
On me, her son and most direct descendant.

XXXIX

It's clear that I was struggling to cope.
  And where was Julie when I needed her?
Close by my side, supporting me? Well, nope.
  Much as I wished and prayed my Julie were,
She wasn't. There was very little hope
  Of any help from her I must aver.
No, Julie made a huge contribution,
But to the problem, not to the solution.

XL

She said she had been asked by her employer
  To research current trends in respite care.
I was suspicious (could that be paranoia?)
  It seemed unlikely. (Am I being fair?)
She told me they now wanted to deploy her
  One weekend down in Nottingham, for there
A flag-ship respite scheme operated
Which Nottingham Council had created.

XLI

She said she'd have to go down Friday night
  To observe it working on the Saturday.
To me that somehow didn't seem quite right.
  I couldn't see the reason she must stay.
It wasn't far. She could get there alright
  And then see all she needed in a day.
I wondered was the true explanation
That Julie had arranged an assignation?

XLII

It all seemed clear. I feared that must be it.
  The evidence against her was emphatic.
I'd challenge her, invite her to admit
  The reason she'd been restless and erratic.
The jigsaw pieces seemed a perfect fit.
  The showdown when it came would be dramatic.
It was. The vehemence of her denial
Forced the abandonment of Julie's trial.

XLIII

She said I was untrusting and suspicious
  And jealous without any cause to be.
My current accusations were pernicious.
  They'd weaken our relations dangerously.
The lover she was meeting was fictitious,
  An obsessive husband's jealous fantasy.
She swore there was no other in her life
And that she'd been a loving, loyal wife.

XLIV

She forced me on the back foot. In the wrong
  I was once more. The tables had been turned.
It seems I had things muddled all along.
  I was the guilty one. I should have learned
That's where we husbands properly belong.
  She went off for her weekend. She returned.
I thought we ought to try to sort things out.
I felt we had a lot to talk about.

153

XLV

But Julie didn't. That was obvious.
    In her eyes all the love we'd shared had gone.
In fact she felt we'd nothing to discuss,
    The bonds between us had become undone
And now there was no future left for us.
    It seemed to me her heart had turned to stone.
I begged, I pleaded, but my Julie said
It was too late for that. Our love was dead.

XLVI

I'd killed it. All my fault. That was her view.
    Perhaps in some ways I had been remiss.
Be even so, accepting that as true,
    How could it possibly have come to this?
There surely must be something I could do
    To change or challenge her analysis?
She was in error, clearly quite mistaken.
A wrong turn in her reasoning she'd taken.

XLVII

For Julie next suggested we should part,
    But not till after Christmas. A reprieve?
Perhaps by then she'd have a change of heart?
    I hoped so. But my wife felt, I believe,
The New Year was the time for a fresh start,
    So that's when she'd decided I should leave.
It suited her and though I might demur
What mattered most was what was best for her.

XLVIII

But for the moment we would leave things there,
    Since neither of us wanted to proceed,
In limbo, unresolved, still in mid-air.
    It was as if a truce had been agreed.
We tiptoed round the crisis well aware
    That once false move on either side might lead
To the whole thing exploding in our faces.
How could we travel onwards on that basis?

XLIX

Just one week later, coming in one night
   From work, my Julie ran up to our room.
She rifled through her wardrobe. 'Thought I might
   Lend Vi a dress...' 'A colleague, I assume?'
She nodded. 'One of these might be alright.
   What do you think?' I didn't dare presume
To offer her advice. 'Posh do, my guess is?'
'Dinner dance.' 'Your best two evening dresses?'

L

'Poor Vi, she can't find anything to suit.'
   For me somehow it didn't quite ring true.
My doubts, there from the start, became acute.
   I felt it wasn't something Julie'd do.
For me it didn't add up or compute.
   The more I dwelt on it, the more I grew
Suspicious, sitting in our bed, quite sure
I knew what those posh frocks were really for.

LI

A love tryst – that must be the reason why,
   A secret meeting one night after work,
But Julie would be wearing them, not Vi!
   (The simple truth glimpsed through the clearing murk.)
'I'm sleeping in,' she'd say, and I'd reply
   'That's fine.' 'He fell for it, the fool,' she'd smirk
As she and lover boy went out to dine.
They'd laugh about it as they sipped their wine.

LII

I couldn't stand for that, or let it pass.
   I took it as a personal affront.
How could she be so brazen, bold as brass,
   So underhand while seeming so upfront?
She must think I was stupid. Yes, alas
   She obviously did. To be quite blunt
She clearly thought I might moan on a bit
But that she'd simply get away with it.

LIII

I got up out of bed. Oh I was riled.
  I felt the scales had fallen from my eyes.
'You're meeting someone, aren't you?' She went wild.
  She swore my accusation was all lies,
Foul lies. She cursed me, called me names, reviled
  Me, 'Jealous bastard!' Then, to my surprise,
My wife stepped closer to me, swung a punch.
It hit me on the cheek. Now came the crunch.

LIV

I grabbed her by both arms. I pushed her down
  She struggled but I forced her to the floor.
'Tell me the truth, you bitch!' She'd never known
  Me be aggressive in this way before.
It frightened her, I think. The fact I'd shown
  I could be marked a watershed. What's more
I'd never be forgiven. Not for this.
No, things had now gone seriously amiss.

LV

So I let go. I left her lying there,
  Stalked off to sleep alone in the spare room.
I heard her sobbing, and was well aware
  Of what I'd done. I sensed impending doom.
The prospect simply filled me with despair.
  Sentence would follow swiftly, I'd assume.
Next morning she informed me I must leave.
No chance of an appeal or a reprieve.

LVI

I had to go immediately, get out.
  I argued I'd got nowhere else to go.
I'd think of somewhere, Julie had no doubt.
  No pity or compassion did she show.
She clearly didn't give a toss about
  The fact we'd just moved in three months ago,
Or that the kids would pine and miss their dad.
I should have thought of that. Tough shit, too bad.

LVII

So I was banished. It had been decreed.
  A *fait accompli.* Nothing I could say
Or do would change it. Nothing I could plead
  In mitigation would hold any sway.
Far better, frankly, simply to concede,
  To leave, head-bowed, and sadly make my way
To a camp bed in my mother's sitting room
And sink into an all-pervading gloom.

LVIII

Depressed? I'll say. The next few days were hard.
  In hopeless pleading much of them were spent
Which Julie simply chose to disregard.
  No sign at all she'd soften or relent
As I had hoped. I found myself debarred
  From home and hearth. My empty evenings went
By parrying my mother's endless questions.
'What can we do, dear?' I had no suggestions.

LIX

I'd have to move, I realised, or go mad
  For Julie wasn't going to take me back
Just yet. If that thought left me feeling sad
  My mother's input had me on the rack.
She tortured me, made things, already bad,
  Far worse, turned every shade of grey to black.
I had to get away, spend time alone,
And so I found a bedsit of my own.

LX

By now I understood my Julie's view.
  I had destroyed our happy family.
That's what she told me so it must be true.
  The break-up and the pain were down to me.
I'd ruined her life and the children's too
  With my unreasonable jealousy.
I'd poisoned everything, and turned it bad.
I'd wrecked our marriage. Julie said I had.

157

LXI

But still at times she needed me, it seemed.
  The ties between us weren't yet severed quite.
If she wanted something from me or deemed
  That I could be of service, then despite
The fact I was no longer much esteemed
  By her, she'd ask. She broke the bathroom light
While trying to change the bulb. She wondered if
It was the sort of thing I'd help her with?

LXII

And like a fool I'd readily agreed,
  Another opportunity I'd missed.
I didn't even make her beg or plead,
  Just told her I'd be happy to assist.
(I hoped by being helpful I'd succeed
  In winning back her love. Yes, that's the gist.)
I volunteered to go and sort it out
Next day when no-one else would be about.

LXIII

It was quite eerie, opening the door
  And entering our home. I stepped inside
And standing in the hall tried to ignore
  The pounding of my heart. Preoccupied,
Forgetting what it was I'd come here for,
  I stood a moment lost in thought, then sighed
And dragged my mind back to the task in hand,
To fix the bathroom light fitting as planned.

LXIV

I climbed the stairs, I checked the broken light.
  It didn't work. I went to fetch a chair.
I stood on it. I reached the thing alright.
  The cover seemed stuck on. A screw head there
Which wouldn't turn. No, it was really tight.
  A small screwdriver? Must be one somewhere.
I thought I'd seen one. Where? (A moment's pause.)
Perhaps in Julie's dressing table drawers?

LXV

I went to look, I never even thought
   I shouldn't, or that doing so was wrong.
A Posidrive was what I really sought,
   And so I cast aside each silken thong
And lacy bra. (What memories they brought.)
   But did a small brown envelope belong
Among such treasures? It seemed out of place.
I'd better open it though, just in case.

LXVI

Two folded sheets of A4 it contained.
   An e-mail print out, by the look of it.
I read it slowly, puzzled, till I gained
   A sense of what was being said. Oh shit!
'My darling Donny, how I miss you.' Pained,
   Perplexed, I soon grew angry, I admit.
Who was this darling Donny Julie missed
So much, and when precisely had they kissed?

LXVII

Her e-mail bore a date two weeks before.
   She'd sent it in reply to one from him.
I read them, then re-read them both. I swore.
   I had to face the facts. The facts were grim.
The two of them were lovers, and what's more
   They'd planned it all, not acted on a whim.
Despite her past denials, it appeared
It all had been exactly as I'd feared.

LXVIII

I staggered backwards, sat down on the bed.
   I couldn't quite believe it, yet I knew
I must. Illusions shattered, dreams all dead,
   There in my hand the proof that it was true.
A thousand angry thoughts now filled my head.
   But what, I wondered, was I going to do?
For finally these e-mails had supplied
The evidence to prove my Julie'd lied.

LXIX

Who was this donnyjohnny@hotmail
    With whom she'd had criminal conversation?
I mightn't yet have every sordid detail
    But I'd enough to back my accusation.
This time no flat denial would avail.
    She couldn't claim this was mere speculation.
These e-mails proved it. I'd confront her, yes
And finally force my Julie to confess.

LXX

I did that night. I told her what I'd found
    And bluntly asked her what her e-mail meant.
Speechless at first, she didn't make a sound,
    Then suddenly all hot and red she went.
Poor Julie cornered, stammered, looked around,
    That she'd no place to hide was evident.
She said she was embarrassed, now I'd named
Her lover. (I think she meant she felt ashamed.)

LXXI

I asked her how she'd met him. He'd been thirty,
    Deejaying in a club in Middlesbrough.
Just fifteen, under-age and rather flirty,
    With all the morals girls had in Gomorrah,
Young Julie was fair game. She liked it dirty.
    The seeing-to he gave her had been thorough.
Hence Julie looked back in recollection
On Donny and that night with some affection.

LXXII

She told me how he'd found her through the net,
    How sorry he had seemed that they'd lost touch.
It was, she said, a source of deep regret
    To Donny, who had loved her very much.
(To me this sounded juvenile and wet –
    a chat-up line, though rather naff as such.)
His whole life had been blighted till the night
They'd met up on that social net website.

LXXIII

And so, of course, they'd started corresponding.
   And then quite soon they had arranged to meet.
In Nottingham they'd obviously been bonding,
   'Oh Julie!' 'Oh my Donny!' What deceit!
She'd thought about, but then ruled out absconding.
   No, I would have to go. That would complete
Her happiness, for Donny could replace me.
I wondered how she'd had the nerve to face me!

LXXIV

That's what the last few months had been about.
   Before her darling Donny could move in
She had to force her horrid husband out.
   No wonder I had felt I couldn't win.
That's why my marriage ended in a rout –
   So their cohabitation could begin!
For months my Julie'd looked me in the eyes
And boldly told me, well, a pack of lies.

LXXV

But I suspected Donny too was lying.
   His promises were what she'd hoped to hear.
You cannot really blame the bloke for trying.
   He'd whispered honeyed words into her ear.
They'd done the trick alright, there's no denying,
   Helped him achieve his aim it's pretty clear.
But were his aims what Julie thought they were?
Did Donny really want to live with her?

LXXVI

He'd a sister down in Watford and a child,
   Was working still as some sort of Deejay.
He wouldn't give all that up. Julie smiled,
   'He's moving up to live with me in May.'
Poor Julie. She was totally beguiled.
   'You're certain?' 'Absolutely.' 'Well, okay.'
I doubted it, but didn't contradict her.
To me it seemed that Donny'd simply tricked her.

LXXVII

It sounded pretty much as I'd expected,
　A hackneyed mix of cliché and romance.
His one true love; his fear he'd be rejected;
　Their sweet first kiss; that secret, furtive glance;
A hidden passion smouldering undetected
　For all these years. And then, as if by chance,
Re-kindled in an instant, re-ignited
Online one night on Friends Reunited.

LXXVIII

What woman could resist that skilled depiction
　Of her as Goddess, first love, lost love, Muse?
My Julie couldn't. Her lifelong addiction
　(And this, I'm sure, won't come as headline news)
Has been to Mills and Boon romantic fiction.
　She fell for it (I'd ask you to excuse
My cynicism) hook, line and sinker.
Too easy for Donny to hoodwink her.

LXXIX

She should perhaps have done more to resist him.
　As much her fault as his I have to say.
But Julie couldn't. No, for once she'd kissed him
　Her moral compass seemed to go astray.
She'd then done all she could do to assist him,
　Conspired with him and helped him get his way.
No, certainly my Julie wasn't blameless.
Duplicitous she'd been, and rather shameless.

LXXX

I knew the truth now. That was some relief
　For, finally, even I had come to see,
Although it only brought me pain and grief,
　My wife no longer loved or wanted me.
That I could win her back was my belief.
　There surely was a way? There had to be.
I couldn't face the fact that we were finished.
I had to hope but hope was soon diminished.

LXXXI

No, we were doomed. Our marriage was undone.
    Julie'd withdrawn her love from our account.
I knew she had. I checked. It was all gone.
    She'd taken everything, the whole amount
And then invested it instead in one
    She'd opened up with Donny. Tantamount
To fraud on his part, I'd claim, for in the end
He'd never pay the promised dividend.

LXXXII

Just as I thought, he never would deliver
    On all the empty promises he'd made.
He always had some excuse he could give her
    Why once again their plans must be delayed,
And he couldn't move up North to live with her.
    His daughter, the recession... He displayed
Some skill in coming up with different reasons.
Their details seemed to vary with the seasons.

LXXXIII

Poor Julie, blind or blinkered, couldn't see
    How Donny had been stringing her along.
His 'one true love' became his fuck buddy,
    Love's anthem turned into the same old song.
And she accepted it quite willingly,
    Unable to admit she'd got it wrong,
Till in the end he'd found a younger lover
And changed his Facebook status. It was over.

LXXXIV

By then, of course, for me it was too late.
    I didn't want her back. The mist had cleared.
I saw her plainly now, my former mate.
    The love I'd had for her had disappeared.
The only thing I felt for her was hate.
    I'd seen how horrible she was, how weird.
I never could forgive her or forget
The part in this played by the Internet.

LXXXV

The worldwide web conspired in our undoing.
   That virtual, cyber world, for now IT
Has made it easier to go a-wooing,
   Yes, you can even do it digitally,
The vulnerable and gullible pursuing
   From the comfort of a chair at your PC.
Self-advertising for the self-deluded,
That's social network sites I have concluded.

LXXXVI

But what begins upon the Internet
   Will perish by computer in the end,
When online lovers find to their regret
   That it was all a game of Let's Pretend,
And they've been dumped by e-mail. And yet
   It wasn't all that hard to comprehend
What he was up to. How gullible she was.
How easily deceived. And all because

LXXXVII

Those online lies, which brought her such delight,
   Looked different on a grey, computer screen,
Viewed secretly, alone, around midnight,
   Too easy to mistake what they might mean.
Illumined by the strange and eerie half-light
   Of wishful thinking and what might have been,
Like moonlight on a stretch of North East seaboard,
The words tapped out by Donny on his keyboard

LXXXVIII

Seemed somehow fairer than they really should.
   In fact she took them at the time for true.
It's plain, with hindsight, she'd misunderstood
   What Donny at his end was trying to do,
Imputing motives to him far too good,
   Though I'd have thought it hard to misconstrue
What he was really after. It was sex.
That's all that Donny wanted from my ex.

LXXXIX

And it was almost bound to end in tears,
  I'm told in fact it nearly always does.
That is the usual outcome it appears
  Of extra-marital, adulterous
Affairs. Their legacy can last for years.
  I have to say it still impacts on us.
In all our children, sadly, I've detected
The scars that signify they've been affected.

XC

And as for me, well I've been devastated.
  In fact my world will never be the same.
My happiness has been obliterated,
  For which sad fact my Julie is to blame.
Her fault alone our marriage terminated,
  A responsibility she can't disclaim,
Although she'd clearly like to if she could
And claim instead she's been misunderstood.

XCI

And has she made me any reparation
  Or offered an apology? Of course
She hasn't. No, it's no exaggeration
  To say I've seen no signs of real remorse.
She still denies she caused our separation,
  Or that of all my ills she is the source.
She won't accept the blame, or my reproof.
She's still determined to deny the truth.

XCII

It's me who has to pay her maintenance.
  No wonder I'm still angry at her guile.
No nunnery for Julie. Not a chance,
  Repentance and reform are not her style.
Though she misled me in a merry dance
  All I still get from Julie is denial.
She now believes the version she's created
From which her sins have all been expurgated.

XCIII

And as for Donny, I despise his sort,
   Self-centred hedonists, you know the kind,
Who'll never spare even a single thought
   For the broken hearts and lives they've left behind.
It's just a silly game to them, a sport,
   And once it's done they put it out of mind.
No, Donny's never for a moment paused
To think about the hurt and harm he's caused...

XCIV

'Oh come on, Alf. You're crying. Don't take on so.
   I'm sure what you have been through has been rough,
But really, there are limits Mr Onso.
   It's time to call a halt. Enough's enough.
It's over, Alf. Forget it. Julie's gone so
   There's no point dwelling on it. Yes, it's tough
But just accept it now. Your ex is gone.
What can you do? Get over it. Move on.'

XCV

'That's just what Julie used to say to me.
   "Move on now, Alf." But I was fifty-eight.
Move on to where? With whom? Seriously,
   Could she not see, can you not, it's too late?
It isn't going to all end happily.
   Love doesn't last forever, but the hate
Which has replaced it looks as if it might,
So I'll hang on to that if that's alright?'

XCVI

'I'm sorry, Alf, that's sad, but even so
   I think you've told me nearly all you can.
We'll leave it there. No, really, I must go.
   I've other folk to see. Yes, that's the plan.
There's lots of other stuff I need to know
   To get a rounded picture of our man.
I'll talk to former friends and cronies, but
I'd like to thank you, Alf, for your input.

XCVII

'I will. Thank you. A pleasure, Alf. Goodbye...'
  Thank God that's over. Now back to the car.
I hate it when a cuckold starts to cry.
  Pathetic and self-pitying they are.
Is he so blind he really can't see why
  She left him for another man? Bizarre!
A puzzle still to him, but plain to us.
In fact I'd say it's flaming obvious.

XCVIII

Just look at her. I've got a picture here.
  I took it from the Donny Johnson file.
Hot stuff! Deep cleavage, nicely rounded rear.
  The miniskirt, the bright, seductive smile.
What's on her mind I'd say is pretty clear.
  And I'll be talking to her in a while.
Yes, she's the next appointment on my list,
An interview that isn't to be missed!

XCIX

I have to say I'm looking forward to it,
  To hear her version of what in fact befell.
Excited at the prospect? Just a bit.
  I could be wrong, of course, it's hard to tell
But when I phoned her, yes, I must admit
  We seemed to hit it off. We got on well.
Some sympathetic interest and who knows?
We'll have to wait and see just how it goes.

C

Mind you, it's probably long out of date,
  The photo that she sent him. There's a chance
That Julie will have put on lots of weight
  And that it now bears no resemblance
To her at all. I'm several years too late.
  I bet she won't be worth a second glance.
No, she'll be bitter, middle-aged and fat
For Donny's conquests all end up like that.

JOHN LUCAS

Don Johnson; Restaurateur

I

One day, as per, Don woke up in a bed
    That wasn't his own, clocked the room's Che poster,
Some artsy photos of a mouthy head
    Looming though smoke, then heard a pop-up toaster
And coffee grinder tell what lay ahead
    – Thanking the girl whose name would be at most a
Guess – Janice, Jean? – and knew he'd have to change
As the poet said from seeking such a range.

II

In that last week alone he'd failed to score
    Once only, and that was when, unable
From drugs of choice to know a great deal more
    Than that he lay beneath some kitchen table,
He'd yawed to what he thought was the front door
    And pitched into a room, where, dank parable
Of some failed god, he'd fallen like a comet
Then woke next morning soaked in his own vomit.

III

Now, fumbling to the bathroom for ablutions,
    He knew the time had come for taking stock.
But what could cure his dissolute ways? Solutions
    Were what he craved. Restraint? I wouldn't mock
Those who vow conversion to a Puritan's
    Strait life is through excess, it's not a cock
And bull story, how the wild Augustine
Handed his spurs of *chevalier d'outrage* in

IV

Before becoming frankly eremitic,
    Thus keen to barricade the primrose path
Against each errant – Hell the diuretic
    He forced on all. But then the aftermath,
Of setting fire to every heretic,
    Is, I would say, *de trop,* likewise the bath
Of acid, though while men dissolved, confessing,
Pious prelates offered the Church's blessing.

171

V

Don had no wish to ape Savanarola,
　　He liked the flesh, found joy in food and drink,
Felt mild contempt for every holy roller
　　Who warned him that he trembled on the brink
Of bottomless perdition. (Any stroller
　　Round London's parks and public squares would think
These many stare-eyed prophets of our doom
Were prompted more by gloating than by gloom.)

VI

Still, shower-fresh, he knew he had to call
　　Time on this weary, flat, and stale routine
Of sex and rock and roll. He'd break its thrall,
　　Throw off his sable *ennui,* and begin
To find meaning where the intellectual
　　And workday world were one. But how? Get clean
'Away from Cobbett's scrofulous "Great Wen,"
"Satan's Drawing Room." (There was more smoke then.)'

VII

'"The man who's tired of London's tired of life",
　　Well, maybe, but for Don the signs were clear
And pointed to elsewhere. He'd seize a knife
　　And cut the strings that bound him to his drear
Routine. Thus Don, who liked the storm and strife
　　School of acting, staunching a manly tear,
Consents in Earls Court no more to abuse
'My days in a grey haze of pot and booze.'

VIII

Observe him, then, abandon his bed-sit
　　That afternoon. Adieu to the Kings Road,
To all the luvs with whom he'd scored a hit,
　　Jules, Toby, Jade, Miss Moggie, Mr Toad –
Adieu. The anthem fades. This daylight flit
　　Promised the pleasures of an open road.
And so, albeit with some trepidation,
DJ fared forward to St Pancras Station.

172

IX

Once in the Booking Hall, he joined a queue
  Where each one fixed his eyes before his feet,
And no-one spoke, until at last, 'Where to?'
  Where to, indeed? A question to defeat
The unteleologically minded. 'Waterloo?'
  'You trying to be funny, sunshine? Beat
It, squire. We're Mainline, not the Underground.'
A message in those words! Don stared around

X

Then – 'Nottingham, one way.' What made him choose
  That town, he wondered, sipping rancid beer
In the *Shires*, St. Pancras' bar, a place to lose
  The will to live, he thought, then shook with fear
As cloacal smells came drifting from locked loos.
  Were corpses left to rot here year on year?
Could this place be an ante-room to hell?
And were those clock chimes or a Passing Bell?

XI

Recovering, Don asked to see the menu.
  The barman gawped. '*Menu*? Here's what we've got.'
'Here' was an ancient glass dome. Even you,
  Mark A., who drank your horse's stale, would not
Have risked the so-called cheddar blotched with blue,
  Ham slices slimed with what resembled snot,
And least of all that purulent pork-pie,
'Wonder to all who do the same espy.'

XII

'Thing is,' the barman said, 'they're here for ale' –
  Nodding to where a line of topers leant
Against each other, lock-jawed, deathly pale,
  As if this was their place of banishment,
The last chance bar, where they must needs bewail
  Like some poor Arab tribesman and his tent
Their shiftless plight. And just then, 'Nevermore,'
One wretch declaimed and toppled to the floor.

XIII

Aghast, Don thought again, why *Nottingham?*
  Ancestral voices calling him? No way.
He knew it was *un moment fou,* a whim
  To cast himself adrift, to seize the day
Presented by his going on the lam,
  Where hopes, though few, might never gang agley.
Besides, he'd heard – who hadn't? – that the city
Was full of girls street-wise and more than pretty.

XIV

And now let's cut to meet him on the train.
  What has he brought to read? *Saturday Night
And Sunday Morning?* No, Nor yet *The Rain-
  Bow,* nor *Harris's Requiem,* it's light
matter he wants *en route,* not for his brain
  To be fired up by those he *knows* can write.
So no *Start Somewhere,* no *Hosanna Man,*
And above all no glance at *Don Juan.*

XV

Two hours of brochures, then it's journey's end.
  Soon enough, Don stands in a market square
Whose high-domed Council House seems the pretend
  Capitol of some Baltic Province where
Outlaws are dropped down caves while folk descend
  In hordes to celebrate an autumn fair.
(From which you'll guess that while in transit, Don
Learnt something of the city. Now read on.)

XVI

That evening, hoping to find a restaurant
  Not smothered in puce flock or wan bamboo,
Its stainless cutlery less *très elegant*
  Than *tres* Home Stores, and one without a view
(Hung skew-whiff) of the Sphinx or hierophant
  Chits in chitons outlined against the blue
Acropolitic air, or Notre Dame,
He sank in banquette gloom. 'For this I came?'

174

XVII

He muttered bleakly, having spurned the food
   On offer in each pub he'd tried, rejecting
The pickled eggs in kilner jars which stood
   Murky on fag-scorched bars as though expecting
No-one to plumb their depths – that hebetude
   (Or do I mean hebona?) where the sting
Of blind-worm lurked, prompting the Don to swear
He'd learnt at last the meaning of Despair.

XVIII

Now, prodding pinguid chips, a kiln-baked steak,
   Those lead-shot peas and sump-oil gravy – Berni
Catering For *YOU* – No, mate, there's *your* mistake,
   Don thought. Then *PRESTO!* Suddenly, this journey
Made sense. *Shazzam!* He'd start a bistro, make
   The town a Five Star treat for Egon Ronay.
Possessed, he tried out names. *Don's Grub Galore,*
Don's Diner, Don's Delight, Don's Dindon D'Or –

XIX

Well, give it time. 'Oh, look, you've hardly started,'
   The waitress said who came to take his plate.
Don met her gaze and all at once his heart did
   The flutter-bang he knew had sealed his fate.
She stood, a Galatean caryatid,
   High-busted, broadly hipped, her smile elate
As though he'd brought new purpose to her life.
He saw no wedding ring. So, not a wife.

XX

At least not yet. 'Your name is?' 'Cheryl. You're
   Not from round here, are you?' 'No, but I
Think I'll stay awhile. My barque's touched shore
   So many places, I need rest.' A wry
Shy smile to let her know that even more
   He needed solace and some company.
He flicked a lock of hair from his creased brow
And sighed as one awaiting Charon's scow.

XXI

'Found anywhere to stay?' Don seized his chance.
   'Not yet. I wonder…. Could you recommend…?'
He looked, she looked. And then and there romance
   Took wing. 'Sit tight until the evening's end,'
She told him. 'We'll be closing soon.' Forbearance
   Was what he'd earlier vowed. But vows will bend
Under love's heat, and Cheryl's eyes, her smile,
Showed celibacy here was out of style.

XXII

And so it proved. For later, snug in bed
   Post-coital, Don told her of his plan.
'I'll make this city understand "well fed"
   Is neither wodge nor stodge. Out frying pan!
Death to prawn cocktail, tinned cream, sliced white bread.
   Long live ratatouille, *riz* and good French *vin*.
I have a dream. Say, will you help me, Cheryl.'
And she, borne upward in his arms – 'I will.'

* * *

XXIII

Fast forward now some months. It's opening night
   At Nottingham's new bistro. These soigné
Diners, the *Post* reports, express delight
   At Mme. Cheri's décor, while the sommelier –
Didier Jean – guides patrons through the bright
   Crisp wines (*Appellation controllé*)
Acquired from the remotest Dordogne *caves*.
Begone *St. Nicholas* and Spanish *Graves*.

XXIV

Begone, too, oak and teak. Here, all's stripped pine,
   Rush matting, chequered cloths from Habitat,
Wrist-testing cutlery, carafes of wine
   (Green, warty glass), bread board and seeded plait,
Plus prints by Mocha, Moreau, Klee, and Klein,
   Le Déjeuner sur L'Herbe and *La Grande Jatte*.
No wonder Cheryl's pleased. Her cup is full,
And Don's in tow, no longer on the pull.

So, for a while, it proved. The *Canarde Bleu*
  Was full most nights and diners came from far
To try 'the earthy, chthonic, *echt* milieu'
  As the *Observer* called it. In the bar
A swing quartet played Django, fairly true
  To the originals, although the star
Proved the *chanteuse* whose vibrant, husky vowels,
As Lawrence might have said, fluttered Don's bowels.

XXVI

But that same writer's *noli me tangere*
  If not on Cheryl's lips was what she meant
When warning of the serious danger he
  Was in of losing both balls if he went
Looking for *amuse-bouche* with strangers. She
  Murmured, cleaver in hand, 'Who pays the rent
Can stop the tune. And Don, my honey lamb,
You lack the cash to play the big I Am.'

'A broken dandy lately on my travels
  You mean.' 'Perhaps, though I'll not rub it in.
But here's the deal. For business' sake your revels
  Now are ended.' Don took that on the chin
As local hero Bendigo did when levelled
  By knuckled luck. He'd shake his head and grin,
Then get back on his feet, resume the fight,
And never blame his fall on some god's spite.

Not boxing, though, but cricket was the sport
  Don loved. '76 saw him at Trent Bridge
To watch Windies v England, a cohort
  Of cannon-fodder led by Greig, whose language –
He vowed to make Viv 'grovel' – was the sort
  That had Don begging Viv to prove the savage
Master of high sixes. Viv's sword-blade blazed,
And Greig abandoned hope, aspermed, abased.

XXIX

Don's delight, that, and as the decade passed
   Meals were *gratis* if he thought well enough
Of those who'd sample his cuisine. The cast
   Of *Pravda* and *Comedians* got free scoff,
So did Ken Colyer's Jazzmen on their last
   Slipper Go-round. And even Brian Clough
Was rumoured to have supped on *coq-au-vin*
One night, "And not too many spuds, young man."

XXX

That was near the 70's end, which Don,
   Not fond of fondue, cursing kipper ties
And Heath's shark-grin, was happy to see gone,
   Although it kept to last satire's surprise
Of Thatcher preaching Peace, what time the *Sun*
   Lit up a government whose ermined lies
Proved Greed was Great and Public Good a chancre
That threatened the hale life of every banker.

* * *

XXXI

Time for a change, Don thought. Cheryl did, too,
   Although she had a different change in mind.
A shock to Don, who'd on the whole stayed true,
   While buying bin-end bargains made him blind
To Kurt the sous-chef's brute charms, though he'd rue
   Such bleared vision, finding himself behind
The curve of Cheryl's needs. For now it seemed
Kurt was the consummation that she'd dreamed.

XXXII

They planned, she said, to start a bar in Crete,
   And Don was welcome to the *Canard Bleu*.
She'd let him pay her once he'd made ends meet,
   For Cheryl, as we know, was D.J.'s banker
And cash wizz at the bistro, and now sweet
   Hot Kurt had made her soft as melted Anchor.
She kissed Don, left, he conquered agony,
Then tore the place apart in frenzied glee.

178

XXXIII

Out went scrubbed pine, in came smoked-glass and steel,
  Plus new décor in muted blues and greys.
And prints? Marc? Rouault? Rothko? Masereel?
  "NO!" The consultant's power-suited gaze
Met Don's. "Tell me, who'd want to eat a meal
  With angst or worse staring him in the face?
The suits we're aiming for have attitude.
Do give some thought to what best sets the mood."

XXXIV

"Mood?" She sighed. *"Ambience!"* That gave Don pause.
  Risk full frontal with an Ecdysiast?
(Lord B. liked Turkish ladies, though their flaws –
  "Sacking" rivals, for one – brought him at last
To plump for Venizianas or, the cause
  Of his demise, Hellenes.) Encomiast
For women as Don was, they failed to please,
Green-sandal shod with tented dungarees,

XXXV

Though, as was almost said by Rosalind
  When Jacques objected to her nomenclature,
"I had no thought of pleasing thee in mind",
  And in the new decade much *haute couture*
Was seen, Don knew, as something less than kind
  By women who rejected sex allure
As *démodé,* though what they got was less
Sane than Miss Most-Strict, cane-primed governess

XXXVI

Complete with cuprous hair and sharkfin nose,
  Vitreous eyes and teeth, those rat-trap lips –
She seemed the work of one of Archimboldo's
  Animaphoses in which swedes and turnips,
Pumpkins, carrots, and gourds were swapped for those
  Steel images that help us get to grips
With what Ortega called Dehumanis-
Ation of Art in life. So, no surprise,

179

XXXVII

The '80s proved his worst fears right. First came
  "The Mad Monk" Joseph, Norman "Boot Boy" Tebbit,
Panting to offer service to their Dame,
  Then Howard, hissing through his days, the rabid
Hezza, slime-soaked Baker, and, past shame,
  And worse than Rack-man Ridley, Howe who bleated
Lies for Ally Saddam – I quote his words –
"Not gas but bee-swarms killed 5,000 Kurds."

XXXVIII

Parkinson, too, his pursy mouth an anus
  Through which crap squeezed its way, until – there is a
God I sometimes think – this true-gel Janus
  Got with child an aide who, though no Clarissa,
You'd think would not play Moll to one as vain as
  This crock of unction, sump oil Cec., all sa-
Ponacious smarm? Say, Muse, how could she manage
To lie with what no pig would take as pannage?

XXXIX

— Though this, I know, 's little to do with Don,
  "I like to speak and lucubrate my fill".
But there's one theme I can't expatiate on –
  She-Who-Must-be-Obeyed's heir, that mandrill,
That monkey-businessman, her simian son,
  Whose "Backing Britain" Arms Deals let him fill
His piggy bank, for which a grateful nation
Made him a knight, which in Don's estimation

XL

Out-Lehrered Lehrer.) Now, back to the advice
  His cool consultant ordered. A flow chart
Was flipped to show him how to match the price
  Of goods to bums on seats, "and from the start
To maximise potential." In a trice,
  A flash of teeth, she'd shown him where *her* heart
Was to be found, how busily *she'd* range
To seek her true love on the Stock Exchange.

XLI

Hardly the basis for romance. But Cheryl
  In going made a gap in D.J's life,
And perhaps, briefly, Sue might do to fill
  His bed. She liked his pitch. "Though never wife
I'll be to any man, for where's the thrill,"
  She asked, "in habit?" Then, sternly, "and I've
This warning, Don. Don't think my stripy suits
Mean that I favour handcuffs, whips and boots."

XLII

Nor did moody murmurs move her, she said.
  Her talk was flowcharts, over-head projector,
Management stress – or how to keep your head
  When others' fell. She purred of Venn and Vector
And, always open her side of the bed,
  Books extolling growth in the private sector
Alone brought on those acquiescent groans
Concupiscent as seventy-six trombones.

XLIII

No wonder their affair was brief! Her "Good"
  Meant "Caring for One's Self". The Iron Lady
Was Virtue's Model. Her firm rectitude
  When faced with destitution – charity
Was, she said, proof of decrepitude –
  Showed Don to be a niminy-pimby. He
Vowed that though he paid full dues to Bacchus,
In politics he took his cue from Gracchus.

XLIV

"Who he?" Sue asked. "The people's Tribune," Don
  Explained, "who argued land should be distributed
In equal shares. Naturally, he was soon
  Murdered." "Quite right, too." For Sue attributed
Such talk to what she labelled "red subversion,"
  And wished all those who spoke thus would drop dead.
That hour, therefore, she packed her bags and left.
And for a day Don felt himself bereft.

XLV

But come the next, his thoughts had turned to food.
   "Try fusion" Sue had murmured late one night,
Words which her lover first misunderstood,
   Though sneers of cold command soon put him right.
"Not now, my dear, I may not be a prude,
   But, Don, you hardly stir me to delight –
That more than hint of garlic's some repellent!
I've never fantasised about a peasant."

XLVI

"A fig for Fusion," Don muttered. So, too,
   He dealt with thoughts to try *nouvelle cuisine*.
Not for our Don a blend of shredded *choux*
   With salmon morceau poised on one mung bean
And garnished with a ghost of tinctured *roux*
   To keep the pectorals of power men lean
While lunching over contracts thought propitious.
Don favoured menus that would please Apicius.

XLVII

But where to find them now? Where's Beeton – binned!
   Where's Grigson – grilled! Where's David – dumped!
                             Where's Leith –
Lost for all time! Where's Carrier – cooked! Who's conned
   Hearth-lessons Harbon taught – No-one! Where's Heath
(Ambrose, that is, not Edward, not the spurned
   Leader who fell, gnashing those grille-like teeth
Through which he'd forced his rhetorician's "Who
Rules Britain?" and the Brits replied, "Not you.")

XLVIII

All gone, the chefs of yesteryear, and gone
   Those dishes planned to fill a manly torso,
Lancashire Hotpot or Beef Wellington,
   With napery at knee or neck, the more so
As Clubs acquire the habit of *bon ton*
   And conversation turns to hound and horse, Oh
Empire Pudding, Stilton, Port and Brandy,
And in due season, keep a posset handy.

XLIX

Don shuddered at the very term. Yet, speak,
  Memory, he said, summon *my* favourite dish.
And there on Friar's Lane at once a Greek
  Taverna was his dream, and oh, a wish
Come true, it seemed – or could it be a freak
  Of light? – No, it was real, and though suspic-
Ious of forms seen at midday he dare
Believe this figure crossing Market Square

L

'D prove real. "Maria," he called. And it *was* her.
  Cloud of black hair, proud eyes, olive complexion,
And ample bust. How could he not remember
  Months that they'd spent together (on reflection
He thought they'd run from June to mid-September,
  That long-ago romance in – was it Sounion?
Or Skopelos? No matter.) "Ah, my dear,"
He said when he could speak, "what brings you here?"

LI

"And who might *you* be?" Then, to use a saying
  As lost to past times as "That's all my eye
And Betty Martin" or "We'll go a-Maying",
  The Penny Dropped – "It's *Don*." Though from her cry,
So muted, it would seem he was displaying
  Scant evidence of what had made her sigh
That time, long past, he'd fanned her to desire.
Still, e'en in our ashes lives their wonted fire

LII

Etcetera, and, spurred by hope, "Maria,"
  The Don confessed, "I dream of a taverna,"
Then, seized by hope, "I plan a new career.
  With you as guide, I'll prove a willing learner
In mastering Greek cuisine. Within a year
  At most I'll make the place a steady earner,
With specialties perhaps like moussaka
Certain to earn at least one Michelin star."

LIII

And speaking thus he led her to a bar
   Where she could tell her story. First, the pain
That followed on their week in Ithaka
   (So *that* was where!) For cure, she'd left to train
In Athens as a nurse. And there, a doctor
   Wooed and wed her, then brought her here to gain
Knowledge of northern ill and epidemic,
While Hans became – ho hum – an academic.

LIV

But now, Maria said, bored by society
   Where Hans cursed others' Grants and his own slights,
where green-eyed envy, drip-full to satiety,
   Caused him despair, dyspepsia, sleepless nights,
Ulcers and umbrage at the impropriety
   Of Honours lost, she'd ball a pair of tights,
She sometimes thought, and as an antidote
To such self-pity, ram them down his throat.

LV

"Then leave him, come and live with me, Maria,"
   Don urged, and, nothing loath, she, "Lead me, Maestro."
They hand in hand with wandering steps drew near
   His place while Don took thought how to pursue
His latest dream. And once inside, "My dear,"
   He said, "how would you favour *D.J.'s Kastro*?"
"No!" Maria was firm. "Something unique
We'll have. *Kathemera*. Open all week."

LVI

That was unique? But buttoning his lip,
   Don drew Maria to him, "S'agapo,"
He murmured and she, smiling, "Let me slip
   Out of this old *foustani*. Half a mo."
Now, Muse, be dumb before the heady trip
   The lovers took that day, their mounting O-
Blation to Erotica on what Cole Porter
Called gossamer wings. No doubt it was a snorter,

LVII

But – modesty's my *forté* – I'll descant
   Instead on how Maria, Don's bright star,
Beamed full upon him as he learnt Levant-
   Like dishes spiced with minted arakas,
Thyme, basil, oregano, oh, enchant-
   Ing scents and savours succulent. *Tra-la!*
Ecstatic Don! He conjures cunning plates
For opening night on which the city waits.

LVIII

It comes! And with it comes a contumacious
   Restaurant critic. Now, to say that Don
Refused to show civility or gracious
   Profile would be wrong. Still, he laid on
No special dishes, though the farinaceous
   Came to the fore that night like a *Mouton
Cadet* he had small use for, being keener
On *lefko topico* – that is, retsina.

LIX

It worked! Night followed night, the place was packed
   With those who, having read the man's encomia
For *Kathemera,* chose now to retract
   Their previous praise of Thai, while Don's superior
Pikilia made certain to attract
   Those short of cash. And for his *papoutsakia*
Some diners vowed to sacrifice their lives,
Though others, less expansive, offered wives.

LX

In jest, of course, and Don, in jest, replied
   That now was not the time for contemplating
Night errancy, besides which, he was tied
   To his Maria: all these years of waiting,
And now, as Midland men say, his "true Bride"
   Had come to him, too late, perhaps, for mating,
But he and she could breed a reputation
With locally sourced meals offered the nation –

LXI

For Don had signed to write a weekly column
   In one of the top glossies: and a book
Of *Greek Delights* soon followed. Suited, solemn,
   Don graced the cover, while Maria, "Cook
Of the Year", posed with a tray of *stollen*.
   (Not Greek, of course, but in the withering look
Maria cast toward the rubbish bin
She aimed to show how Athens saw Berlin.)

LXII

A problem, though. Some diners found it diff-
   Icult to speak the menu. *Where* did stress fall?
Don watched one groan and sweat then ask for *Stiff-*
   Ado, meanwhile another tripped on *Kol-*
Okathakia, as with handkerchief
   He mopped his brow and muttered, "fuckin' ell,
All these tongue-twisters and we're meant to pay!
I'd sooner have a Chinese take-away."

LXIII

'What's to be done?' Maria asked, and Don,
   Whose love of jazz was constant, shouted "Good
God, I know – how's this for inspiration?
   If music be the food of love, let food
Be named for music. Punters'll know their ration
   – *Moschari*, say – as 'Sentimental Mood',
Or *Bamies* – "Billie's Blues". Well, will it work?"
"As well as calling Sophocles a Turk,"

LXIV

Maria said, but seeing Don's perturbation,
   "Ok, O Kirios, try it for a week,
And who knows – if any explanation
   Is needed, we can tell them it's all Greek."
Don's hunch proved right. Without a reservation
   No-one could get a table and all speak
Of *Kathemera* as *the* place to be seen,
Even if you're uncertain what you mean

186

LXV

When ordering your meal, something I've found
   In other Greek tavernas, though who cares?
Not Don, for sure. His barque safely aground,
   He's host to folk he likes, though when T. Blair's
Office called up no table could be found –
   "All taken," Don said smoothly. "Oh, and there's
No chance he'll get one. Tell him that Maria
Would rather I'd a dose of gonorrhoea."

LXVI

For Don, though ageing, won't sing Gaudeamus
   With lying statesmen, comminates all those
Who stash their ill-gained loot in the Bahamas,
   Thinks Kate as sexy as elastic hose,
That fashionistas aren't the cat's pyjamas,
   Knows "noble blood" is not "seen in a nose",
And, though it's topped by crown or tulipant,
Knows cant for what it always will be – CANT.

LXVII

Maria, too, would choose a Souliot fate
   Before she'd bow the knee to those whose fame
Fans her to rage. See her haruspicate
   Kotopoulo while murmuring name on name
Of media tarts! Watching her extricate
   Liver and lungs, Don knows his dauntless dame
A match for any hero of Greek myth,
And not someone you'd want to tangle with –

LXVIII

(Apologies for such a rhyme, *epat-*
   E in spades.) Where was I? Yes, her worth
As Bouboulina's shade matched Don's éclat –
   And then, her kitchen skills! Oh, how the earth
Moved when she gave him *kleftiko*, though that
   In time would add some inches to his girth,
So (speak it softly) while in bed still able,
He ofttimes chose the pleasures of the table.

* * *

LXIX

And there I think we'll leave our blessed pair.
   Did Don remain for long a restaurateur,
Or did the two, as some allege, repair
   To country parts and take up literature?
(But Don would never wish to ape Hilaire
   Belloc's belief in nature as a cure
For social ills. He's no faux-primitive,
Though keen on love that's uninhibitive.)

LXX

Well, let them go, it's better they be free
   To fade from sight and thus avoid the curse
That's wished on many by biography,
   That insolent intrusion, where the hearse
Has scarcely been unpacked before you'll see
   A headline – NOW AT LAST. **THE TRUTH.** Averse
From such vulgarity, I'll spare D.J.
The spite of hacks. Then up, Muse, and away!

AMIT MAJMUDAR

I

Charms and the man I sang, but I would fail
  My epic models – *Odyssey, Aeneid,*
Et cetera – if I didn't send my pale
  And trembling Hero, by poetic fiat,
To gawk and gossip in the flaming hail.
  If Juan must descend to rise, so be it:
And should my critics claim I've lost the dare,
I bid them – *vide infra* – join him there.

II

And as for whether I've procured the rights
  To conjure this posthumous vision, dream
Of Juan's afterlife, presume to write
  In Ariosto's rhymes on Dante's theme,
Forget it's me – instead, take in the sights
  As I hear tell of things I've never seen.
Besides, it's not like Milton laid an eyeball
On Baal pouring Beelzebub a highball.

III

We last saw Juan shaking hands with that
  Commando, crosseyed ever since the Falklands,
Who'd shown up raging at our Hero's flat –
  With three prostheses quite the dead man walking,
His breath so sulphurous it killed the cat.
  Juan, in spite of all his Richard Dawkins,
Was dragged down to the nether lands – and damn
Your doubt, I don't mean Delft or Amsterdam.

IV

I must suspend my disbelief describing
  The landscape where he found himself. Just think
Hieronymus Bosch on psilocybin:
  A vision far too intricate for ink,
Much less an amateur who's been imbibing
  A greater Poet's long-unfinished drink.
When left for dead on that infernal ground,
Our Hero slapped his sleeves and looked around.

V

The weeds beneath his feet were Mary Jane
    (Not asphodels, that cannot get you high),
And here were poppies promising no pain,
    A field of blue where users got to lie
Like lotus-eaters, or bureaucrats in Spain,
    Siesta endless under an endless sky.
Juan believed the lush outskirts of Dis
A Blessed Isle whose cash crop was bliss.

VI

But he was quickly disillusioned by
    The vision of a tar-black, waddling bird
Whose body had been able, once, to fly.
    Some naked children clicked as if to herd
The gull, if that is what it was... but why?
    He staggered, horrified, from what occurred:
The imps had brought a matchbook, and they lit
The tarred bird in the slick that covered it.

VII

'Forgive the devils,' said a voice beside him.
    'They're only boys, and starving for a lark.'
A tourist needs a resident to guide him:
    In Dis a tourist's doubly in the dark,
And though its spires flash like thorny diadems,
    I've found there's never anywhere to park.
With sound convention I'm no-one to quibble:
It's time that my Aeneas met his Sibyl.

VIII

Of course, the guide in question was a man –
    I should have likened him to Virgil, but
We rhyme not as we wish, but what we can.
    He wore a coat of 19th-century cut:
Taut at the shoulder-seams, it strained to span
    The Lord's love-handles and his drinker's gut –
And yet his face! Nay: *visage!* So celestial
It would have left the angels looking bestial.

IX

'Are you,' gasped Juan, 'the poet of *The Giaour*?
　Fever of Europe! Genius of the Age,
Driving your stanzas ninety lines an hour!
　You – faced with Critics, or an empty Page,
Or even Turkish warships – didn't cower
　But, pacing Missolonghi like a cage,
Perished for Greece – the Greece that Britain's wan
Young tigerlilies merely rhymed upon.'

X

'Funny,' said Byron (for it was the Scot),
　'I'm famous – infamous? – down here for *Cain* –
While if you go topside, you're like as not
　To hear my work "in the satiric vein"
Is best, while all the rest is period rot.
　Who knew that Keats's Cockney Odes would reign,
While poet-scholars, from a sense of duty,
Would slot me nothing but "She Walks in Beauty"?

XI

'I, too, am thrilled to meet you, I must say –
　Your tireless two-hundred-year-long bender,
The way you've scarcely aged, like Dorian Gray –
　That fateful Handshake – quite the bender-ender!
I've watched you, Juan, watched you night and day...
　Mostly your nights, of course, in all their splendour.
Don't look surprised: Your amorous attainments
Regaled us all – such epic entertainments!

XII

'As for your run-in with that vet, who pincered
　And dragged you from your Holland Garden flat –
A man with symptoms like a package insert –
　How could a fellow have avoided *that*?
That madman could have killed you with a tin sword,
　And well before your body went to fat.
The old commando had a mind of slaughter
For decades – ever since you dumped his daughter.

XIII

'...Not that you remember what her name is.
  The greatest lovers aren't very good
With little details, not if they are famous –
  We'd maintain all our girlfriends, if we could,
But that's an awful lot of seats at *Les Mis*,
  And good luck monitoring each one's mood –
Violet wants her hand held, meanwhile Valerie
Is angry that her ticket's for the gallery.

XIV

'You must have guessed the nature of this place,
  But fear not: Satan long ago declared
His torturing a sinner just obeys
  The Will of God and, ever since, has cared
For us – indulged us, really – so our days
  Are spent in sinning on a scale we dared
Not try on earth. Blaspheming's so habitual
It's grown as dull as any sacred ritual.

XV

'We use the terms of virtue when we swear,
  So that we argue shouting *Bless you!* back
And forth while making crosses in the air
  (The gesture's grave, a personal attack).
But generally we're friendly. Everywhere
  Likeminded sinners sin together, packs
Of killers hacking at each other then
Comparing wounds before they kill again.

XVI

'The thieves have all the coins they wish. They fill
  Their pockets full and gather in a crowd
Where everybody picks his neighbour's, till
  They shake their pockets out and laugh aloud.
We've seven Vaticans on seven hills
  And Senates to accommodate the proud.
The covetous get everything they covet.
It's hell all right, but home – and hell, we love it.'

194

XVII

'And how about the – er – promiscuous?'
    Asked Juan, with a nervous grin. 'Do they
Amuse each other, deep in this abyss?'
    Lord Byron grinned. 'We get our share of play.
They've got a nightclub here in downtown Dis
    Where trust me, Juan, you'll enjoy your stay.
You've never seen the calibre of misses
As those I'll show to you at Beatrice's.'

XVIII

His whistle conjured up a coach and four;
    This old conveyance seemed a little odd
To Juan. 'With hellfire snuffed out for
    All time,' said Byron, 'gasoline's outlawed.
For years, we've sent our stockpiles topside. War
    Would die out but for fossil fuels and God,
So Satan, cultivating war, sows oil wells
In deserts, Bibles in five-star hotels.

XIX

Considered geographically, our sky
    Is earth – this *is* the Underworld, remember.
The smog was like Los Angeles in July,
    The snowing ash like New York in September.
Apparently, asthmatic succubi
    Were letting fires dwindle to the ember.
The sky topside is filthy too, and finite –
Good thing the ozone layer's got a skylight.'

XX

They passed an SS-Obergrüppenführer
    And Mississippi slaver – over grapes
And Brie discussing, with convivial furor,
    Whether the blacks or Slavs were truer apes.
One slit his neck to prove his blood was purer
    Then poured it like a syrup on his crepes.
The spot was Hell's most popular café –
Pol Pot and Stalin shared a canapé

XXI

As well as stories of their favourite slaughters,
  Two lifetimes of accumulated wisdom
Exchanged across a pair of sparkling waters.
  As for the rest, too many lunched to list 'em
(A list would read like History's police blotter).
  Two Huns stepped out: Alas, the carriage missed 'em.
The riders couldn't look for very long
Because of how quickly the carriage was tearing along.

XXII

'But justice...' Juan murmured, '...for what they did...'
  'Are lovers just,' said Byron, 'when the love
Is gone? Are *courts* – that jail a coloured kid
  (A pinch of powder in a bag's enough)
While silver-haired execs, with millions hid
  Offshore, go free? Are things so just above
(Where God, supposedly, is seeing all)
That you're so shocked when Satan makes the call?

XXIII

'Hell's job, my friend, was outsourced long ago –
  To earth. The gnashing teeth and beaten breast,
The so on, so forth, lash and heat and woe,
  The fire pit, dark wood, and all the rest
Were staffed and stocked with us. Wouldn't you know,
  We the people – *human* demons – prove the best
At making other people shake and howl.
We trump the torments dreamt up in a cowl.'

XXIV

And yet (thought Juan innocently) hadn't
  There been some killer parties even then,
Though military-minded midgets maddened
  Mitteleuropa? (And then – did so again?)
Sometimes your face might look a little saddened;
  You'd spin a record of *La Belle Hélène*.
(Though for a pick-me-up, no score compares
To the overture of *Orphée aux Enfers*.)

XXV

'Jean Dindon' had the canny luck to witness
    The death of Civilization... from Geneva,
And back when Hitler raved of racial fitness
    Was high out West on *cannabis sativa.*
Thanks to a forged passport, which proved his Britness,
    'Johnson, Donald' never did receive a
Draft card, while in the Maoist Fifties, 'Dong Jong'
Observed a purge up close – that is, from Hong Kong.

XXVI

No use explaining his voluptuary,
    Ascetic distance from this-worldly griefs
To Byron – who was revolutionary
    In deed and verse, not just in his 'beliefs.'
For Juan's heart was in his Bloody Mary
    While Byron's was among his Grecian chiefs.
Unlike most noblemen in his milieu,
Though he attended balls, he had them too.

XXVII

A theatre – at which the damned might catch
    Die Hard, or *Die Hard Again* – neighboured the steel
And glass headquarters of the *Dis Dispatch.*
    Look, there was Ixion on a ferris wheel;
Two sahibs, off to watch a cricket match;
    A vast Financial District – with a patch
Of grass and benches, where the Fraudulent
Could eat panini while they hedged and lent.

XXVIII

He only glimpsed the City. Icarus,
    The coachman, held his cap and began to whip
The horses so hard, Juan didn't miss
    Combustion engines on their breakneck trip.
The nightclub's sign said 'Paradiso' – this
    Was where the steeds, stopped, hung their heads to drip
Exhaustion on the kerb, sweat-blind, whip-wary.
Established 1321: B. Portinari,

XXIX

A plaque announced. Above the portal:
   Abandon all clothes, ye who enter here.
Juan was hardly shy, but his immortal
   Spirit was skittish till the Scottish Peer
Divested all his vestments with a chortle
   Almost childlike to Juan's ear.
Ladies, if you must drop your eyes, then please do,
But when in Dis, one does as the Diseased do.

XXX

Now Juan, gasping once more, pointed down –
   For shame! not where you're thinking, *lower* – crying
'Your foot, Milord! It's fixed!' The faintest frown;
   And then a gentle nod. 'For all their trying,
London's surgeons failed. But my renown
   Had travelled distances beyond my scrying,
And when I reached this city, Satan's own
Physician cracked and realigned the bone.'

XXXI

They'd just ventured into the noise and flashing
   When an Italian vixen threw her arms
Around the naked Poet, fairly crashing
   Against him. Juan marvelled at her charms
And rather minimalist sense of fashion,
   But in the Club beyond, among the swarms,
He made out wedding gowns, some thongs, a sundress –
A dozen styles of dress and semi-undress.

XXXII

In fact, the only ones who stood by, bare
   And forked, were both men, just his Guide and he.
Our Hero blushed, a colour very rare
   On Juan's cheek since 1823
But flattering, apparently, for their
   Insouciant Hostess licked her lips to see
This Latin Lover modestly as Adam
Concealing treasures where she knew he had 'em.

XXXIII

'I'm Beatrice, and this is Paradise,'
   She said. 'You know me, maybe, from the Poem
An old Admirer wrote to praise my Eyes?
   My friend, consider Paradise your home.
Plenty of pleasures... though excuse the mice.
   It's hard to keep them from a catacomb.
In time, I wager (though we'd never rush you),
You'll grow to love the way their whiskers brush you.

XXXIV

'If ever, as a Virgil-bludgeoned boy,
   You wondered just how hot it gets on Venus
Or what cup size compelled the sack of Troy,
   My club's your college. *This* Romantic genius
Has graduated (Georgie, don't be coy!)
   Cum laude – Magna – though our profs are keenest
On freshmen, which is why I'm thrilled to see so
Astute a student enter Paradiso.

XXXV

'I offer nymphs from Ovid, nymphets out
   Of Nabokov. You'll have Scheherazade
For a thousand nights – or one; Héloïse without
   Her habit, rosary, or jealous God.
You're one who likes to make it new, no doubt:
   I'll find you Starlets – look at Georgie nod –
Like Brittany Murphy, or Brigitte Bardot.
They won't just wink and kiss their hands – they'll blow.

XXXVI

'They'll sell their bodies for a song, my Sirens.
   And this historical extravaganza
Will expand your knowledge – as it expanded Byron's –
   You too will be devoted to *la danza,*
A *danse macabre* though it may seem, requiring
   More women than can fit inside a stanza,
Lovers of Dukes and darlings of the media,
And even one who prompted a *Commedia.*'

XXXVII

The Bar was serving everything from whiskey
    And rye to Hennessy, from 'shrooms and quaaludes
To hits of heroin. He thought it risky –
    But Byron counselled that he in no way should
Hold back from using – or from getting frisky,
    'Cause after all – the past is but a prelude.'
The lines he did off Beatrice's thigh were
Like all of Byron's other lines inspired.

XXXVIII

The ladies, too – Empresses Theodora
    And Josephine, among those Juan knew
On sight – were smoking up, while Petrarch's Laura
    Was way too wasted for a *How d'ye do.*
The loudest lady there was Ibsen's Nora,
    Who'd gotten soused, but only like a true
Bourgeoise, that is, she'd downed Bacardi Breezers
In quantities enough to bring on seizures.

XXXIX

It seemed that Byron drank to work up bravery,
    Thumping his chest like someone mourning something.
Now Juan felt his spirit somewhat wavery,
    For parties were supposed to be a fun thing.
He headed – like a free man off to slavery,
    His body everywhere a strangely numb thing –
Out onto Paradiso's dance floor, where
The ravers whipped him with their raven hair.

XL

He felt like Pan upon an orange urn
    Approaching nubile naiads, nothing loath,
And for their part, the women seemed to turn
    By heliotropic instinct to them both.
And Juan, getting close, could now discern
    A chancre on a lip, a flattened growth
Upon a bosom otherwise alluring.
(Some beauty marks grow lovelier with curing.)

XLI

A Hindustani Begum in a sari
   Mistook him for her lost Angrezi beau,
And Juan fled her – straight to Mata Hari,
   Whose writhing felt like snakes. He trod her toe,
A great *faux pas*, but as he shouted 'Sorry!'
   She gripped his waist and dropped into a slow
Gyration. When she flashed her covert eyes
He saw that great Spymaster, the Prince of Lies,

XLII

Leering at him from deep inside these hotties
   Bumping and grinding on the strobe-lit floor,
One Spirit in one thousand female bodies
   (Or is that *mille e tre*?) all moaning *More!*
He'd loved his share of ladies, true, but not these
   Demonic damsels and historic whores.
It seemed Tussaud's ensemble went from wax
To flesh and had concerted an attack.

XLIII

So now, converged upon, he caught a smell...
   Eau de toilette? Mortician's formalin,
More like it, mingled, mangled with Chanel.
   Speaking of whom: Coco Chanel was in
The house tonight, and looking less than well,
   Unsteady as a drunken skeleton
In pitch-black shades, determined to be fairest,
Draped like a hangar with Milan and Paris.

XLIV

Our Hero, wanted *oh* so bad, began
   To ricochet from Lana Turner with
Her maggot smile – to the blistered tan
   Of Jackie O. – to Ishtar from the myth,
Grotesquely breasted – to beheaded Anne
   Boleyn and Catherine, who I think was fifth,
A choker set strategically in place,
A red horizon in a cloud of lace.

XLV

And here was Edna St. Vincent Millay,
 Who groped him at the volta of his pelvis,
A Siren who sang – and was – a wild lay.
 She jumped on him and clung, light, almost elvish,
But Juan shouted, swatted her away.
 She started raging, stomped, and called him selfish,
Then scanned the prospects in that hot environ
And stalked across the floor to target Byron,

XLVI

Who at that moment fondled Antony's Queen,
 Scarce noticing the asps that twined his forearm.
When Edna moved in, there was quite a scene –
 Lucrezia Borgia showed up, for a quorum,
But Byron, as they clashed, escaped between
 And shimmied through that harum-scarum forum
To wretched Juan, who had once been swimming
And now had drowned in women, women, women.

XLVII

'How do you like the Party, Juan? Quite
 The centre of attention you've become!
That old babushka – watch out, she likes to bite –
 Is Catherine the Great. My rule of thumb
Is forty Major Figures in a night,
 But you're already doubling that sum!
I wish you, Juan, all the luck in cramming a
Cool hundred in by midnight. Luck and stamina!'

XLVIII

Don Juan, crawling from a pair of Livias
 And kicking off a grunting Amy Winehouse,
Was far too petered out to feel lascivious,
 The formalin still stinging either sinus,
His body bumped and ground down till oblivious
 By half a hundred partners, plus or minus.
'O Byron,' he beseeched, 'O Lord of rhyme
Who slept with all the Muses in your prime,

XLIX

'If this is fun, by all means call me boring!
  If this is partying, then call the cops!
I think I'm done, at least for now, with whoring.
  You've handled this how long? I give you props.'
His guide guffawed. 'Poor Juan! You're ignoring
  Lord Byron's Law: The Party Never Stops
Until the Break of Dawn. This music's on
4 eva, playa. Here, there *is* no dawn.'

L

And Juan witnessed in his master's eyes
  A laughter shading into pure despair,
His hard Byronic laughter, that disguise
  By which the tears are masked and teeth are bared,
Delighting in bedevilling device
  Tossed off at top speed with an offhand air.
They might have said more: – But the slender hands
Dragged Juan moaning back into the dance.

SINÉAD MORRISSEY

And money, that most pure imagination...
Byron, *Don Juan*, Canto XII, 2, 7.

Part One

I

We need a hero. The time is out of joint,
  has burnt its fragile socket, while for the Mayans,
who read their dazzling mountain stars like newsprint,
  transcribing mankind's pre-allotted lifespan –
by 2012, there's simply no more of it.
  God's eighteenth-century clock has winded down.
We're at the end, or so the websites warn us,
of everything we know and value precious.

II

I'm usually unconvinced, convinced instead
  that end-of-history talk is soon demolished
by history's own refusal to be led
  into some silent terminus. Things may not flourish:
we may be colder, hungrier, more upset
  by the growing list of what's been taken from us.
But even lame, thin, choking and at variance
with the riches of before, we'll falter on regardless.

III

Now I'm not so sure. Take this week's news:
  a cataclysm, a Herculean storm
unlike anything even Al Gore lent shape to
  is closing in, caused partly by a shifting jet-stream,
partly by the pole-ice melting through –
  a rough beast rising as the oceans warm.
We watch its blue-white swirl by satellite
on flashy CNN, like spies on our own planet.

IV

We watch it hit. They've timed it to the second.
  A waterproofed and clearly mad reporter
getting tossed across a junction by the wind,
  then back again, up to his calves in water,
tries to speak to us but his voice is drowned.
  The anchorwoman smiles and leaves him there,
shuttling between the leaning trees and the signals
as the rain rolls over him and the picture fails.

V

By morning, we're in Aftermath, a Birdseye view:
   parks and streets submerged in the ravaged cities –
sheets of pewter sea blown into a new,
   transplanted element; kilometres of debris.
The northeast national grid has blown its fuse.
   The graces we now live by – transport, electricity –
that house us all in rooms of heated glass
lie savaged and defunct as the cable telegraph.

VI

And how much will it cost? Dear Lord, the cost...
   Tens of billions, according to *The Guardian,*
on insurance claims alone for what's been lost.
   Since the financial crisis, we can't imagine
what so many profligate zeros, nestled close,
   reproduced like cells, have come to *mean* –
they march across our headlines, black and crass,
and always with a minus sign attached.

VII

A little while ago in Houston, Texas
   three awfully clever men invented something
very bold and deft and half-miraculous:
   a fresh, *creative* way to run accounting
(and why not?) whereby losses make a plus.
   They made wealth up: income, future earnings,
so that, sign without a signifier, wild
in its own unfettered realm, money multiplied...

VIII

... until it crashed. O what a falling off!
   While thousands lost their pensions, they went to jail
in handcuffs, though sadly not for long enough,
   and not before their brainchild had gone viral.
Soon debt became a bargainable stock
   and the trick with debt, how it loves to dive and spiral,
a ballooning asset. Champagne baths on Wall Street,
the fizz of endless cash and nothing cheap,

IX

not even escorts, a 'legitimate' expense,
   and certainly not the cars, the drugs, accessories
for adventure sports, the loft apartments.
   But holes are holes, no matter how unholily
they may be cloaked with crafty argument,
   and Enron's falling off just mere pinprickery
compared to the current void. A chasm splits
the contours of the earth. We're staring into it.

X

Like Attack of the Giant Crabs! The Killer Spiders!
   (small and normal creatures malformed by radiation)
all the hidden less-than-zero numbers,
   tired of being barred, like ruined cousins,
from civilised conversation, staged a takeover.
   We're starving, they announced, *and we are Legion.*
The mega-banks went first: their secret debts
devoured them from within, then spat them out.

XI

The other banks we salvaged with our taxes.
   And for what? Their doors stay double-bolted
while talk of what we haven't got in practice
   is all the rage since money's lack revolted.
Nothing's offered: no credit, ready cash,
   no sweet forgiving margin; those evicted
from the homes they can't afford, who bought too late,
live someplace other than on ghost estates.

XII

The outlook's bleak. We're inside a climacteric
   our baby boomer parents never dreamt of
who grew up in the groove of post-war pop music,
   who always had a job, who shared their love.
As weather forecasts grow apocalyptic,
   as doubting politicians lose their nerve,
as markets tumble, as what we're told we'll owe
engulfs our children's children – we need a hero.

Part Two

I

A Judge? A Pope? A President? Not likely.
   Four years ago we thought we'd found a true one
when Obama won the White House. His wife was pretty,
   his daughters tall and modest; his speeches shone
like electroplated costume jewellery
   with glittering abstract nouns: *justice, freedom…*
But the poetry of campaigning got rearranged
as prose once he took office. Little changed.

II

Someone close to power but not wet-through
   with it; someone honest, wry, congenial,
who's commonplace enough to not be deaf to
   the voice of that most abstract noun, the people.
No banking magnate, no plane-and-shipping guru,
   no prophet of a lizard nation, no angel –
but best of all a mirror or a silver screen
we catch our captured selves reflected in.

III

Enter Donald Johnson. At sixty-three
   childless, virile, handsome, single, rich
with all the things he's done and where he's been
   (Australia, Budapest), still sleek and boyish,
still dynamic, still brim-full of bewitchery
   with women (who are still the ones to ravish
him) and who has recently found employment
as an attaché in the European Parliament.

IV

To such a skilled adventurer, Belgium is dull
   (with compensations: waffles, chocolates, beer
so fine he quaffs it by the tankard-full,
   mussels steamed in wine, shallots and butter,
stupendous *frites*) but on the whole he's grateful –
   a job's a job and he isn't getting younger.
He has a tiny flat above a park
and visits, *le weekend, Les Museés des Beaux-Arts.*

210

V

Work's a doddle. The mechanics of the Union
   grind and turn, down miles of spotless corridors
in countless shiny rooms. A gravy train
   for every sort of bureaucrat: directors,
policy advisors, inventors of Eurojargon
   (*Flexicurity, Acquis Communautaire*),
advocacy officers. The EU's sound:
it's well-oiled and its wheels go round and round.

VI

He breakfasts with the Secretary at nine.
   He de-briefs after meetings those beneath him.
He drafts agendas, often before the deadline.
   He sets up conference calls in French and German.
He tracks reports and checks if stats align
   with various previous member-state projections.
He leaves at ten, to dine and then to bed
sometimes alone and sometimes with a friend.

VII

And then things change. The map is not the territory
   and metaphor, like language, leaves a gap
between the thing described and its new summary.
   So when things change, metaphor plays catch-up.
A greased machine? The EU-as-a-Body's
   more apt now its economies are crap;
it ate a lot, in what they termed 'expansion',
then instantly fell foul of such infection

VIII

it threatens to expire... The U.S. sneezed,
   the EU caught the flu: national debts
so vast (and growing) they betray disease,
   rising unemployment, frozen assets,
tottering banks and shrinking GDPs.
   The five most gangrenous toes on Europe's foot –
Ireland, Italy, Portugal, Spain and Greece –
are losing blood and blackening from necrosis.

IX

Surgeons stand ready, scrubbed and dressed in green.
  Austerity! Austerity! – the answer
backed by Merkel, Europe's undisputed Sovereign –
  has gripped us all ('we're all in this together')
but is gripping some like a slip-knot at a hanging.
  Austerity the 'Fury' with 'abhorrèd shears'
who 'slits the thin-spun life' – the dreadful price –
the cutting off the nose to save the face...

X

It's Monday morning, dim with Brussels rain.
  November 12th. The Secretary's serious.
He doesn't want to deal with the campaign
  on Donald's list (a biodiversity crisis)
and stares into his coffee. News in from Spain
  is dire, but the news from Greece disastrous
as Austerity cuts deep, cuts deeper still...
He wants a witness, someone with the skill

XI

of staying low, anonymous and watchful,
  to gather notes and keep him up to date
on how the current measures have proved harmful
  (beyond the TV, papers and debates
in the two parliaments) to 'ordinary people'.
  He spreads his hands. 'I'd like to delegate
this research trip to *you*, Mr Johnson.'
Call it a hero's quest, call it a mission –

XII

Donald coughs and nods. Outside the window
  cherry trees in rows are almost bare:
the last of their scarlet/golden leaves to go
  before the winter, flash their burnished fire.
His ticket's booked. He'll leave for Greece tomorrow.
  The bleeding South. He's never been before
(but knows Lord Byron died there). He thinks of sun
and olives, wine with resin... Revolution.

Part Three

I

Brussels' airport's busy with arrivals –
    a crisis brings the margins to the Centre
like supplicants to Rome. Its polished hall
    of cafés gleams and hums. Spice-in-sugar:
the caffeinated jazz of morning travel
    sets Donald tingling. He buys cologne, saunters
towards his departure gate, checks his watch,
then thinks of white geese ranged around a trough

II

with held-back wings as he stares at the jets outside.
    Hardly anyone's flying to Greece. No tourists.
No families steering buggies loaded high
    with snacks and nappies. No propertyists.
A bored EU official scans the sky;
    another suffers questions from a journalist
and by the entrance, a woman on her own
stands scrolling through a document by smartphone.

III

Donald looks again. Too long ago
    an interpreter for Russian sent a text
which conjured up the dear, well-worn scenario:
    dinner, drinks, a so-what-happens-next...?
Perhaps a month. He mouths a warm hello
    across the seats, but she only seems perplexed
and looks away. She's dark, composed, allusive.
This only serves to make her more attractive.

IV

The cabin's almost empty. Mozart trills
    to a frothy, crested peak – and down again.
Scattered heads observe the safety drill.
    Then the roar and lift of flight, the seat-belt sign
clicks off, and she's suddenly beside him in the aisle,
    asking if she can join him. Donald feigns
surprise and says of course. Not *over*-gleefully.
She stretches out her hand. 'I'm Persephone.'

V

She stows her laptop, feathers out her hair.
   He asks her if she makes this journey often.
She turns her gaze to his. 'Once a year.'
   They order wine – a lull before the conversation
loosens its tie and runs. 'Every winter,
   from November to February. I live in Athens.
And you, Mr...?' 'Johnson. Call me Donald. Please.'
All is good. The flight's as smooth as a Baileys;

VI

clouds are massed like floss beneath the wing-tip;
   sun is streaming in; she's friendly, smart,
with brilliant teeth and slightly glossy lips
   and could sweeten, not just the clockwork start
to this morning's flight but the whole brief trip...
   He muses on seduction, its lines, its parts,
its dartings forth, its keeping some things buried,
and mentally marks a tick for 'clearly interested'

VII

as he listens to her talk. She talks a lot.
   And so the game of Working-Out commences.
She laughs and volunteers that she's a Eurocrat:
   a Master's in economics, fluent French,
a decade's stellar service (which makes her what,
   thirty-five or six? – not, he thinks, on balance,
disturbingly his junior) and sent to oversee,
each winter, changes to the EU C.A.P.

VIII

in her own benighted country, on which she's expert.
   She wears no ring. 'It must be hard on your husband
when you leave?' She shrugs. 'He tolerates it:
   since we met, it's just what's always happened.
We lead our Belgian life, easy, quiet –
   not volatile, not raw-edged or impassioned –
and then I'm gone, and our winter lives are different
and we never ask precisely how they're spent.'

IX

A husband – damn. But O the little thud
    in Donald's groin as she scurries to dispel him!
She's said enough, she's said more than she should
    if Donald doesn't rush to state his freedom
just as obviously. The flurry in his blood
    engulfs his knees. Is it the Sauvignon?
Is it the sun-drenched cloud-scape for a view?
He turns to her directly. 'I want you...'

X

and there's a moment then – she holds his stare,
    not moving, calm – and he listens to the engine
through the floor, and feels the pulse of her,
    as though they'd touched already, as though she'd spun
a web of silk and drawn him in. He falters,
    flutters closer (her mouth is slightly open)
and they kiss: a single quivering kiss,
and he's weirdly trapped like a climber in a crevice

XI

as something rank runs through him, something cold
    from caverns too long shut to wind and light
deep inside the ground, where little grows
    but the thousand-year-long creep of stalactites
and fishless rivers carve out limestone folds
    and viaducts, and nameless shapes take flight –
He pulls away. The world is bright and stable:
here are his hands, here is his tray-table,

XII

there's a suited woman smiling her assent,
    looking (slightly) embarrassed by his haste
but not affronted; they've started their descent.
    The seat-belt sign clicks on. 'That's a foretaste,'
she offers softly. Then she gathers her equipment
    and is gone – as though he dreamt her face,
her lips, the untold clammy depths of her...
Her perfume fills the air. Donald shudders.

215

Part Four

I

What is it we fear? We fear the loss
　of whatever it is we've set about our hearths
to keep life's slicing cold at bay: a house;
　a food supply; coins that hold their worth
from one day to the next; a health service.
　We fear the loss of a perpetually generous earth.
We fear the end of buses, the closure of stores,
we fear a return to conditions between the wars

II

when ragged men in lines brought all they owned –
　a battered bowl and spoon – to public kitchens;
when governments were fractured, jelly-boned,
　and hostage to a mass, enraged sedition
that ushered in such darkness, light was doomed.
　We fear a return to the Old Road into London
where mothers left their babies in their hundreds
to die of cold and lack of Parish funds.

III

In 2012, on the 13th of November,
　all over Greece – in Athens, on the islands,
in the agricultural north – Loss is Ruler
　and only the slick and sheltered rich withstand
its hunger. Every flat, every schoolyard and taverna
　plays its host, and should the honeyed Sirens
still exist, their singing would be rent
with Greece's wailing, and turn into lament.

IV

The airport's crazy. Just the day before
　a budget slashing billions, yet again,
from salaries and services was deplored
　around the Chamber, then passed by a squeaky margin.
Another national strike looms like a downpour.
　The rush to leave in advance of a total shut-down
is panic-stricken. Donald doesn't feel well.
He takes a taxi to a moderate hotel,

V

showers, cleans his teeth, and falls asleep
  in a room that's beige and redolent with smoke
and dreams a lake. He's standing ankle-deep
  and then he's flailing underwater and he chokes
and then he stops. He looks. Trapped – in reeds –
  a long-haired, staring girl... He jolts awake.
Outside on the street, two men are arguing.
Their voices play like scales: rising, falling,

VI

rising... It doesn't end. The clock says eight –
  he thought it would be earlier but the difference
in the hour? How did he sleep so late?
  The room is dark. Headlights' luminescence
moves around the walls. He needs to eat,
  shake off the wide-eyed girl, experience
the city in the evening, start making notes...
He stows his wallet and his phone inside his coat,

VII

ignores the lift, trips down the dusty stairs,
  and is in the lobby, striding towards the exit,
when he sees her – straight-backed in an armchair,
  waiting. She's changed: no longer in a suit
but in a dress, not wearing make-up, older.
  He'd told her nothing, now he thinks of it:
nothing about his life, his job, the reason
for the trip. Did she *follow* him?

VIII

'Mr Johnson...' She's stood to stop him leaving.
  He brushes past. 'I'm here to introduce
you to the current facts. My car is waiting.'
  And the strangeness of the day – its working loose
of steady, regular stuff (read *sleep* and *kissing*)
  like a tongue around a half-extracted tooth –
goes up one notch. He finds himself disarmed,
inside her car as the door is being slammed,

217

IX

Persephone beside him in the back,
   a wordless driver skulking in the front,
the night, both brightly lit and densely black,
   unravelling by his window, and what he wants
to say – *how dare you* – vanishing like a snowflake
   on a spit. He tries to speak but can't.
Athens seems normal: lovers hand-in-hand;
illuminated bars; tobacco stands –

X

like any typical European capital
   with tree-lined avenues of modern flats;
market squares packed tight with canvas stalls;
   displays of jewels and shoes and sequinned hats
gleaming in the darkness; a City Hall
   fronted by gushing fountains. Though there are rats:
he spots one as they angle round a corner,
flashed up by the headlights, then another –

XI

then another – fast and fat and freakish –
   running out of pipes or into drains –
the streets are twitching. Tottering piles of rubbish
   begin to catch his eye. They turn again
into a major thoroughfare. He hadn't noticed,
   but garbage bags are everywhere: thrown
in heaps round litter bins, clogging doorways –
the refuse of a city, left for days...

XII

'Welcome to the Winter of our Discontent.
   It's lasted years but now it's getting worse.
We borrow double, for every Euro spent.
   There's a bottomless pit in place of the public purse
that can't be filled, though each successive government
   tries its best. This is our constant curse,
like Sisyphus.' Sirens tear the air.
She leans forward in her seat. 'Syntagma Square.'

218

Part Five

I

Syntagma Square, Syntagma Square's on fire
  Boots and batons, petrol bombs and bricks
They've strung up Merkel's portrait on a wire
  They've burned the German flag for bitter kicks
They've dumped the Euro symbol on the pyre
  and asked police to suck their fucking pricks
It's blazing, it's amazing, it's awhirl
with teargas and cannons, down in the underworld –

II

What do you get if you slice a loaf in half,
  then half, then half again? Answer: hungry.
What do you get if you lay off half your staff,
  the public civil servants of your country,
then threaten to axe the rest? Wheat from chaff,
  or the sudden, icy plunge into 'mere anarchy'?
You face two doors: an 'out'-door and an 'in'-door;
their signs are hidden, but both of them are trapdoors –

III

Eight little Indians, gayest under heaven –
  (seven little Indians, chopping up sticks)
one went to sleep, then there were seven –
  (one chopped himself in half and then there were six)
And there's never any chance of getting even
  And the wings to lift you out of here are wax –
One little Indian, left all alone,
he went out and hanged himself and then there were none –

IV

The roar increases. A camera crew retreats.
  The riot squad advances like a wall.
Huddled against Persephone, Donald sweats.
  He doesn't want to stay with her at all
but there's smoke and screaming out there on the streets
  and he doesn't know the way to his hotel...
As though she's made her point (or read his mind),
she clears her throat, the car backs round a bend

219

V

then screeches off, untouched. They roll along
      past empty restaurants, strings of shuttered shops,
an ambulance growing fainter like a song
      on a turned-down radio, until it stops.
Persephone says: 'Disorder will go on –
      they'll broadcast it as students versus cops –
but it's everyone. The people have no choice.
They're damned already.' Donald finds his voice:

VI

'Where are we headed to next?' 'A quiet place –'
      (O the relief of that!) – 'to a garden.'
They're there in minutes: a residential space
      between two railway lines, overgrown
with weeds and shards and dubious sorts of waste –
      the kind of neglected bypass, Gypsy-rotten,
where immigrants begin their new existence
overlooked by us. Except there's silence:

VII

'no lights on in the flats; no smells of cooking;
      no children on the swing that someone's improvised;
no beat-up vans or bikes, no tethered washing.
      'Who were they?' 'These were Syrians, terrorised
by Assad, and his overindulged-in bombing
      of hospitals and schools. But Greece is immunised –
Europe's most porous border no longer leaks:
we round them up and house them all in concrete,

VIII

thirty to a cell – Iraqis, Afghans –
      and if they come by boat, our coast patrols
do their damnedest to ensure they never land.'
      A train grinds by, transparent as a fishbowl,
its passengers bright and separate, elsewhere-bound,
      who stare ahead. The wind is moaning cold.
A front door hanging slant like a flap of skin
bangs and bangs... Persephone sits waiting.

220

'There's one last site, a temple, we should visit –
    out at Sounion. Let's get started.'
And they drive. He finds her stern and forthright:
    the woman on the plane, a lie imparted
according to his known pre-requisites;
    a satin mask. *Among the dear departed,*
she shall reign: cruel, true, unwavering;
she carries out the curses of the living

upon the souls below and knows no anguish...
    This rings inside his head like burning scripture.
Soon Athens' dish of radiance is eclipsed.
    The road winds up through trees, they park, and there –
a roofless columned hall upon a cliff,
    the sea beneath – a drop of sixty metres –
sighing on the stones. 'Lord Byron came
and in the marble chiselled out his name,

XI

'But to us this place is famous for Aegeus –
    father of Theseus, who forgot to change his sails
from black to white. Although he returned victorious
    from the labyrinth, his father thought he'd failed:
he glimpsed the ship and, frenzied with distress,
    jumped from the cliff and gave this sea its name.'
Donald surveys the wide and smooth Aegean,
the temple's broken tribute to Poseidon,

wind plucking at his coat and at his hair,
    and wonders why they're there. 'Since last year,
suicide in Greece has grown more popular –
    wives and daughters, sisters, nephews, brothers –
instances have doubled. Some favour here:
    it's desolate and high, without a barrier,
and, like Aegeus, they strew the sea beneath them
with what is left when all their hope is done.'

Part Six

I

And yet the wretched truth is this: Byron
    might summon a hero (however much he meant it)
to play the leading role in his *Don Juan,*
    to be seduced and fight; we cannot.
To be lucky both in war and amongst women
    in nineteenth-century Europe *could* have cut it
(even if, in Juan's case, it didn't) –
for royalty was useless (the hapless Regent),

II

untrammelled aristocracy in its cups,
    and the old bone-house of influence, glued
with noble blood, finally coming unstuck...
    One could be dashing, magnetic, brave, imbued
with rhetorical gifts and almost incredible luck
    and make things happen – a King's false pledge come true;
a fairer treaty drafted; a people freed.
One could be dramatic. God knows change was needed

III

and God knows change is also needed now –
    but the new bone-house of influence's been rebuilt
with corporations' cash; it won't allow
    outsiders to invade; it's defended to the hilt
and ruled by those with savvy media know-how.
    Governments bow to Businesses; Businesses sit
secure behind closed doors and ruminate
on how to best direct affairs of state.

IV

We might run our story's *dénouement* as follows:
    like scenes of Dickens' Ghost-of-Christmas-Present,
Persephone's display of Greece's sorrow
    works its full effect: Donald's incandescent.
He hurries back to Brussels, his soul aglow
    with a people's underserved and cruel treatment
at the hands of the prosperous North... He barges in
on the Secretary's weekly Eurocrisis meeting,

V

demands an instant audience, *tête à tête,*
   and there unfurls a tale so sad, so shocking –
of a country where, if EU terms are met,
   everything goes to the dogs: law, policing,
the vestiges of a shredded welfare net
   to catch the unemployed and stop them starving –
the Secretary sighs. 'It's just as I suspected,'
he says when Donald's finished; 'It must be stopped' –

VI

and while he's on the phone the camera switches
   to other phones which ring along the chain
in quick succession: a woman frowns, then flinches;
   a man listens, bangs his desk, then dials in turn
to his own boss higher up... And so, like stitches
   cast on one by one, what Donald's seen
accumulates its own materiality,
grows real and vivid, felt; and in the sanctity

VII

of the EU's topmost echelons, in blood-wet gowns,
   Austerity's merry surgeons down their scalpels.
Let's say we discover a brand-new Maynard Keynes:
   A no-one up to now, a minor detail
in the ECB's machinery – good on loans
   and fiscal policy generally – who has an apple-
moment, an insight, a hot Eureka!-flash
and proposes simply *giving* Greeks more cash,

VIII

to spend just as they like, side-stepping banks.
   What would happen? The banjaxed wheels of commerce
could re-start; handouts be outflanked
   by the sale of goods; an ever-increasing workforce
pay their taxes... Who forms a one-man think-tank,
   which quickly grows and soon becomes the source
of *the* most radical EU plan in years:
a means for Greece to thrive without arrears

223

IX

...But this is fancy. Donald wakes once more
  in his muted room at nine the following morning.
She must have dropped him back; he can't remember.
  His head is sore. The day is waiting –
a whole bright day to walk about without her –
  and he's glad: her doleful talk of keening,
of savagery set loose and baited traps
has made him sick and might not quite be accurate –

X

Greece could shine completely differently
  in daytime. And he's starving. The breakfast's good
(yoghurt, honey, fruit and fried *halloumi*)
  and puts him in an optimistic mood,
fuelled by several cups of shot-gun coffee.
  He feels the way he usually does abroad:
inquisitive, free, undaunted, at his ease,
alert to pretty women (who aren't Persephone),

XI

ready to explore. There's no museum staff,
  which means the great Acropolis is shut,
as is the home of Agamemnon's mask,
  of Santorini's frescoes, Nestor's cup...
But there are ships and islands. To Aegina perhaps?
  The ferry smokes, the anchor gets wound up,
Piraeus shrinks then falls off the horizon,
Donald inhales the salt of the churning ocean,

XII

seagulls scream and dive in the ferry's wake,
  the winter sunlight's pale but trails its touch
abundantly, everywhere he looks,
  in the white waves' ruffled scrim, the masthead's torch.
He feels inside his pocket for his notebook,
  flicks it open. He hasn't written much:
'Athens', the date. Then, to be rid of her,
he adds her name and casts it on the water.

A.E.
STALLINGS

I

Back in Athens now, 2013,
   Less drama on the streets, and more despair.
Bureaucrats get fat when times are lean.
   Police are thick in Constitution Square,
Protests continue, wearied and routine,
   Street vendors still turn out to sell their fare.
Donny looks from his room in the Grande Bretagne.
You still can't beat the view from up here, can ya?

II

There's parliament, the guards everyone mocks
   For skirts and pom-pom shoes. And since it's sunny,
Beyond the Stadium and apartment blocks,
   There's Mt. Hymettus, famous for its honey
In ancient times, and clouds in fleecy flocks.
   It all conspires to turn your mind from money.
Even the protestors, since unemployed,
Decide the day is one to be enjoyed,

III

And furl their banners, pack up megaphones,
   And head for Plaka, some outdoor café,
To get their nicotine or caffeine jones.
   Without the tear gas, somehow it's blasé.
The Plaka cats slink by, all skin and bones,
   On Byron Street, where Gypsy urchins play
(Or rather Roma Children) *Zorba the Greek*
On old accordions that wheeze and squeak,

IV

Some tourists snap their picture – girl and boy –
   But don't drop them a coin. Isn't it sweet? –
Some local colour. Thus the *hoi polloi*
   Of westerners meander down the street
In flip-flops, seeking T-shirts or a toy
   Or plaster reproductions. 'We have to eat,'
The kids tell Don in Greek, and then they point.
He buys them cheese pies at a sandwich joint,

V

And feeling pleased to have got off so cheap
　　With charity – so fine, in short, and sterling,
So different from when dawn began to peep
　　As last night's hangover began uncurling,
It's always easier to sow than reap –
　　He thinks he'll have a drink. But then a purling
Vibration from his trousers starts to presage –
His Blackberry's turned on – an urgent message?

VI

A friend from school's in Athens to deliver
　　A talk at the Residence. Lord, what a bore.
Ex-pats and diplomats, and many a silver-
　　Haired matron well-preserved. He knows the score.
And how the wine won't flow. It makes him shiver.
　　It's like a nightmare he has had before.
But then the postscript: 'Did I mention Alice
Will be there?' His friend always was a phallus.

VII

He's just the type who'd smilingly correct your
　　Grammar, Greek or English. How it vexes,
And now he'll have to hear the bloody lecture.
　　The problem with Don's history with sex is
The past is never past – it's still conjecture.
　　It seems that every spot is marked with exes.
He'll stop and have a glass or two of raki.
And seven sharp, he'll be in Kolonaki.

VIII

The evening is in honour of Cavafy.
　　Some anniversary – sesquicentennial –
Of birth or death? Well, soon he should be off, he
　　Thinks, or he'll be late. He'll shower, then he will
Put on a fresh shirt, down a quick Greek coffee.
　　The faint anxiety he feel's perennial.
It suddenly occurs to him that's why
He's seen lines of Cavafy flashing by

IX

On trams and buses, his one day of leisure
   Between dull meetings. They all seemed to say
'I'll hand my body over to sensual pleasure'
   Or 'I'm not in the mood to work today.'
Poetry being the only national treasure
   The politicians could not give away,
And not a day goes by the parliamentarians
Do not misquote 'Expecting the Barbarians' –

X

(Rae Dalvyn's version's clear if not sublime.)
   And now we find him at the Ambassador's house
Just late enough in Greece to be on time,
   No worse for wear after an infamous Grouse,
And only a few grey hairs beyond his prime.
   He greets the young Ambassador and his spouse –
Two elegant young men. Well, wouldn't you know it –
A nice surprise, especially for the poet!

XI

And during the long lecture, strong and dry,
   (He's thinking of a Bombay Saph martini),
A phantom from his past catches his eye,
   His heart too. Now he's back in Santorini
It's 1980, and a girl walks by
   In a laconic take on the bikini –
The black volcanic sand, the pristine water.
It's Alice to the life! No, it's her daughter,

XII

That's Alice next to her, he realizes
   The handsome, well-dressed matron with fine bones,
A handsomeness that shines through time's disguises.
   God, it's Shakespearean how beauty clones
Such copies of itself. He hates surprises,
   How iron hunkers at the heart of irony.
He looks up at the portrait that's so Byrony –

XIII

The Phillips' portrait, where the poet's dressed
   Like a brigand from Albania. Don's not certain,
His memory's elliptical at best,
   But he thinks that it was kept behind a curtain
Till his daughter came of age. She'd be distressed,
   Or corrupted? It sets poor Donny's head to hurtin',
To think of Byron's daughter – few would dispute her
As first programmer of the first computer.

XIV

How far away computer science seems
   From some Romantic, dressed up like a chief
Of a wild tribe, his eyes alight with dreams,
   His brain astir with rhymes, leaf after leaf
Of far-flung travels. Now it's Facebook memes
   That leap from mind to mind. Ah well, in brief,
The poet strove with fate, while all along he
Would die in the salt flats of Messolonghi,

XV

But maybe there's an epic to be written
   About the daughter – the computer age
Spawned by Lord Byron's offspring – Don's half smitten
   By the idea, a brilliant one – the page
Seems to compose itself – till truth, hard-bitten,
   Reminds him how absurd it is – to wage
A poem of that sort, one you could win with,
You'd have to be a woman to begin with!

XVI

After the talk and concert (strings and voice,
   Some settings of Cavafy, hardly mellow,
Sung by a young soprano, curious choice,
   Who, marvelous to say, could play the cello
And accompany herself – *amen, rejoice* –
   Modestly hiking up her skirts of yellow
To draw the bow – a goddess, if you please –
While the cello swooned between her slender knees),

XVII

The evening gets off to the social stage.
    Armed with a brace of drinks, he seeks out Alice.
She doesn't seem surprised about his age.
    Her gaze is cool, without a trace of malice,
As if she'd never fly into a rage
    To rival Queen Medea, played by Callas.
'Come by tomorrow night,' her smile's a frown –
'Let's catch up.' And 'My husband's out of town.'

XVIII

Next evening. And there's a single light he
    Thinks not man-made, that man-made light can't mar –
Venus, Lucifer, or Aphrodite
    As she is known in Greek – the evening star,
Vespers, Hesperus. She is all mighty,
    The goddess who controls us from afar,
By whose attentions we are doomed and flattered.
She gathers everything the dawn has scattered:

XIX

Rumours come home to roost; and some come true,
    The homeless man resumes his bench in the park
Beside the church; the bills again come due,
    And care renews her argument with cark,
The protestors come home, and strikers too
    Like children after school. All days go dark,
And all the golden promises of dawn
Are called in when there's nothing left to pawn.

XX

Well *she's* done well, Don thinks, more grand than quaint,
    A neoclassical on a cobbled street,
While one graffito marring its fresh paint
    Says, 'Kill your inner cop.' It seemed discreet,
But when he rings the bell, he sees it ain't –
    A servant answers, and he wipes his feet.
And when he walks into the humble palace,
The woman waiting for him isn't Alice.

XXI

Penelope, she says, voice like a charm.
   Her hair's a waterfall, dark brown, with henna,
Her eyes – where has he seen them? – getting warm-
   er, yes, against a gold ground in Ravenna.
Earrings cascade, some bangles cuff her arm.
   Stay for a drink, she says. He musters 'ena' –
She laughs and switches languages, a solace:
His Greek is rusty, and her English flawless.

XXII

She seems, indeed, an actress in a scene.
   Her eyes, yes, are imperial, defiant,
Her smile's archaic, stained with grenadine,
   (Her arms are long, and golden-hued, and pliant),
Her shoes are Louboutin, her dress is green.
   As if she were a patron, he a client,
He feels that he has come to beg a boon,
But that he's come too late, or else too soon.

XXIII

The coffee table's marble, and ionic,
   A column capitol, an ancient vase,
Sits under glass, and here's a gin and tonic.
   'At where', he says, 'd'you say your mother was?'
'She's at our other house in the Saronic.
   Why do you ask?' He coughs, and says, 'Because…'
'And you're a friend of hers from way back?' … 'Yes' –
He'll leave the year an algebraic guess.

XXIV

The talk starts small, moves on to current events –
   The rapper who was murdered by a gang
Of neo-Nazis. She grows flushed, intense –
   Her mother's girl – more aria than harangue –
'Any good?' Don asks. 'His talent was immense.'
   She moves a large dog and an ancient tripod
To find some gadget and plugs in her iPod

XXV

All pretence to his Greek must fall away,
  It's fast and slangy, though he thinks the meter,
Might be driving fifteeners. What to say?
  She looks triumphant at him. You can't beat her
For silent eloquence, so he gives way.
  It's not exactly rock and roll, or lieder.
It's isn't the kind of Greek he's learned to master,
His understanding blurs as it drives faster:

***

The trials of Greece, the trials of Greece,
  Where tragic Callas thrilled the nation
And shrill Mercouri would not cease
  To ask for the repatriation
Of Elgin's – there translation garbles –
Let's just say Greece has lost her marbles.

Muses of Ritsos and Cavafy –
  Seferis, Palamas, Elytis –
Have they all gone for Turkish coffee?
  Or Nescafe? How bitter-sweet is
Poetry and song – but lo,
Who shut down public radio?

The mountains look on Marathon
  And Marathon looks on the bay,
Olympic venue ten years on
  And nothing's gained, and all to pay.
Security still has its demons
Despite those hefty bribes to Siemens.

Persia now is called Iran,
  Darius has long turned to dust,
Cyprus nixed the Annan plan
  And no-one takes her banks on trust.
Austerity is blind, or deaf,
And Freedom is the IMF.

In Constitution Square, conveners
  Deliver megaphonic sermons
In the traditional fifteeners,
  Or blast Philippics on the Germans –
Occupation come full circle –
It's all so murky, call it Merkel.

(You know the joke – it's rather droll –
  Ms. Merkel visits this fair nation
And when guards at passport control
  Say, *name?* Frau Merkel. *Occupation?*
She laughs a little – here's the sting –
And says, '*Nein*, I'm just visiting.')

A day late and a euro short,
  The IMF admits mistakes –
Although it's too late to abort.
  No bureaucrat exaggerates –
Austerity, youths in capotes
Will tell you is, in Greek, *litotes*.

But blame the politicians too –
  Who were too busy getting rich –
Byzantine teams of Green and Blue –
  To notice the old bait-and-switch.
No longer can they flaunt their lots:
The dry docks chock-a-block with yachts,

Though hardly any go to jail,
  Each party quick to grant asylum
So that, when it's their turn to fail,
  And their own newspapers revile 'em,
They wriggle out of the kerfluffle
The decks are stacked that parties shuffle.

Give me some ouzo, or retsina –
  With no receipt, or VAT.
When Xerxes sat on Salamina
  And watched his tubs sink in the sea –
He didn't know to thank his luck.
Who runs this country runs amok.

The unemployment rate is rising,
  While pensions sink and prices spike.
What is the use of moralizing?
  Let's have a drink, and go on strike –
A poet's strike. That's what we need!
They'll beg us for the latest screed!

Even graffiti has to rhyme,
  Even the anarchists must scan!
The fascists chant in perfect time –
  As do the lefties, to a man
(or woman) – slogans, cries, and curses –
What is a protest sans the verses?

234

Yes, thanks, I'll have some ouzo yet —
　　A liquid pure and clear as Lethe,
Until some water gets it wet
　　And it goes cloudy underneath. The
Problem churns and gets no better:
The ouzo just keeps getting wetter.

On Byron Street, the T-shirts sell
　　With slogans from Thermopylae.
300 Spartans went to hell
　　That Greeks (Helots aside) be free.
There's money, if the mint will make it —
Let's tell the Troika, come and take it!

The isles of Greece, the isles of Greece,
　　The Greeks will sell them, one by one,
And hope to buy a little peace
　　By auctioning the sea and sun.
No war has been their fate, but tax,
And greed, and debt, and Goldman Sachs.

Europe, thy very name is Greek —
　　You were a princess once, and fair,
Wide-eyed, perhaps. A little weak,
　　But everyone has flaws to bear.
The promised trip was wonderful;
But the ride you were taken on was Bull.

***

XXVI

Or something like that, all the while he looks
　　At Attic landscapes, peasants in native dress
19th century oils on wire and hooks.
　　A watercolour Lear. A shepherdess.
Antiquities in bookcases, and books
　　On vellum, from before the printing press,
And priceless kilims. Well, you get the gist.
Was Alice's husband also on the List?

XXVII

The List Lagarde – that is, of tax evaders,
   Or suspected tax evaders, with a stash
Of moolah in Swiss Banks? No doubt she'd paid hers –
   That's what she'd say, her smile cinched like a sash.
He thought of banks, and of the fourth crusaders,
   Who half-way on crusade ran out of cash,
And helped themselves, as to an ATM,
To all the treasures of Byzantium.

XXVIII

The furniture's all poised to pounce on claws,
   Bronzes, antiquities, great carven chests,
But it's the painting opposite that draws
   His gaze – two maidens, with their perfect breasts
Bare, in some era innocent of bras.
   They're pouring wine a lounging man ingests –
Perhaps he's had too much. He isn't young.
He wants to ask about the picture, hung

XXIX

Beside a sketch ascribed to Gregory Corso.
   He's puzzled. Is this fellow Dionysus?
He's got grey hair, despite his muscled torso.
   The girls hardly seem Maenads. One entices
With smiles, and sweetly, how the other pours so.
   Then Don snaps back to speaking on the crisis.
But while he babbles on, and downs his drink,
His gaze goes back, and he begins to think

XXX

He understands what's hanging on the wall
   Despite the drapery, the wine – it's not
From classical mythology at all –
   The half-clad maidens in the pleasant grot,
The drinking, bearded man; it's Biblical;
   These are Lot's daughters; they're seducing Lot.
While somewhere underneath the sky's cold vault
A woman's bitterness is turned to salt.

XXXI

Not that Don is some expert on the Torah.
   But now he sees a city that's on fire
In the corner – is that Sodom or Gomorrah? –
   The lewd, deluded girls, besotted sire.
He takes his leave. He's half-way out the door a
   Moment later, 'Sorry I must retire,
It's getting late.' 'Oh do come back some other
Evening.' 'Remember me to your mother.'

XXXII

Good God, his life's a farce – that summer, Zea,
   They'd camped beneath the stars, the sounding voice
Of the sea – (he'd broken up by then with Lia;
   It was before he'd taken up with Joyce.)
It's like a scene straight out of *Mamma Mia* –
   They'd both agreed abortion was her choice.
He works out that the age would be just right.
A close escape. He strides into the night.

XXXIII

But it's a night of tensions and unrest.
   There's something in the air, a stinging haze
Of tear gas. Still, he likes such evenings best –
   It reminds him of his journalism days.
It clears his head and sinuses. He's dressed
   Too formally to riot. But he strays
A little closer, seeing a street battle –
It makes the rusting sabre in him rattle.

XXXIV

He'll go no more a-roving though – it's late –
   He'd best be getting back to the hotel.
When he visited back in two-thousand eight,
   And that boy got shot, and suddenly all hell
Broke loose – the rioting did not abate
   For a fortnight. Many buildings were a shell,
The dumpsters turned to toxic plastic braziers.
The unrest made a fortune for the glaziers.

237

XXXV

He'd found himself one evening rather deep
  In Exarchia, nervous, sure, but not scared stiff.
A fellow drove up in a shiny jeep,
  Said, 'Burn it,' to some anarchists. 'As if,'
They answered, as he drove off with a beeeep,
  And set fire to another garbage skiff —
Insurance? Or late payments? Either way,
The driver learned anarchists don't obey —

XXXVI

Like those fierce folk in Crete or in the Mani,
  (He thinks of Paddy Fermour's anecdotes...
Sans Horace.) Shit. He can't be lost now, can he?
  The city's changed. A homeless man with totes
Goes shuffling by. A thin young Pakistani
  Wheels by a grocery cart of cans. Some coats
Piled by a closed-up shop that once sold rugs
Turns out to be some teenagers on drugs,

XXXVII

And everywhere, graffiti, politics:
  Leonidas's 300, they had balls,
The Parliament's 300, though, are dicks.
  He's pleased to think that he can read the scrawls
Of Greek spray-painted over broken bricks,
  The writing, as it were, that's on the walls,
The way austerity leads to despair.
He's ended up near Koumandourou Square,

XXXVIII

Where shops are boarded up and scraps of trash
  Blow down the street. He needs just to relax. He
Pats for his wallet, to make sure of cash,
  And starts to scan the streets to find a taxi.
That's when he hears the footsteps and the crash
  Around the corner, and stops in his tracks. He
Isn't sure at first just what he's seeing —
Some skinheads, and a dark-skinned young man fleeing —

238

XXXIX

The Pakistani kid he saw before?,
  He's been roughed up, but not too hurt to run,
And his escape is followed by a roar –
  They're cursing and they're laughing, having fun,
And corner him against a boarded door.
  Donny shouts – what else is to be done?
The kid slips from their grip as the men turn,
And Donny thinks, *Christ, won't I ever learn?*

XL

I'm too old for adventures of this kind,
  Surely a taxi will heave into view.
He fumbles for his phone, but he can't find
  The damned device. He's left it in the loo
At Alice's humble mansion. She won't mind.
  He stands there waiting for the other shoe
To drop. To run away would be the surest
Path to 'Fascists Beat Up British Tourist.'

XLI

The men wear black and gold, like centipedes
  To advertise they're dangerous, with candour.
Not the brightest sparks the nation breeds.
  The logo on their shirts a black meander –
A swastika bent out of shape. One leads
  The others, and they call him Alexander.
'And who are you?' in taxi-driver Greek.
For a moment, Donny is too scared to speak,

XLII

He finds his way is blocked now by a car.
  I'm nobody, he realizes, rife
With doubts – but they have no doubts who they are.
  And there are fists, and maybe there's a knife.
Don thinks about a kouros and a star –
  Of Rilke's sonnet. 'You must change your life.'
He's known it for a while. A kind of silence
Comes over him sometimes, a dream of islands –

XLIII

He'll buy a place next to the sea, and learn a
  New instrument – the lyra? Maybe he'll write
That novel he's been thinking of. Or turn a
  Diary into memoirs. That's all right.
A song, he thinks, from a nearby taverna
  Comes drifting out like smoke into the night.
Comes thickly trickling out into the dark,
Or something's tricking – it leaves a mark

XLIV

On his shirt, like that night Alice threw her wine –
  More beautiful the crazier she got –
And he'd deserved it to – he'd been a swine.
  When they were drinking wine, they always fought,
And they were always drinking. But it was fine –
  It was always fine, till one day it was not.
That's how all things go bankrupt, years, then months,
Gradually, as someone said, then all at once.

XLV

And now the music's singing in his ear –
  He cannot move, as though tied to a mast –
Except he's on the pavement. It's so clear,
  A poem, perhaps, he'd heard, far in his past,
It's not austerity, but it's austere,
  The sirens sing, an ambulance drives past.
His anonymity, he thinks, protects him,
And then the music comes inside and wrecks him:

XLVI

I'll find another land, another shore,
  There has to be a better place than this –
That's what you said, and what you've said before,
  When one by one dreams died, or went amiss.
And so the years rolled by, score after score,
  It's not too late, you say, to seek your bliss,
But you've failed everywhere once you have failed.
All roads are dead-end roads. All ships have sailed.

GEORGE SZIRTES

I

Why would anyone go to Budapest?
  Why Juan in particular? Who knows?
Maybe it's simply boredom with the West
  As concept, ideology, or pose,
Why else desert the Island of the Blessed
  With all its shops and malls that never close?
It's boom time in the gardens, all is fine.
The calendar says 1989.

II

No, really, what's the big attraction here?
  The Cold War still feels cold as does the weather,
The smogs of January make a blear
  Welcome and the wind is like wet leather
Stinging the skin of cheeks both front and rear.
  You long for kisses lighter than a feather
But while Hungarian women may be beautiful,
Arriving at this time feels somewhat dutiful.

III

Well, things must change, of that we are assured.
  The ground is shifting under the world's feet,
The sickness of the age may well be cured
  Within a year or two as two sides meet –
But then again may not. We're not inured
  Against the cold and fate remains discreet
Regarding its affairs and often covers
Its tracks more skillfully than Juan's lovers.

IV

Juan, this time, was working for the press,
  Not permanently – he just liked to linger
At one or other convenient address,
  So took up a position as a 'stringer',
A jargon term, I know, yet nonetheless
  The right one so don't point that ugly finger.
The word comes with a decent etymology.
In any case I offer no apology.

V

A little silver now in Juan's hair
   Added distinction to a handsome figure
Kept trim by exercise. It isn't fair,
   Friends whispered while remarking on his vigour
In pursuing, if no more, some new affair.
   He ate and drank with a most perfect rigour.
He loved wine but he'd given up on porter
And always swore by hock and soda water.

VI

He took rooms on the fifth floor of a block
   Of Thirties vintage, one without a lift.
He ran upstairs as if against the clock
   And those below looked out to see him shift
At such a rate. It comes as quite a shock
   To folk more used to saunter or to drift
At the exhausted end of a hectic century
To meet someone so oddly unsedentary.

VII

The block was full of lovers and assignments.
   Hungarians and desire are close-knit neighbours.
Communal living encourages alignments
   And there are times when, far from rattling sabres,
Next door is busy working out refinements
   Of seduction and you hear his noisy labours,
His form of hammering or manual drilling
Which always sounds so charming and fulfilling.

VIII

Of course it isn't man and wife at play –
   The man may be a different man, the wife
May have her husband nights, the man by day
   But it is, I think, the general rule in life
That fidelity works out the other way.
   And male desire trumps all. The city's rife
With stories of affairs we shouldn't wink at
The man being the one to throw the sink at.

IX

A man may leave his wife, it's not unknown,
  To go off with another woman, younger,
Less disputateous, less familiar-grown.
  It is a sad dimension of male hunger
Whereby the woman suffers hurt alone.
  It's not just the desire for bunga-bunga
But for the ever new. It's dreadful really.
I say it now, in public, and quite freely.

X

But no, that is not Juan's way, not quite.
  It isn't him I mean. This verse won't carry
News of his wedding, nor would it be right
  For such a person to get up and marry.
Despite the good such men might do at night
  They're not much loved by Tom or Dick or Harry
Or any husband, in the inglorious
Ranks of the tired and uxorious.

XI

So where is all this going? My old habit
  Of digressing means you will sometimes get lost.
The fact, dear reader, is I'm used to rabbit
  On and there are moments lines get crossed.
If once you see a narrative line, grab it
  And try to hold on tight, don't count the cost,
Because though you might trip on an enjambment
There's something in this style that's rather lambent.

XII

Once he'd unpacked his case he took a walk.
  The old façades were, many of them, crumbling,
The blackened surface scrawled over with chalk
  The trains under the pavement faintly rumbling,
Cracked limbs of statues hung on a wire stalk,
  And every thoroughfare a ghostly mumbling.
Other cities may be equally vaunted
But no great capital feels so oddly haunted.

XIII

Ah Budapest, you louche imperial city,
   Not quite *your* empire, not entirely yours,
I would not call you altogether pretty
   And yet you're beautiful despite of wars,
Maybe precisely because of them. A pity
   You had to be bombed and shelled but Time abhors
A beauty without blemish and prefers
A city full of scars to make it hers.

XIV

Myself, I'm of Time's party. Pretty girls
   Are two a penny and I've seen a few,
With bobs, with hairbands, crewcuts, bangs and curls
   And yes, they're cute enough but all too new.
Give me the older woman's eyes, the whirls
   Of fortune in her gaze, how she looks through
The world and pities it, and I am moved.
Look at my backlist and the matter's proved.

XV

Have I mentioned the smog yet? And the cold?
   I see I have. The mighty Danube flows
past triumphs and defeats. Its tides have rolled
   through several bloody centuries, God knows,
its people brave but rarely self-controlled.
   A fuse somewhere is lit, the river glows,
And pretty soon it's bring on *War and Peace*,
As you may read in Claudio Magris.

XVI

Things were brewing again: old leader gone,
   Reputedly mad, a new leader installed,
The Party on its treadmill, carrying on
   Without much sense of purpose. Life had called
Time on something, something had had its run,
   But what it was who knew? Careers that crawled
Up bureaucratic ladders hesitated,
Looked vulnerable, far from armour-plated.

XVII

Moscow behind it, Gorbachev, *glasnost*,
  A European house to loiter in,
A new investment (never mind the cost),
  A place to practice *perestroika* in
To which hardliners found no firm riposte
  And therefore ripe to 'string' or Reuter in.
(Such rhymes, dear reader, are my patent system,
And though you might dislike them, I would miss them.)

XVIII

Juan's politics? Libertarian?
  Left wing or right wing? Sitting on the fence?
Maybe simply humanitarian?
  Red-blooded certainly, at times intense,
More carnivore than vegetarian,
  And yet ironic, even calm. His sense
Of the ideal could be at times pragmatic,
His judgment though was quick, some say erratic.

XIX

Erratic, reader, not erotic. There
  His judgment was what it was, so let it rest.
I don't think it's a secret we should share
  But keep it, like good friends, close to our chest.
Enough to say that something in his air
  Touched a deep chord in many a female breast:
Some mothered him, some called him in a crisis,
Some loved his virtues, some preferred his vices.

XX

But as to vice there is a common store
  In any capital and you may find
Budapest to your taste. It offers more
  Than others of the pornographic kind,
An industry the state was ready for,
  Though you, reader, may be of purer mind.
When all is said and done, some people thrive
By filming sex while other couples swive.

XXI

Money is money, and industry a boon,
　　Whatever field it is that you excel in,
Profit, like fat is liable to balloon
　　And any sport is good that you do well in.
Good patriotic sex is like the moon:
　　It has its dark side. It's a place you dwell in
For a brief while and hope to leave it wealthier
Though relatively few depart much healthier.

XXII

And what's with *swive*? I realise it's dated,
　　But has, I think, a gentle Saxon sound,
And reader, would you not be educated
　　In matters where much cruder terms abound?
I like to see the act thus elevated.
　　I like my coffee too quite finely ground.
I like toast burned, I like a spicy curry.
I like enjoying food and hate to hurry.

XXIII

But this was winter, life was on the move,
　　And Juan understood the pulse of change,
He had his contacts of which some might prove
　　Useful across a wide political range,
And once he'd settled down and found his groove
　　He might find hidden treasures, rich and strange.
Full fathom five thy Marxist fathers glitter,
But here they're so much rubble among litter.

XXIV

Day by cold day some fresh item of news
　　Appeared in the press. Clearly wheels were turning.
More ground was broken. How to read the clues?
　　How does the land lie when the stomach's churning?
Which of the useful contacts could he use?
　　And what old truths were only fit for burning?
I know U-turns are chiefly for denying
But history has its own ways of replying.

XXV

Consider the contacts: K the journalist,
   Economist F, ex-minister V,
Authors B, Z and H on the black list
   Of oppositionists who might be free
But under surveillance... others I have missed
   Might turn out to be important, we shall see,
Keep your eyes open, keep your ears pinned back:
Get news where you can, in pubs, or in the sack.

XXVI

He needed an interpreter. The Magyar language
   Isn't difficult, any baby can master it,
But seems to cause a fair amount of anguish
   To visitors who go there seeking after it.
Having arrived you wouldn't want to languish
   At the bar listening to foreign laughter, it
Would leave you puzzled. Languages and Juan
Were old companions. He loved to try a new one,

XXVII

And had in fact picked up more than a smattering
   But not enough to tell the delicate shades
Of meaning as a stream of words kept clattering
   Past him. Language is a knife with many blades.
People were nice and what they said was flattering
   As far as he could tell, but much evades
Amateur linguists, declaring itself plain,
Which, heard just once, you must hear through again.

XXVIII

A friend in Prague had ventured some advice.
   Hedi is brilliant, eloquent as Wilde,
Efficient as the Stasi, as precise
   As a Cartier watch. Everything is filed
In that beautiful head of hers. Besides, she's nice
   Company, her clothes perfectly styled,
Her ear for velleities quite impeccable,
Besides which she is rumoured to be sackable.

XXIX

Ah Hedi, tall and slender, cheekbones sheered
     To knives, her eyes two deep and icy lakes.
Rooms fell silent whenever she appeared.
     Elderly gentlemen would get the shakes,
And one, they said, set fire to his beard
     Lighting her cigarette. No-one mistakes
Such signs for short sight, DT, or senility.
They may in fact be symptoms of virility.

XXX

So let us place her in her modern flat
     In a leafy part of Buda. She has money
From her ex, an old-time aristocrat
     With a literary bent. Her alimony
enables her to engage in this or that.
     There's never any need for parsimony.
For now she is an intepreter-translator,
She might be anything she fancies later.

XXXI

She has, as we'll discover, politics
     Quite of her own but let's not get ahead
Of ourselves. It is impossible to fix
     One's attention, as I think I read
In Yeats, one's mind on such a dangerous mix
     Of interest and desire. One can be led
Down highly confusing corridors and passages
And fail to pick up the most simple messages.

XXXII

Juan in the provinces, now back in town,
     Juan filing incidents he heard about
From cabbies. Juan getting it all down
     In black and white, putting the word about
on Moscow, Washington, St Stephen's Crown,
     Anything worth waxing faintly absurd about.
But pretty soon he realises Hedi
Is what he needs, so he rings up the lady.

XXXIII

The name is Juan, Don Juan, he utters
    In his best and most mysterious manner.
I've been expecting you to call, she mutters.
    Let's meet for drinks downtown in *The Red Banner*.
Such irony! The red flag rarely flutters
    At night in Pest. It takes a Party planner
To set it up on ceremonial occasions,
The rest is all excuses and evasions.

XXXIV

And so they met, what else did you expect?
    Adventures? Yes, but as romantic fiction.
What's that term? 'Politically correct'?
    To me the twin terms are a contradiction.
You want a hero? So do I. Expect
    Some derring-do, expect intimate friction,
Expect some matters of the heart and flesh,
Though politics and romance rarely mesh.

XXXV

What happened at the meeting? Yes, the drinks,
    And yes, some conversation, at first wary.
There's something about alcohol that links
    Complete strangers together, which is scary.
Beer swears, gin glowers, but a good wine winks
    Complicity and sparkles like the fairy
On your Christmas tree, and how pleasant
To contemplate the unwrapping of a present.

XXXVI

But hold your horses, reader! Juan's way
    Was not to rush and make an awkward pass,
Nor could you call Hedi an easy lay,
    A woman of the intellectual class
Who knew her worth, however she might stray
    From Party principles on a full glass,
Such principles need constantly revising
And sometimes gaps themselves are tantalising.

XXXVII

So February. March, the first big date –
   The 15th – with its annual demonstrations
Commemorating 1848,
   Complete with strict policing operations.
One must distinguish 'the nation' from 'the state'
   As from 'the people' but this year relations
Such as these have grown a mite confusing.
And much depends on what terms you are using.

XXXVIII

A vast and unofficial crowd moves down
   The unofficial street, while the official
(Less vast and mobile) trudge along through town
   Feeling a touch unloved and interstitial.
Juan is there with Hedi, having grown
   Dependent on her sharp ear. I could wish all
To go well with such a couple, and it might.
They seemed to get on pretty well last night.

XXXIX

The city has been tense since the New Year,
   There's always a nagging fear of the unstable.
'But what if Gorbachev should "disappear"
   And a hard man smash his fist down on the table
Declaring: Enough!' says one. 'In that case, dear,
   The table breaks, that's all.' There is a Babel
Of voices out there of unequal quality.
Few in the street yet talk of a new polity.

XL

Hedi with Juan, Juan with Hedi, weave
   Their way through the most intricate of mazes
Of dissidence and officialdom. They leave
   With new ideas and try to follow phases
Of the national mood. What then to believe?
   It's the uncertainty that most amazes
A waiting world once sure of its polarity.
Is this a cause for terror or hilarity?

XLI

No violence yet and no police reaction.
    The weeks go by and time appears elastic.
The Party's splitting: there's the diehard faction
    And a mild-mannered, pragmatic, faintly plastic
Bunch of liberals whose real power and traction
    Might turn out to be rather more fantastic.
Remember '56? It's not forgotten.
Was it the great revolt or something rotten?

XLII

It was, I believe, not Churchill but Martini
    Who told us history's written by the victor.
Yes, but the bottle of fizz contains a genie –
    Der Sieger schreibt (in German) *die Geschichte*
Is the title of his book. It isn't steamy.
    The man's a scholar not, like me, *ein dichter* –
And genies write their own rules once they're out
So who laughs last is open to some doubt.

XLIII

One night after a bout of hectic pleasure
    Hedi remarks to Juan *I have met a*
Young lawyer who is something of a treasure.
    It would be useful to get to know him better.
He'll be a force I think by any measure.
    I suggest we meet. I've written him a letter.
There's something of the emperor in his air
And he does have the most gorgeous head of hair.

XLIV

Juan had never heard of him but nodded.
    A breaking story adds to the excitement
(Not that a year in Hungary ever plodded.
    From public order acts through to indictment,
The country leapt whenever history prodded)
    And later wondered what news of this night meant
In terms of Hedi and the head of hair.
Every dalliance has to end somewhere.

XLV

Dalliance, such a sweet word, don't you find?
  One dallies here or there like some *flâneur*,
Lost in the streets of love, half-deaf, half-blind,
  Tuned to the pulse of life, feeling it stir
Like blood, or something vaguely of that kind,
  Recalling a half-glimpsed beauty, dreaming her,
Meanwhile time passes, you've written a line or two
Then, disappointed, strike the whole thing through.

XLVI

Never do things by halves. The months flew by
  '56 was declared a revolution
By a minister, almost on the sly
  But perfectly timed in its execution.
Dubcek on TV. A regular supply
  Of ever wider debates on constitution.
Scribbling his notes Juan inclines to hear
Hedi's metatext whispered in his ear.

XLVII

The Fourth of April, First of May, and soon
  We're straight through spring. The age of grand parades
Is past, a dizzy world attends on June.
  June, and Juan in fashionable shades,
Hedi in silk on a silky afternoon,
  A boy slides by them on his roller blades,
The underground is playing Sam Fox hits,
And even the classy are decked out in glitz.

XLVIII

The lawyer's out of sight and nothing's changed.
  Hedi and Juan are a constant pairing,
Their meetings regular, readily arranged,
  And if there's any news it is for sharing.
Small tokens of affection are exchanged
  But both maintain an independent bearing.
Relationships are complex, we enjoy them
Until some force within strives to destroy them.

XLIX

June 16th. The great reversal comes.
  The dead are disinterred and celebrated.
Vast crowds gather. Bring on the muffled drums,
  Ring out the bells though thirty years belated.
Read out the names, and do the dreadful sums.
  Make speeches, sing the anthems of the fated.
There are nerves in the square and little wonder when
It's only twelve days after *Tian-an-Men*.

L

The speeches roll, the world stands on the brink.
  But who's this speaking now, that bright young fellow
With a fine head of hair? Who do you think?
  It is our lawyer, his resounding bellow,
Demanding drastic action. Others shrink
  Into the background. It's a fine and mellow
Evening on which to conclude this solemn session,
The perfect time to make a big impression.

LI

From here things happen fast. The wire is cut,
  A minister snips through the Iron Curtain,
And all is open which before was shut.
  Though one small step for man, this much is certain,
The region haemorrhages, cracks like a nut,
  And that's the DDR gone for a burton!
Ossies flood Budapest. No more closed borders.
The press is there with mics and tape recorders.

LII

And Juan with them, Hedi at his side.
  Excitement mounts, surely there's no way back.
Husak and Honeger rant but can't decide
  On plans of action: Cut the crowd some slack
Or tighten up? Can Gorbachev be relied
  On to restore order, go on the attack?
One never knows when one is over the edge
Or whether it's wise to wait and simply hedge.

LIII

Sing Muse, as Homer put it, of the rage
    Of Achilles, son of Peleus! Do sing,
And yet remember, Muse, to turn the page.
    The Furies are awake and on the wing
Indulging in their sprightly badinage,
    But simply circling, moving in a ring,
And frankly, Muse, you're being indecisive.
Surely it's up to you to be incisive.

LIV

The city seethes, the temperature keeps climbing
    And life is dizzy. Hedi sometimes misses
Their meetings now. She had such perfect timing
    Before, but soon she's back and it's all kisses.
I'm tempted to compare a kiss to rhyming,
    A kiss recalled when Juan reminisces
May be romantic but not sentimental
Yet such things hurt and are not incidental.

LV

One night she speaks, it's Hedi I mean, of course,
    Her tone more sharp, of what should happen now.
We know that government requires force,
    A nation has to be driven like a cow.
(Juan interjected, 'Not a horse?')
    You need to keep an eye on the highbrow
Who tend to lack in patriotic feeling.
Juan watched the light move on the ceiling.

LVI

What we need is national consciousness,
    The sense of what a true Hungarian is.
A stirring show of folk in country dress,
    A revival of old fashioned courtesies.
What is one Jew or Gypsy more or less
    When it comes to claiming tribal loyalties?
She spoke in measure like a Party chairman,
As if she were that splendid-head-of-hair-man.

LVII

Well, no, that is not fair. She may have picked
   A phrase or two from him but Hedi's mind
Was still her own. She hesitated, flicked
   Her hair back in the knowledge she'd defined
A clear position, and looked very strict.
   (There had been times when she could look quite kind.)
Ah, blood and honour! A mischievous mythology
Bubbling to the top as ideology.

LVIII

It is the shadow of a troubled region,
   The region's troubled. Shadows pass across it,
Its enemies are powerful and legion,
   There's always one or other keen to boss it.
It's not like being Swedish or Norwegian,
   There's little here to curl up with and cosset,
Except Hedi, now in a different orbit.
So Juan understands but can't absorb it.

LIX

For weeks they hardly saw each other. Hot
   Afternoons grew close, flirted with thunder.
Things change whether we want them to or not
   And what was intimate is blown asunder.
Any firm course is very hard to plot:
   Who knows what stays afloat and what goes under?
We meditate on history's calamities,
On liberty, and in what a fine jam it is.

LX

The world is stirring now, the dominos –
   You will recall the old strategic game –
Are on the point of falling. No-one knows
   Where they should run or whom to safely blame.
To fall may be better than to come to blows,
   But wasting forty years does seem a shame
My own years, reader? They go on for ever.
You can't go a whole lifetime boxing clever.

LXI

Then X returns, back from the USA
  Together with family. Juan must relocate.
He packs away Hedi's presents. *Toujours gai,*
  As the cat once said and an old reprobate
However young he feels, knows how to play
  The game, and that it's good to remonstrate.
The woman who leaves you is likely to prefer
To think that you would kill yourself for her.

LXII

The old world's passing, practically gone.
  The Twentieth of August! Fireworks!
St Stephen's Day! The fly-past! All that *son*
  Et lumiere. The great city perks
Up after a season of sluggish sun.
  The night draws in. The party spirit lurks
In villas, on the embankment, and explodes
Over the packed and melancholy roads.

LXIII

Explosion on explosion. Light for hours
  Of night! It's dizzying and transformational.
The human mind is in hock to the dark powers
  Of the grandiose and the irrational.
Here is a symbol locked inside the showers
  Of red and white and green, the national
Colours of 48, the last great glorious
Revolution that failed to be victorious.

LXIV

Time for Juan to go. Look, there's the moon!
  It's clouded, and listen! there is the first clap
Of thunder that means the end of summer. Soon
  The slide to autumn. Juan feels the slap
Of the wind, and here's a child with a balloon,
  And then another with more balloons that flap
And fly and vanish. Give me the bag, says Juan
I'll blow a new one for you. And he blew one.

N. S. THOMPSON

Now, for my part, I heard he took a trip
To Italy, apparently to guest
At some gigantic discothèque, all hip

With suntanned bodies, spiked gel hair and pressed
Together in a tangle, similar to...
Well, funny come to think of it – you guessed –

The very beaches where they shun the view
Of white waves and prefer to surf the swell
On gently frying bodies – wouldn't you,

With all that naked flesh on which to dwell? –
Or rather have to stride over instead,
Lying stretched like fallen angels on the hell

Of burning sand... And, hell, my face is red
As well. It seems that Dante's terza rima
Has lodged into a groove inside my head:

I think that this should be ottava rima...

I

So let me start again! He took a trip
   To Italy, did 'DJ', out to guest
In one of those vast discothèques so hip
   With mingled dancing bodies tightly pressed
Together, packed as if about to strip
   For Spencer Tunick's great ensembles, undressed
In public places for a camera's eye
To take them as one mass of flesh. I fly

II

A little from truth here: unlike Tunick's folk
   (Whom one sees turning purple in the cold)
Among this mass there was no room to poke
   An arm out of a top or calmly hold
A bottom in its underwear. No joke
   Among this swaying mass of bodies rolled
About avoiding arms and legs of those
Who seemed to want an exit from their clothes.

III

And set inside this heavy metal box,
   Complete with gantries round it spaceshipwise,
A fleet of consoles that would rival Spock's
   Aboard the plastic Starship Enterprise
That boldly goes between the plastic rocks
   Of space... but crewing *this* ship as it flies
Through inner space stands someone magisterial
To take off into sounds ethereal.

IV

Ethereal? A super techno mix
   Laid down on orange vinyl for the crowd
Is music for the sphere of light that picks
   Its spangled way to girders, light allowed
To float and travel as it tries to fix
   Itself to solid surfaces, a cloud
Of, yes, ethereal meteors that showers
This tiny planet, dappling it for hours.

V

And here to conquer it stands Captain Don,
    The Don, our Donald Johnson, the Dee Jay
From England, fortunately with something on
    In simple fashion in a simple way,
His jeans two hundred pounds (to us, a con),
    Designer T-shirt half that... who could say?
His trainers seemed to show no signs of wear.
Why should they? We know DJs walk on air.

VI

So, Donald Johnson, having been flown in
    Across the blue Tyrrhenian Sea to Pisa
Was checking out which playlist he should spin
    And wondering how his new remix would please a
Lively young crowd in Tuscany, a gin
    And pineapple drink worthy of a Caesar
Beside him when, all of a sudden, space
Seemed to enclose *him*: wrapped around his face

VII

Appeared to be a velvet bag for shoes
    And something more like metal in his side.
Relieved of his dilemma what to choose,
    He saw that there was nothing to decide.
The offer one not easy to refuse,
    Especially seeing that his hands were tied,
His slender body pushed out through the crowd
Left in the dark and looking rather cowed

VIII

By half a dozen men in stocking masks
    Who menaced them with Uzis to impress.
The kind of group that never stops and asks
    For your consent, or even lets you dress,
But moves in silently... and so its tasks
    Are all accomplished pat (and leave no mess).
This gang of kidnappers had paid the house
To stage this little coup, but had the nous

IX

To know the foreigner might not agree
　　To being sold off to another party,
Political or celebratory;
　　Also the crowd, so innocent and arty-
Looking one moment, could turn nastily
　　Against a sequestration – even tarty
Girls have been known to cut up rough and poke
An eye out when they could not see a joke.

X

So in the utter darkness of the hall
　　Whose lights mysteriously had been put out
To shield eyes as our hero took a fall,
　　And bundled off before there was a shout
(Or folk thought they were at a punk masked ball),
　　Don was escorted to the world without
A by-your-leave but with designer label,
His techno mix still spinning on the table.

XI

As for the rest, his little bags of tricks –
　　That is, three heavy laminated cases –
Were following behind, brought by the six
　　Who took the trouble to disguise their faces
Despite the dark. These beefy mavericks
　　Were swift executors but knew their places,
And sat Don in a helicopter seat,
Handcuffed and bound, while they took to their feet,

XII

Off in the armoured 4 × 4 they drove
　　And roared off to the South behind the flight
Which landed in a sacred shady grove
　　Miles south of Naples in the starry night
Beside a villa painted white and mauve,
　　Which awful colour scheme was kept from sight
By walls of ferro-concrete twelve feet high
In case the locals or police should pry.

XIII

This villa was luxurious, its doors
   Were steel, its roof bombproof, a bunker lay
Well-furnished underneath its marble floors,
   Complete with gym. Proprietor: Bébé.
A hideout for her secret paramours
   Whose orientation you could never say.
But certainly there sat beneath the gloss
The daughter of a *Camorrista* boss

XIV

Who had decided she would like to hear
   The latest vinyl that was going down
And so had engineered the bright idea
   Of borrowing a Dee Jay of renown
And have him guest at what she hoped would be a
   Fantastic celebration for uptown
Entrepreneurs in real estate and – prime
At that – but you could also call it 'crime'.

XV

As two dark shapes emerged from olive trees
   And bundled Donald, dazed, out of the seat
He was surprised to see a light chemise
   Step from the pilot's suit, two slender feet
Slip out of boots with customary ease
   And into sandals for the dark retreat,
But most of all what made him stop and stare
Was from the helmet came a shock of hair

XVI

The gleaming yellow of a buttercup.
   But strong hands bent him down beneath the blades
Still spinning to a stop, then pushed him up,
   Supporting him. The couple of shapes in shades
Then carted him as if he were a pup
   From that far field of Enna into Hades
Behind the iron curtain of the shutters
Whose strength was that resistant to bolt cutters.

XVII

Don wondered, as he followed in the head
  Of hair, if he was in for something sweet
Instead of ending up – as he thought – dead.
  Then thoughts of home along the winding street
Towards the Downs outside of Leatherhead
  Turned to this chick he was about to meet:
A chick who was mature enough to fly
And sure enough, he thought, not to play shy...

XVIII

So anguished thoughts of Brenda and their kids
  (About whom he kept quiet from the fans)
Now vanished with the thought that he was quids
  In with this beauty who had shot his plans
To pieces – cutting up a storm amidst
  The heaving mass of real and sunbed tans,
And squashing out his half-day on the beach
Sipping a white rum in a sling of peach

XIX

Before the flight home... well, there was no hurry...
  His life was comfortable in his bungalow
Set safely on a rolling hill of Surrey
  Where an extension served as studio
And evenings they could order in a curry
  And add some yoghurt made from sheep to go
With it, both were bovine-intolerant
(I have confirmed this with a confidant).

XX

But once inside the marvellous marble villa
  The supermodel-looking slinky girl
Slipped off and left him standing by a pillar
  To watch her strip her clothes off and then twirl
Into a bedroom, while the tall gorilla
  With hands on him and grin of toothy pearl,
Beneath the *keffiyeh* draped around the shades
Sported like certain armies on parades,

XXI

Was nodding to the other and the steps
  Down to the secret basement and the gym.
Between this pair of shrouded demireps
  Both under orders to take care of him
He shuffled to a whiteness of the steppes
  Blinded by spotlights he could wish would dim
And, shackled to a light bed in the glare,
They simply wandered off and left him there,

XXII

His hands and legs restrained by cable ties...
  And in that moment all his fears came back,
He looked into his captors' deep dark eyes
  Now they were bringing up the largest rack
Along with others of a different size.
  Were these the instruments to make him crack?
Was that low table there a waterboard
And what were those large straps and orange cord?

XXIII

Our Don began to sweat, his mouth was dry,
  His body shaking at the thought of what
Was coming next: *we have your children, why*
  Will you not pay the ransom, we have got
The evidence against you... 'Hey, don't cry...'
  He raised his hands to wipe away some snot
That trickled from his nose. What had he heard?
An Afro-Caribbean voice? Absurd.

XXIV

'Not crying,' Don said, snuffling through his nose,
  Still far too scared to ask why he was there,
But now supposing he was one of those
  Unfortunates kidnapped, held in a lair,
Until... one figure turned away to pose
  And, stretching out its arms without a care,
Unwrapped the scarf, unbuttoned the fatigues...
What was this, blackmail? One of those intrigues

266

XXV

To be recorded for posterity
   Or rather for extorting loads of cash
To be consigned with swift dexterity
   Or compromising shots of whip and lash
Would find themselves with some celerity
   (Not even shielded by a false moustache)
In every Continental magazine
And English tabloids calling him 'obscene'.

XXVI

Don swallowed as he watched what happened next,
   A gleaming back emerging from the zip
And naked muscles bulging out when flexed,
   But round and smooth across a curving hip
Placed in a lacy tanga. Most perplexed,
   Don shook himself and tried to get a grip,
But then the other figure grasped his arms
And Don, spread-eagled, heard the loud alarms

XXVII

Scream that he was a plaything and was dead.
   Then shackled by two different set of cuffs
(Light plastic, actually, so he later said)
   By this strange pair of swift professional toughs
Who gave him no time to propose, instead,
   A much more friendly strategy, out puffs
A chest that gained attention as it first
Stood up and made his shackles nearly burst.

XXVIII

A rippled body round two muscled breasts
   Which sported two fine golden nipple rings
Subjected the large frame above to tests
   Which conjured in Don's mind fantastic things,
The sort of hidden mental palimpsests
   Of adolescent pages with no strings
Attached. Yes, this lithe female body builder
Attracted him so that he could have filled her

XXIX

Neat shining shaven head with abject pleas
  Not for the sexual pleasures of the flesh
In one long sultry afternoon of ease
  Where they could let their thoughts and feelings mesh...
But rather friendly chats with herbal teas
  And scones and jam and fat-reduced *crème fraiche*...
Or was it hearing English in that voice
That made his palpitating heart rejoice?

XXX

The lady said her name was Violet
  Which Don, head musing on his fantasy,
Misheard as 'Violence' and urged her get
  Some painkillers. He was not man to see
An opportunity go west, but set
  A limit on the... Would they both agree?
Of course they would, and urged our Don to smile,
Calm down, relax, for they would take a while...

XXXI

Meantime, the other lady dropped her veil,
  Not Caribbean this time, but a Serb,
And as she stripped Don found himself exhale
  As she dropped on him offering some herb
Or other from a little pipe: 'Inhale,'
  The dark lady, whose muscles were superb,
Commanded, as she stretched in her crow's nest
Above him and, well, you can guess the rest.

XXXII

And so that morning Donald woke up sore,
  His clothes dispersed, a buzzing in each ear...
'I see they treated you just like a whore,'
  Said Bébé, eyes wide, almost in a leer
To see how far her girls went to have more
  Than she could offer for a strict career,
Helped by what made a man stand up for hours
Above his natural reproductive powers.

XXXIII

She tutted seeing him in disarray,
  Sweat-soaked and fluid-soaked and much abused,
His hair a spiky mess of gel and spray
  Below where Adrijana was amused
To paint the Serbian flag... I cannot say
  Precisely where the aerosol had cruised
But lines that showed remarkable control
Suggested that the flag once had a pole.

XXXIV

Appropriate as latter day Bond girl
  In white designer catsuit (zipper, gold)
Our Don winced as he saw her French lips curl
  And shrank to see the spidery arms unfold,
The zip was coming down, his mind a whirl,
  Disaster, Don thought, he was pigeonholed
As nothing more than sexual pleasure, man
To be a flagpole for a Serbian.

XXXV

His captor strutted round and boldly stared,
  Don thought she might produce a riding crop
And stimulate the parts the girls had bared...
  Good God, did women not know when to stop?
He left the pointed comment undeclared,
  In no position, left without a top
Or bottom and quite naked for his pains,
But still secured by little plastic chains.

XXXVI

'You must get up now,' she said, '*Sbrigati!*'
  The Don's mouth so dry he could barely speak,
His brain still whirling... Oh, hot diggety,
  What was he in for, could he take a leak,
He could, but for a technicality.
  She passed a jar and promised not to peek,
While Don, still thinking of the bodyguard,
Tried all he could but found it rather hard.

XXXVII

She clicked her fingers and the girls appeared,
  Both smiling, looking fresh as daisies, plied
With muscle-pumping hormones. Donald feared
  Again his male performance would be tried
And photos taken that would not be cleared
  By him or by his agent, multiplied
In countless images the gutter press
Would never ever con... But I digress...

XXXVIII

The bodyguards wore scrubs, unlike the boss –
  Not *the* Boss, but his daughter, you recall –
(Here I can understand a reader's loss
  Of memory listening to this free-for-all)
And picked our hero up like candyfloss,
  Still hobbled, placed him in the shower stall
And like two *yuna* girls in Old Japan
They soon had Donald scrubbed up, spick and span,

XXXIX

Then dressed him in a jumpsuit all his own,
  Bright orange, short sleeves, V-neck, showing off
His manly chest. From Donald came a groan,
  What he was wearing clearly made him scoff:
Would looking like a convict set the tone
  For him? This was the pits, the very trough
Of fashion... '*Shuddup*, this is techno art,
Cretino, now you dress to play the part!'

XL

Don swallowed as they added a moustache
  With Superglue: '*Perfetto*', they exclaimed,
And had him pirouette with some panache
  And giggled when he heard somebody named.
Then Bébé said that it was time to dash,
  They knew the penalty if they were blamed
For any hitch in Papa's special *festa*,
To which they were delivering the guest, a

XLI

Famous Techno DJ from foreign parts
   Who happened – with the hair below his nose –
Not only to be dear to all their hearts,
   But also when he struck a certain pose
With music that was climbing up the charts
   To be a look-a-like to one of those
Whose members now were sadly found to be
A few remaining parts and all at sea.

XLII

So quickly given helmet and a jacket
   (The former for no trouble with the cops)
And promising that he would earn a packet
   If he would play and pull out all the stops,
(They knew they had a way to make him hack it)
   They might include him in one of the ops
She and the Boss were hoping to create
Which he in England would legitimate.

XLIII

Oh, no, thought Donald, he would not be made
   To help these criminals in Italy
To get a toe hold in the substance trade
   No matter how they charmed or wittily
Persuaded... He knew what would never fade
   Was how he had been treated shittily
(He blushed to hear the word escape his lips).
Then all four pulled on straps and did up zips

XLIV

And Don was chained onto the pillion seat
   Behind the Serbian astride a large
Ducati M900 Monster, neat
   Machine (a V-twin) and she was in charge,
Roaring off fabulously, looking sweet
   Around the curves (not hers) and on the marge,
Behind them Bébé taking Violet,
Bent forward in a curious tête-à-tête.

271

XLV

And so they raced towards the lovely coast
  And ended somewhere near Agropoli,
The afternoon so hot it made them toast,
  And Don's mouth watered thinking 'broccoli
And pasta' which both he and Brenda most
  Appreciated, no monopoly
Of vegetarian tomato sauce
For them, they liked a varied diet, of course!

XLVI

Bikes skidding on the gravel, they were met
  By hefty men in shades, the ones who first
Took Don away, gun toting, the sextet
  Whose very high dramatic entry burst
Among the dancers of his opening set.
  This time they offered juice to quench the thirst
And, even smiling, offered Don his box
Of music; Don smiled back and checked the locks.

XLVII

Another hand offered his bags and gear
  (And one more false apologetic smile),
But gaining some possession over fear
  And quickly picking up on this gang's style,
Don gave a look as haughty as King Lear
  And motioned they should follow Indian file
Behind this extra special foreign guest,
No matter how ridiculously dressed,

XLVIII

Bringing the boxes, bags, the gear and glass
  That tinkled pleasantly with cubes of ice.
And there was Xanadu: an underpass
  Led through a grotto into paradise,
More properly the Underworld – its class
  Of citizen was, well, not very nice,
But Orpheus received a warm applause
Appearing with his train like Santa Claus,

XLIX

Bearing his early precious acetate.
   But this was not the reason. As I said,
He heard the echoing claps appreciate
   And realized the image of his head
And shoulders in the jumpsuit of a State
   Pen was the mug shot of the *Capo* dead
And lost at sea for his attempt to muscle
In on Camorra clans and in the tussle

L

This errant Mafioso and his members
   Discovered this Camorra (as it's known)
No pushover and now were floating embers
   Or single limbs and torsos or fly-blown
Beneath a landfill site no-one remembers
   Was once the villa where he held his throne.
Once so informed, the Don surrendered to
The cheers and whistles for him and his crew.

LI

They made a flourish to release his hands
   Which Don held up and clasped in victory
As if he were the owner of the lands
   About him; sadly, for this history
It is as well the reader understands
   That his compliance was no mystery:
The Don was working for a clan of dons
And had no time to weigh up pros and cons.

LII

And all that Don could see beneath the palms
   And mushrooms of umbrellas was a crowd
Dressed up for Sunday and for singing psalms,
   Dark suits and jackets (*no* T-shirts allowed),
Dark glasses, dark looks, women with the charms
   Of superstitious cults around them, proud
Of having men who would take care of them
By offering that extra special gem:

LIII

A string of cultured pearls, a diamond,
  So long as it was costlier than the mistresses
Received... and felt that they had not been conned
  Out of their true deserts, for their distresses
Came not from feeling small fish in the pond
  But when they saw a young thing's lustrous tresses,
Ankles and deep-glossed lips used as the foil
For what they knew came not from honest toil.

LIV

To Donald they looked like a pack of toads
  The rows of glassy eyes, unfathomable,
The women draped in jewels under loads
  Of make-up. Were they trying to be dull,
Decked up in so much stuff, the signs and codes
  Of life provincial, faces like a skull,
Expressionless and so devoid of life?
How to excite a *Camorrista* wife?

LV

Don looked down with dismay at what he had,
  His 12″ vinyl (Best Extended Club),
His acetates and mixes: things were bad
  And he risked much more if he played them Dub.
This was a situation and was sad.
  He asked a waiter for a syllabub
(Well, 'pointed' really) then called Bébé loud
And clear. 'Some Easy Listening for the crowd?'

LVI

She nodded, standing by with her two guards,
  The only blonde, the only one in white,
But not a soul in all that pack of cards
  Would dare to criticise the neophyte
With MBA and business models, yards
  Of black-and-white predictions for, despite
The fact the family business was in crime,
It sought to have a business paradigm.

LVII

This was the way the world was shaping, risk
   Aversive, even in the Underworld
Where Orpheus pointed out the kind of disc
   He had and sadly, *de profundis*, twirled
The spoon round in his syllabub, but brisk
   The lady was and with her fingers curled
Commanded Adrijana to her steed
And bring *musica leggera* with due speed.

LVIII

'They want Domenico Modugno, these
   Guys, or at least they look as though they do...'
Said Don. 'Well, I want you to try some cheese,'
   Said Bébé, pulling out a jar. 'Now chew
And tell me if you think that it would please
   The English public. This is something new
For them.' 'What is it?' Don asked. 'Buffalo
Milk mozzarella... well, *è buono, no?*'

LIX

And on the words that followed, Donald froze...
   'We have a product we should like to place
With you and what my market research shows
   Is we could market, too, a pizza base.
You're vegetarian, everybody knows...
   Your daughter has a very pretty face...
I know you would not wish to hurt a hair
Of her, so help us win a market share...'

LX

'Aha, non-bovine dairy products now,'
   Scoffed Don... that is, after he had scoffed the ball
Of mozzarella... but his brow
   Was knitted, swallowing hard. 'I thought that all
You wanted was a DJ who would wow
   The party...' Then he stared out at the wall
Of all-too-solid flesh and solid figures,
The silence breaking into several sniggers.

LXI

But in came Adrijana like a breeze
  To save the moment, although not the hour,
Clutching her helmet and brand new CDs
  The audio supplier was glad to shower
On her for Bébé, anything to please
  The gentlemen of honour with the power
To distribute some wealth out to the poor
Albeit breaking down a person's door.

LXII

'I'm sorry you're bovine-intolerant,'
  Bébé whispered and nodded vigorously,
'You know, we had it from a confidant...
  We always research sources rigorously.
Ebbè, it's no use being arrogant
  Or keeping to your secret covetously,
We want you to promote it, strike a chord
And you will have a generous reward...'

LXIII

'Don't tell me, let me think... Oh, yes, my life
  And adulthood assured for both my kids,
Free pass for continued living for my wife,
  And guarantee our lives won't hit the skids
(You'd even try to sell the afterlife!)
  And we will not end up two invalids?'
'*Si, si.*' 'Then, *done!*' Don offered one free mitt,
The other had a syllabub in it.

LXIV

'Truly, I am one of the lucky ones,
  Bovine-intolerant, but buffalo
Is fine for me and Brenda, same response
  For both our children, we knew long ago
That we could take it... And so, did your dons
  Or you come up with this idea as one to go
With?' 'Actually, it was me, I chose the field,
The studies talk of buffaloes' high yield...'

LXV

And all that afternoon so hot, they talked
  Of this and that, statistical reports
And market trends and when the markets baulked
  And how to smuggle in and out of ports,
It was quite fascinating... Donald chalked
  It up (his interest, that is) to sorts
Of feelings that he had for James Bond girls,
These retro ones, cat suits, and butter curls...

LXVI

Meanwhile he changed the easy listening, time
  To time, and no-one cared among the troops
Assembled for this dress shirt pantomime
  To celebrate a *quondam* Don with scoops
Of choice *gelato*, the champagne sublime.
  Occasionally he mingled with the groups,
Who smiled politely when he played *Volare*
Delighted they could hum and sing: *cantare*...

LXVII

Ôh, ôh, ôh ôh... But idylls have to close
  Just as the Don was starting to relax
Among the men in ties and girls in bows,
  He was informed they would be making tracks
Quite soon, there was no time for changing clothes,
  This time he would be playing to the max,
A VIP reception held in Rome
And after which they would escort him home.

LXVIII

So Bébé radioed her pilot in
  And Don was left free at both feet and wrists
To scramble to the helicopter's din
  And, ducking, made a gesture with his fists
Up, hoping this would please his new-found kin
  Remaking themselves as industrialists,
These criminals now on the side of law
Acting exactly as they did before.

LXIX

Perhaps this was an index of the age,
   Thought Don, his eyes closed to the chopper's blades,
Still mesmerized like someone on the stage
   Not by this latest of his escapades,
But by the thought he could be all the rage
   In orange jump suit, moustache and some shades...
In his home market there could be a gap
To put a certain something on the map.

LXX

He drifted with the clouds, what few there were,
   Then noticed they were coming in to land,
His thoughts now settling on to Bébé, her
   Gleaming white leather suit, the skin he planned
To unzip and to taste... but then the blur
   When he hit on reality and canned
The pleasures he eternally deferred.
Beside him now, that very lady stirred.

LXXI

'Okay, a car will take us to the club,'
   She said, once all the helicopter noise
Subsided, giving both her cheeks a rub
   As best she could to keep her feminine poise
While Donald, who had snuggled like a cub
   Beside her, felt the harder hands of boys
(Well, men) who led him from the heliport
Not far away from where St Paul once taught...

LXXII

O how the august colonnades of Rome
   Had hosted most of history's fine words!
Now overlooked by cupola and dome
   Mere backdrop for a scattering of birds
And tourist photographs in Ektachrome.
   But Donald was not set down for the herds
Of gaping culture vultures, he was there
To liven up a party. Yes, but where?

LXXIII

A limo whisked up to the melting kerb
  Leaving an imprint in the sticky tar,
Doors opened and the scent of wafting herb
  Made Don feel quite relaxed, he was a star
Again, the music pounding with reverb
  As small hands led him to the cocktail bar
Located in the vast interior:
Vodka and ice, fresh from Siberia.

LXXIV

'Really?' said Don. The little Muscovite
  With almond eyes both wonderfully green,
And skimpy costume of a water sprite,
  Nodded, then sat back in the limousine,
Her full lips on the cocktail straw locked tight
  And Donald found that he was squeezed between
A second elfin figure on the seat
Who passed the joint and took her vodka neat.

LXXV

'They are some entertainment for you,' said
  Bébé, lips pursed as round a cocktail straw,
Then smiled, 'Our friends in Moscow... *Straight ahead,*'
  She told the chauffeur, shades down. Then before
He knew it, back seat turned into a bed,
  Our Donald found the Slavic body more
Or less could not help looking sweet
When seen quite naked and, well, *reet petite,*

LXXVI

Not like the hulking brutes with javelin
  And discus that the Sporting Amazon
Of All the Russias used to turn and spin
  And turned him right off thoughts of liaison
With any *—ovas* who would only pin
  Him down and weigh on him a trilithon
Of muscled flesh. With Don thus occupied,
His bedroom antics through the smoked glass spied

LXXVII

Upon by Bébé and the smart chauffeur
  Who saw Nadezhda and Natalya squirm
And twist balletically with hauteur
  The one-way glass allowing them a firm
View of proceedings that the threesome were
  Engaged in, something like a wriggling worm,
Thought Bébé. In her view humanity
Was quite depraved, devoid of sanity.

LXXVIII

Once with a psychopathic relative
  Who beat her mercilessly with a cane
But always mercifully let her live
  So he could then attack her once again:
She had a love life that was primitive,
  And even if she did not mind the pain
When this *paisano* had a mind to cuff her,
She hated seeing her complexion suffer...

LXXIX

So he lies buried in the concrete floor
  Somewhere inside the bunker paradise,
Garrotted with perhaps a dozen more
  Who would not listen to her sound advice
When treating her as if she were a whore
  And so they sadly had to pay the price,
Well, sad for them, but happily for her
Who quickly took the name of 'Leveller'.

LXXX

(I know you would not want me to translate
  Exactly. It would be unethical
And far too dangerous to contemplate.
  It is too early for a funeral –
Well, mine, that is – and I know you would hate
  To have me visiting a hospital
For treatment, flat as a potato farl...
So let's say – shall we? – *grande horizontale*?)

LXXXI

And so, let me repeat, the only sheet
  That Bébé knew was balance sheet, the rest
About her I have sworn to be discreet.
  Besides, the hidden turmoil in my breast
About the lady comes if I should bleat
  More than I should... I would not like to test
Her patience. (Honest, Bébé, you know me,
I'm good. The bank's cashed those cheques happily.)

LXXXII

The place, like nothing Don had ever seen,
  Resembled marble wedding cake outside
With terraced gardens wonderfully green
  Beyond the Seven Hills of Rome, a ride
Of forty minutes in the most obscene
  Positions. Don was up to it, his pride
Took them as simply warmup for the show...
They pushed him out, resplendent in day-glo

LXXXIII

Jumpsuit, back into which he'd quickly zipped,
  The chauffeur led him to a terrace paved
With terracotta tiles where people flipped
  To see the English DJ quite unshaved
Dressed as a convict. Smiling, 'Hey,' he quipped,
  'They let me out for you, the One Depraved
And only English Don! Let's hear that bling
Go rattling as you make those booties swing!'

LXXXIV

Now this next party meant a special step
  For Bébé – upwards (naturally) – and placed
Her far above the role of demirep
  With which she otherwise might have been faced...
Still dazed, but chemically full of pep,
  Don followed as her white *chaud cul* now raced
Up carpeted back steps, dropped in a stretch
Of Rococo façades he knew could fetch

LXXXV

A patrimony if they were for sale...
　　But these were not for sale, what was he thinking?
The staircase large enough to take a whale
　　Sideways, the marble and the gilt all winking
At him seductively, the flunkeys pale
　　To see his orange jumpsuit and Don sinking
Into a suite of rooms... a discothèque,
Hotel, apartment building? What the heck,

LXXXVI

These buildings held the State and its élite!
　　Don shook hands with them, ushered to the stage
Prepared already with a mixing suite
　　(Attended at each corner by a page)
And soon he had them dancing at his feet,
　　The cardinals and statesmen all the rage
In headlines and political intrigue
And altogether in another league

LXXXVII

From those rough diamonds absurd in silk
　　Suits next to pudding wives also arrayed
In tents of satin and chiffon, the milk
　　Of human kindness never could persuade
Was in the best of taste, but they could bilk
　　Such heavy judgements as they could evade
The tax man, justice and the rule of law...
But Don was then whisked to another floor

LXXXVIII

Immediately he finished his short set...
　　Now he was introduced to deputies
(That is, Italian MPs) and met
　　The escorts for an evening out to please
Them, TV showgirl, hostess and starlet,
　　Exotic dancer... all knew how to tease
The information for a minister
Or bank or business, nothing sinister,

LXXXIX

Merely the usual *aggiornamento*
  On what was happening in the corridors
Of power, tasty as a hot pimento
  Sauce... *salsa, salsa... Hola!* All these whores
Busloaded in were only a memento
  From someone grateful for the dreadful chores
Of legislation, boring tasks that took
The skill of politician mixed with crook.

XC

And naturally night ended with a conga
  And streamers and a youthful belly dance,
A striptease and a sex show even longer
  That seemed to need the novel circumstance
Of champagne popping on a sequined thong, a
  Man doing something naughty on a lance.
It was a far cry from the floors above
Where prelates moved and lips brushed velvet glove.

XCI

Then Don emerged upon the streets of dawn,
  No time to glory in the sights of Rome,
For him it was an English garden, lawn
  And tranquil pleasures waiting him at home
Or so he thought... but home knew better: drawn
  Up by that lawn and angling garden gnome
A van delivered Brenda a container
And sloshing round in it was a no brainer.

XCII

And later, when our Don's feet left the jet
  And private airfield from his special flight,
A chauffeured limousine parked there to get
  Him off again with baggage, all his light
Head now could contemplate was something wet
  And hot, a shower and a breakfast bite
With Brenda, blanking out the deal he made
To enter in the mozzarella trade.

XCIII

Delivered earlier to his bungalow,
  Much to the consternation of his wife
Was one container marked with 'buffalo',
  DOC mozzarella and in red the life
Not of its shelf, but of his family. So,
  Immediately Brenda's thoughts were rife
With her suspicions: what did they contain,
These crazy looking balls? It was insane.

XCIV

She knew it had been one great big mistake
  Allowing Don (this was her word) to guest
Abroad at some great discothèque so fake
  You saw its inside girders. Unimpressed,
At this large chilled container, for the sake
  Of peace at home, Don's Brenda thought the best
Thing she could do, not knowing what it said
Outside the box, printed with LETTERS RED,

XCV

Was ask the local supermarket for
  Advice: perhaps there was a bring-and-buy
Sale coming up and would they like to store
  The contents for her, pending... they would try,
Given that Don would advertise them more
  On air... *Oh, yes, he would!* She breathed a sigh
And drove the carton marked 'Special Delivery'
To them, watched by the man in special livery

XCVI

Who first delivered her the plastic pack
  And now kept up a close eye on events
Not really knowing what was happening back
  In Rome with all those Mafioso gents
['Camorra' really, *ed.*] but he kept track
  And mentioned what he saw – to all intents
And purposes a ready sale, for sure,
By Brenda to a large chain's local store.

284

XCVII

So Bébé nodded happily at the news.
  She liked the feeling that the family
Could rally round Don and would help to choose
  The most appropriate retail outlet, free
Of any interference that would lose
  Them moral standing. But then, cannily,
Inside each ball was nestling like a brain
What Brenda feared: a capsule of cocaine.

XCVIII

Of course the bring-and-buy sale soon revealed
  That there was something extra in the cheese,
But souls in Leatherhead have never squealed.
  Did Bébé mind? Not really, her degrees
Come usefully in keeping her concealed
  From dealings she prefers that no-one sees.
When word got out, she strongly claimed no knowledge
And now professor at a private college

XCIX

She shakes her head and still helps out the bosses
  And puts the venture down as one that failed,
There has to be a time and place for losses:
  Far better to accept them than be gaoled.
She had no time for filthy double-crosses,
  But had to see the venture was derailed
By Brenda and the local bring-and-buy;
To mess with her she would not even try.

C

Did Don confess his multiple misdeeds?
  Strangely, there was no need, immediately
He went into the studio, plugged in leads
  And came up with a clubland classic we
Still listen to from Brighton up to Leeds
  And from that time he has eternally
Been hailed *The Don* and on his sequined cap:
The Godfather of British Gangsta Rap.

TIM THORNE

I

Dear reader, you'll recall we left our hero
  Desiring sudden and complete retirement
From the scene or else we'd rate at zero
  His chances of survival. This desire meant
Flying somewhere. Rio de Janeiro?
  Hong Kong? New York? Of course his chief requirement
Was uneventful and sequestered rest.
Seychelles, they say, is quite by far the best

II

Of all the world's remoter beauty spots
  To hide away in when the mind needs calming.
Luxury resorts and fancy yachts
  Abound and the inhabitants are charming,
The visitors sometimes less so, for lots
  Of dubious types turn up there. It's alarming
To contemplate how wealthy Eurotrash
Can ruin paradise by flashing cash.

III

Donny, while loitering, languid, on the terrace
  Of the Pirates' Arms, a watering hole
Frequented by beachcomber and by heiress
  Alike, got talking with a friendly soul,
American it seemed but, reader, whereas
  Some from that nation tend to think the whole
World is their playground, I've met quite a few
Who're decent fellows, as, I'm sure, have you.

IV

Randy was the name of this young Yank.
  He owned a yacht, a yawl to be precise,
The *Biped Mermaid* was her name, quite swank
  In her appointments. She'd already twice
Sailed round the world, he mentioned as they drank,
  Surviving everything from Arctic ice
To tropic cyclones and lots more beside.
She could take any weather in her stride.

V

'In fact, my friend,' said Randy, 'I'd regale ya
    With many a tale if I but had the time
About how not the slightest hint of failure
    Has ever marked her journeys. She's sublime!
We're just about to sail her to Australia.
    We're taking on provisions here then I'm
Off as soon as I've found a first mate.
The one I had has flown back to Kuwait.

VI

'Some family business there. He had to sell
    Or buy (I'm not too certain) for his wives
Something or other, maybe an oil well.
    Or minor sheikhdom. Just like that, he hives
Off, leaves us stranded, what the hell!
    Some folk can really stuff up others' lives.
I don't suppose...' Donny said, 'I can sail.
My uncle had a yawl, the *Profane Grail*.'

VII

An ocean voyage could be just the thing,
    Our hero thought. They strolled to the marina.
There lay the *Biped Mermaid*. Neighbouring
    Craft, though handsome, all looked somewhat meaner
Next to her. Randy said, 'Wait. I'll bring
    The crew to meet you.' Now DJ had seen her
He loved all forty foot of her, from mizzen
To jib. His wanderlust had really risen.

VIII

He checked her out: mahogany and oak,
    With dacron sails, bronze fittings, stainless steel
Rigging, she was what most seafaring folk
    Would love to sail on. Down to her very keel
She'd won him. Randy seemed a decent bloke,
    So when he came back they soon sealed a deal.
'OK, we sail tomorrow then,' said Randy,
'Now meet your shipmates, Mandi, Candi, Brandi.'

290

IX

Donny felt as if he'd found himself
  Inside *Good As Gold* by Joseph Heller,
A novel that should be on every shelf.
   Seek it at your second-hand bookseller.
But I digress. I must remind myself
   That this is not lit. crit., that I'm the teller
Of a tale, to which I must with haste return.
It's of our Donny's story you would learn.

X

These three attractive women, young, curvaceous,
  Looked up in unison and smiled in greeting.
DJ Donny's smile and nod were gracious
  As he shook each proffered hand, repeating
Each name and managing to keep salacious
  Thoughts well hidden though his heart was beating
A fraction faster than its normal rhythm
At the thought of sharing one small cabin with 'em.

XI

Duly provisioned, early the next day
  The *Biped Mermaid* set out, heading east
Past spinner dolphins frolicking at play.
   The tropic sun shone down without the least
Cloudlet and very soon La Digue, Mahé
  And the whole archipelago had ceased
To be in sight. No tiniest misgiving
Troubled Donny, who just thought, 'This is living.'

XII

That afternoon, sunning themselves on deck,
  Wearing only lotion, Candi, Brandi
And Mandi asked Donny if he'd kindly check
  The contents of a duffle bag that Randy
Had stowed under a transom. 'Just a sec,'
  Said Donny, very pleased to be a handy
Servant to these beauties. He retrieved it
And what he found inside – who'd have believed it?

291

XIII

A little plastic sachet of cocaine.
    From within the cockpit Randy's voice
Called out, 'I guess that out here on the main
    It's not against the law. We have the choice
Whether to indulge or not. It's plain
    That you three girls are dying to rejoice
In a little snort. How about you?'
This last to Don, who said, 'I'd like some, too.'

XIV

They carded up ten lines, two for each nose
    (One for each nostril, you could also say).
Randy said to the girls, 'I don't suppose
    You'd have a fifty-dollar bill.' There was no way
Between their pretty heads and pretty toes
    A pocket could be found. He said, 'OK,
I'll use a hundred.' Then he rolled a note
And sniffed his two lines, every single mote.

XV

Dear reader, it is not my role to preach,
    Or to pontificate on wrong and right.
I merely tell what happened. Surely each
    Of you may (be your morals lax or tight)
Pass judgement, but please, please, I do beseech
    You, not on me, no matter how you might
Wish to shoot the messenger. Just as it
Is I tell it, hostage to moral hazard.

XVI

And so, without regard to long-term danger,
    Dissolving septa, psychosis or worse,
The three partook, then Don, himself no stranger
    To the magic snow, far from averse
To any substance likely to derange a
    Part of his senses, sniffed his share. The curse
Of the moneyed classes has been the description
Of coke by those who uphold its proscription.

XVII

But, as I said, enough of moralising.
  The five of them proceeded to have fun.
The powder was, at first, quite energising.
  They danced, made out, then as the setting sun
Blazed gold and crimson, turning the horizon
  Into a sheet of flame as quickly done
As started (Ah, those tropic sundowns!) dropped
To their bunks and soon all movement stopped.

XVIII

But not for long. Donny felt a hand
  Upon his shoulder as he lay in bed.
Mandi it was. 'I know you'll understand,'
  She whispered, 'But when everybody's dead
Asleep a girl gets lonely.' As her tanned
  Breasts swung gently just above his head
Pity on her plight caused him, though yawning,
To offer company until the morning.

XIX

They snuggled close together. What transpired
  Between them, reader, I'll leave you to guess.
Not much imagination is required,
  I'm sure. Then Mandi's cry, 'Yes, Donny! Yes!'
Must have been louder than she'd have desired.
  Although it wasn't uttered in distress,
It caused young Candi, in the other bunk,
To wake and wonder loudly, 'Have we sunk?'

XX

It wasn't long before she ascertained
  The reason for the noise. She slipped across
The space between the berths. Now the cocaine'd
  Worn off, her mood was black and with that loss
Of joy that coming down brings she complained,
  'It's not fair. Why's it me who had to doss
Down on my own while Mandi got to shag?'
Now, we all know the average sleeping bag

293

XXI

Is hard put to accommodate a pair,
   Let alone three, but where there is a will…
Donny, well-mannered, always glad to share,
   Welcomed and comforted poor Candi till
She was as satisfied as Mandi. There
   The trio lay in blissful slumber, still
As a millpond, even stiller I'd dare say.
Not waking till the dawn of the new day.

XXII

Meanwhile what of the other two? I guess
   You're asking. Curiosity, dear reader,
For all the cats it's killed is nonetheless
   A healthy thing. I've always been a pleader
For knowledge over nescience, I confess.
   And ever since Zeus had it off with Leda
The world has always loved to hear a story
Which dealt in depth with exploits amatory.

XXIII

Suffice to say that Brandi and the captain,
   Having collapsed onto a for'ard berth,
Had spent a pleasant night all tightly wrapped in
   Each other's various limbs. There was no dearth
Of squeals of joy. The query one is apt in
   Such a case to pose, *viz* 'Did the earth
Move for you?' is one that surely oughta
Be seen as figurative; they were on water.

XXIV

The next few days and nights were spent in much
   The same way, though the combinations altered:
Sunbathing, coke, a sip of rum or such.
   The girls' only complaint: the wind and salt'd
Make their skin less than perfect to the touch.
   In rectifying this Don never faltered.
His hands kept busily applying lotion;
The rest of him was peaceful as the ocean.

XXV

But oceans are not always full of peace.
   Strong winds can whip up waves that toss and rock
A craft until its crew plead for release
   From violent movement. Gales can pound and knock
Even the sturdiest vessel. When they cease
   The damage done can sometimes be a shock.
Just such a gale arising quite a stir made
Among those sailing on the *Biped Mermaid*.

XXVI

'Fear not,' said Randy. 'This will soon abate.
   We'll ride it out. This yawl is built so well
There's not a storm could incapacitate
   Her. She's sailed through the hell
Of Cape Horn waters, even through Bass Strait.
   Why this is nothing: just a moderate swell.'
But as he spoke the spinnaker was shredded.
A broadside spun her from where she'd been headed.

XXVII

Donny suggested hauling in the sails.
   Randy, high on coke, said, 'I'll be damned!
This is what sailing's all about!' The rails
   Were by now dipping under as she slammed
From side to side. Then the horrendous gale's
   Fury was joined by rain. The women scrammed
Under the canvas housetop. There they cowered,
Certain the *Mermaid* would be overpowered.

XXVIII

And through all this, what of the vessel's skipper?
   Was Randy standing steadfast in command,
Despite not feeling (like them all) too chipper?
   Well, frankly, no. But you must understand
He thought the thought of sinking with his ship a
   Concept overrated and he planned
If things got really bad then the best thing he
Could do would be to launch the pulpit dinghy

XXIX

With just himself, one other and the coke.
   Which other? That was but a small dilemma.
Candi or Mandi? Brandi or the bloke?
   Any of them would suit his stratagem, a
Plan indeed which virtue-loving folk
   might harshly judge. I'm loath, though, to condemn a
Fellow man for cowardice or greed.
Morally we are each a thin, frail reed.

XXX

The waves (though 'waves' seems too benevolent
   A word) rose halfway up the mast then crashed
Onto the *Mermaid*'s deck. The air was rent
   Not only with the screaming winds that smashed
the rigging and the dinghy, and that sent
   Overboard anything that wasn't lashed
Down tightly (and some that were lashed, too)
But also with the cries of all the crew.

XXXI

For hours that seemed like days, for days that seemed
   Like months, the storm tossed the poor yawl about.
With every thunderclap somebody screamed.
   With every lightning bolt you'd hear a shout.
No nightmare Donny Johnny'd ever dreamed
   Had terrorised him so. There was no doubt.
The motor, lights, pump, radio all gone,
He knew they'd be but briefly hanging on.

XXXII

Too late by far for Randy's planned escape,
   The stricken *Biped Mermaid* seemed just like
Fay Wray when in the grip of that great ape
   Atop the Empire State. No use to psych
Oneself up against this force. No scrape
   He'd ever been in had been known to strike
Such dread and panic into Donny's heart.
Then one freak wave smashed the poor craft apart.

XXXIII

Donny lost consciousness. When he came to
    He found himself clutching a water tank,
Half-empty, floating under a sky so blue,
    So bright, the storm quite spent, while of the Yank,
There was no sign, nor any of his crew.
    He could not see even a single plank
Of the poor *Biped Mermaid*. On each side
The Indian Ocean spread, serene and wide.

XXXIV

At least he had some water. For how long
    He could survive was anybody's guess.
The sun was blistering. What else could go wrong?
    Despair could be expected. Nonetheless,
Our hero's optimism was so strong
    That even these dire straits could not depress
His spirits. His water tank, as you will note,
Was half-*full* and it doubled as a boat!

XXXV

Now you or I, dear reader, would have thought
    The situation hopeless, cast adrift
To be the waves', the winds', the currents' sport,
    But 'seek and ye shall find': he had the gift
Of hope, so, squinting in the sun, he sought
    Some vessel that might offer him a lift
And saw, on the horizon, a small dot
That might, just *might*, have been another yacht.

XXXVI

The dot grew, coming straight for Donny Johnny,
    It surely was a boat, not just a piece
Of flotsam or some bird. Now, all doubts gone, he
    Waved in its direction. Sweet release
From Neptune's clasp was close. The sun still shone. He
    Was sure they'd see him, sure that soon he'd cease
This lonely bobbing on the ocean, soon
Have other humans with whom to commune.

XXXVII

It was indeed a vessel, some small trawler,
    Fishing, perhaps. He cared not from where.
The gap between it and him grew smaller
    Until it drew alongside and a pair
Of figures at the gunwale waved. A call, a
    Hoarse reply from Donny, and then there
He was, wet, hungry, weary, but on board.
His spirits, never low, now truly soared.

XXXVIII

His rescuers appeared to speak a tongue
    Which Donny did not know, had never heard.
These kindly foreign sailors who had sprung
    Him from the jaws of death said not a word
That he could understand: not one among
    Those gathered round him. Donny, undeterred,
With smiles and gestures showed his gratitude,
Also his rather pressing need for food.

XXXIX

And then from somewhere near the vessel's stern
    He heard a voice call, 'English do you speak?'
A female voice. Donny could just discern
    A group: the old, the very young, the weak,
The female, huddling there. 'I try to learn,'
    The voice continued. Eyes downcast and meek
Beneath a hijab, did not meet his, yet
He felt their unseen beauty, black as jet.

XL

'My name is Donny Johnny, what is yours?'
    'Fawziah,' came the answer. Then she looked
Up briefly at him. 'I am here because
    I pay much money.' 'Lady, you've been rooked,'
Thought Donny, looking round. After a pause
    She went to speak again. Our hero crooked
His finger, beckoning her closer. She
Stayed put. 'I am, how you say, refugee.'

XLI

So that explained their miserable state.
  There must have been some sixty of them squeezed
Into a space where maybe seven or eight
  Could comfortably fit. The frail, diseased
And kids among them accounted for a great
  Percentage. Had they all somehow displeased
Their countries' leaders to the point where flight
Was now their only option? It's not right.

XLII

These were the thoughts that spun in Donny's head.
  To his gratitude was added pity.
At brute injustice he always saw red,
  And felt for victims no matter what the city
Or village they were from. Fawziah said,
  'I am from Kabul.' 'I have heard of it,' he
Replied. 'Why did you have to leave?' 'I fought
For the interests of the girls I taught.'

XLIII

Donny thought Fawziah's English fine,
  Though not the very finest thing about her.
Her smile and how it made her black eyes shine:
  Little could top that, but without a doubt her
Sad plight affected him. 'What philistine,'
  He wondered, 'Could so cruelly put to rout a
Teacher just because she took a stand
For her girl students? What a stupid land!'

XLIV

'The others,' Donny waved in their direction.
  'Why are they fleeing? Are they Afghan too?'
Fawziah shrugged. It seemed she'd no connection
  With any of the others, never knew
Their origins. A miserable collection
  Of sad humanity they were, and that is true.
Just then a thin hand suddenly descended
On Donny's shoulder and this chat was ended.

XLV

By gestures it was made perfectly clear
   That adult males on board had their own place.
Women and kids were crowded in the rear
   Whilst men had commandeered the for'ard space,
What's more (and this gave Donny J no cheer)
   Gazing on Fawziah's pretty face
Was not approved of by those in command.
He'd best be patient until they reached land.

XLVI

The captain of this oddly-peopled craft
   Was called Suyadi. Dour-faced and devout,
He made it clear the whole boat, fore and aft,
   Was his domain without the slightest doubt.
Apart from him the boat was only staffed
   By one young lad, smiling, brown and stout,
'Ali,' he said, tapping his own chest, and,
'Bali,' to indicate his native land.

XLVII

Donny feared his half-full water tank
   Was the sole reason he'd been hauled on board.
Their own supply was very low. They drank,
   And ate some boiled rice rationed from a hoard
Which Suyadi controlled. Our hero shrank
   From thoughts of just what might have been. Restored
In spirits by this meagre meal, however,
He gave thanks to his stars or to whatever

XLVIII

Gods may be presiding over fate.
   He rather thought there were none, but was smart
Enough to know he must impersonate
   A Muslim now, and that when they took part
 In prayers, he should seem to participate.
   He'd be mad to upset this applecart.
He watched Suyadi lay out on the deck a
Prayer mat and kneel on it, facing Mecca.

XLIX

At least he faced the stern, so Donny Johnny
  Assumed the holy city of the Hadj
Lay behind them somewhere, whereupon he
  Knelt likewise, having made sure Ali's large
Buttocks hid any *faux pas.* Off and on he
  Glanced up (unseen by the man in charge,
He hoped) to see if he could spot Fawziah.
Alas, it was impossible to see her.

L

A few days passed, all of them uneventful.
  Then one calm evening, soon after dusk,
To Donny's nose a half-forgotten scent, full
  Of earth with a slight harshness like the husk
Of coconut or bark, came. Not resentful
  In the least (though he'd prefer the musk
Of female flesh) he knew that he was smelling
The journey's end. What next? There's no foretelling.

LI

Suyadi cut his engine, coasted in
  To a small creek, then Ali tossed the anchor.
One of the men jumped overboard. His chin
  Was just above the water line, the bank a
Metre or so away. He flashed a grin
  That glowed in the night sky. Now any rancour
Donny might have felt towards Suyadi
Dissolved. This whole adventure was foolhardy,

LII

But worth it just to see that fellow grinning,
  Happy to touch ground in a foreign land
After who knows what hell, but he was winning,
  His broad smile gave Don to understand,
His freedom and a glorious new beginning
  Awaited him, awaited the whole band.
Donny was next to jump into the water;
The other passengers were somewhat shorter.

LIII

They climbed over the gunwale one by one.
   Donny and his friend grabbed hold of each.
Then, giggling as if this were just for fun.
   They were set down upon a tiny beach.
With this disembarkation fully done
   Suyadi left. It took two steps to reach
The shore, where Donny chose at once to steer
Straight for a rock upon which sat Fawziah.

LIV

They looked into each other's eyes. They sighed.
   Was it just relief that made them do so?
You, reader, may think otherwise, and I'd
   Hazard that you'd not be Robinson Crusoe
In thinking that, but they were dignified
   And did not let their baser feelings loose, oh
Dear no, not here, for as you'd expect,
They showed their fellow travellers that respect.

LV

'Suyadi said we wait here till someone
   Comes to pick up us,' Fawziah said.
'But I not trust him. I think we must run.'
   Donny had heard stories of people led
To parlous ends by swindlers, and thought none
   Of Suyadi's ilk worth trusting. If ahead
Lay the wrath of angry immigration
Cops then this was far from a salvation.

LVI

They stole away and found a kind of cave
   Which gave them shelter and some privacy.
Fawziah said, 'I am no longer slave
   To Muslim customs,' and dramatically
Threw off her hijab, letting wave on wave
   Of raven hair fall, tumbling, shining, free.
There's nothing quite as sensual as hair,
Say some, dear reader, be it dark or fair.

LVII

They sat together in that cave a while
  Telling each other of their histories.
Donny, transfixed by Fawziah's sweet smile,
  Often lost track. Forgetfulness would seize
His brain, as if his memory's data file
  Had been deleted. Still, at times like these
It's wise to stem the flow of memory's fount.
Some chapters it were best not to recount.

LVIII

Autobiography's a tiring game.
  Soon all those words had wearied each pure mind.
They fell asleep. Now who am I to blame
  Them if they woke next morn somewhat entwined?
Why, reader, if you think that there is shame
  In such togetherness, it's you I find
Lacking in innocence. Suffice to say
They glowed as they woke to the dawning day.

LIX

As they surveyed the scene by morning's light
  They saw the country's utter desolation.
All that met the eye to left or right
  Was sand and rocks and scrubby vegetation.
Would death by thirst and hunger be their plight?
  However sweet, you can't eat liberation.
While they were pondering how to survive,
They heard a heavy vehicle arrive.

LX

Donny Johnny climbed a stony rise
  And saw a truck and men in uniform.
'The immigration cops: that's no surprise,'
  He thought. 'They've been tipped off.' He watched them
                                                    swarm
Into the bush and heard the anguished cries
  Of former shipmates. 'That seems true to form
For Suyadi, that lowdown, scheming wanker,
Paid by both sides, just like a dodgy banker.'

303

LXI

Having mused thus, our hero slid back down
   The slope to where Fawziah waited, fear
And apprehension causing a deep frown
   Which failed to mar her beauty. 'Ah, my dear,
You'll understand I didn't nearly drown
   To be arrested and imprisoned here.
We must lie low.' He told her what he'd seen.
They piled some rocks to make a kind of screen.

LXII

She needed comforting. His arms were strong.
   Need I, dear reader, tell you more than this?
The time till safety seemed extremely long.
   Must I recount each soft caress, each kiss,
Each breathed endearment? No, it would be wrong.
   Besides, I'm sure there's not too much amiss
With your imagination. Some hours passed
Until they judged that they were safe at last.

LXIII

They vowed to brave whatever might impend.
   Then, hand in hand, they timidly set out
In search of water, food, some kind of friend.
   Heading inland, beset by fear and doubt,
Wondering just how this all would end.
   They guessed the truck's tyre tracks would lead them out
To a road or some manifestation
Of what out here might pass for civilisation.

LXIV

And so it did. Two lanes of sticky tar,
   North-South: our Donny couldn't have been surer.
'We'll wait here for some passing truck or car,'
   He said, thinking Fawziah's looks would lure a
Driver to stop. A van slowed down. Aha!
   Success so soon! Its sign read 'Aqua Pura
Swimming pool maintenance and cleaning service'.
It pulled up. They approached, expectant, nervous.

LXV

'G'day. What's up?' This cheery salutation,
   Followed by, 'Where the bloody hell ya headin'?'
Drew from Donny J, 'Our destination
   Is Fremantle.' 'Well you're in luck. So, get in.
There's a bloody way to go.' The pair's elation
   Lessened when the driver ('Name's Mick') said in
His hearty voice, 'I reckon you should keep
Me entertained or else I'll fall asleep.

LXVI

'So tell me your story.' Donny thought it wise,
   Until he knew Mick better, to avoid a
Factual account. Let's face it, lies
   Can make, if they're intelligently employed, a
Tale seem truer than when one applies
   The facts. He sought not merely to embroider
The truth but to destroy it, thread by thread,
And weave a whole new fabric in its stead.

LXVII

I shall not bore you, reader, with the details
   Of DJ Donny's fabricated bio.
After all, you've had the truth from me. Tales
   Fantastical, owing nought to Clio,
Have no appeal to one like me who retails
   History unvarnished. I wouldn't even try, oh
No, to list his pseudo-souvenirs.
Suffice to say they left bluff Mick in tears.

LXVIII

'Jeez, mate, you've had it rough,' was Mick's reply.
   'I'd love to help you. Ever cleaned a pool?'
Donny said he'd give anything a try.
   'Cash in hand,' said Mick, ''s my general rule.
The taxman needn't know. You'll have to buy
   Some clothes and tucker and I reckon you'll
Need somewhere to live.' He reached into his pants
Pocket, pulled out some notes. 'Here's an advance.'

LXIX

All that day and the next (with a brief stay
   To grab some sleep at a third-rate motel)
They travelled south and as they made their way
   Mick explained to them how very well
Off were the residents of WA
   (Apart from those who had been known to dwell
There for forty thousand years or more)
Thanks to the Chinese need for iron ore.

LXX

'There's suburbs full of multi-millionaires.
   I've customers as rich as all get-out.
They're always looking for housemaids, *au pairs*
   and so on. Your missus there, no doubt,
Could get a job as well. Then all your cares
   Money-wise would just go walkabout.'
Wiping the arses of their bratty kids
Or polishing their pure gold dustbin lids

LXXI

Did not appeal to Fawziah but she
   Kept her counsel. They arrived in Perth,
Spent the night *chez* Mick, then cheerfully
   Just as the sunrise heralded the birth
Of a new day, boss and employee
   Set off, knowing that there was no dearth
Of pools that they could make to look just so
In Dalkeith, Mosman Park or Cottesloe.

LXXII

Mick did the rounds of his rich clientele,
   Introducing Donny as he went.
Each mansion seemed to have a tale to tell,
   A tale of grotesque taste, of millions spent
On sheer vulgarity and size. Could those who dwell
   Among such ostentatious ornament
Be normal humans, Donny asked himself,
Or freaks engendered from excessive pelf?

LXXIII

Next day our hero drove the van around
 While Mick stayed home and did the books. By four
O'clock that sultry afternoon he found
 Himself knocking at the tradesmen's door
Of some *faux château* that would confound
 The aesthetics of Graceland mixed up with décor
By Saddam, all in aqua, gilt and mauve,
The tackiest house in all of Peppermint Grove.

LXXIV

There was no answer, but from by the pool
 A sozzled voice called, 'Here!' so Johnny turned
And there, on a chaise longue, clutching a cool
 Long glass of something pink, could be discerned
The lady of the house. The born-to-rule
 Peremptoriness that comes from wealth unearned
Was clearly in her voice; that single word
Was quite enough to show it, even slurred.

LXXV

'You've come to clean the pool, I gather... Wow!'
 She looked him over, squinting in the sun.
'Come closer. Hmm. I like what I see. Now
 Take your shirt off. Not just anyone
Can clean my pool. You realise I allow
 Myself some extra service, just for fun.
You get my drift?' Donny stood, perplexed,
Wondering what on earth would happen next.

LXXVI

'The maid has quit. There's no-one here but us.
 I'm Jeannie, by the way, but you can call
me Madam or Ms Rhinestone. Let's discuss
 What other small, or maybe not so small
Jobs I might give you.' Then, with no more fuss
 than if she brushed a leaf that dared to fall
nearby, she dropped her swimsuit top and flung
Her arms wide. 'Now, let's see how well you're hung.'

LXXVII

Donny thought fast and came up with a plan.
  'You need a maid. My girlfriend needs the work.
I'll call her now. My phone is in the van.'
  He turned and, with the thought that, 'There's one perk
I can do without,' once out of sight he ran.
  But Jeannie Rhinestone's not someone you irk
Without reprisal. She picked up her Nokia,
Rang Mick and said, 'Your contract's looking rockier.

LXXVIII

'That's three men in a row who've turned me down.
  You'd better hurry and send someone new
Or I'll make sure there's no pool in this town
  You'll ever clean again. I'm warning you.
I need a stud, not some pathetic clown.
  Meanwhile come here yourself. You'll have to do.'
Donny worked the next few hours in fear;
He couldn't wait to get back to Fawziah.

LXXIX

Mick, looking worn out, met him at the door.
  'Strewth, mate, I've got bad news. The Immigration
Came round just as I got home. I saw
  Them take Fawziah for interrogation.
Jeannie Rhinestone's fixed this up, I'm sure.
  What she says goes. She runs this bloody nation.
You knocked her back, which put her in a shit,
So she's found out Fawziah's not legit.'

LXXX

Donny was downcast. Donny's tears were shed
  To think of what awaited that brave soul
Back in a land where ten-year-olds were wed
  To whom their parents chose, and where control
By males was rarely challenged. She had fled
  From what seemed like some archaic black hole
Where ignorance, misogyny and fear
Held sway, and now, to be sent back! Fawziah!

LXXXI

He wept. He sobbed. He called himself a twit.
  He cursed the gods. He cursed his lack of thought.
He told himself he should have grabbed a bit
  Of what La Rhinestone offered. Well, distraught
As he now was, and with the benefit
  Of hindsight he could say, 'Of course I ought
To have done such and such,' but at the time
Resisting Jeannie seemed far from a crime.

LXXXII

Reflect a while, dear reader, on the fact
  That whilst Afghanistan was thought to be
An unsafe place where Taliban attacked
  With suicide bomber and with IED,
Whose own police and military lacked
  The wherewithal to keep their people free
From violence, yet on the other hand
It was considered just the kind of land

LXXXIII

Which people like Fawziah could be sent
  Back to. The logic seems to fail, but I
Have never had the kind of mind that's meant
  For logic, so it's best we say goodbye
To musings of the kind. It's time we went
  Back to where DJ was heard to cry,
'Oh, woe is me! Poor, dear Fawziah! Woe!
Woe, that I ever saw that *faux château!*'

LXXXIV

He carried on like that for half a day,
  But there were pools to clean and cash to earn.
And though he never would forget the way
  His dear Fawziah'd been made to return
He got on with his life and, shall we say,
  With effort overcame the urge to spurn
The multitude of women, semi-clad,
Who lounged beside the pools. Was that so bad?

LXXXV

His skill at doing what pool cleaners do
    Was such that soon his fame spread far and wide.
Mick's business consequently grew and grew.
    He put on extra staff and so supplied
The needs of pools and of their owners too
    From Mandurah to Yanchep where beside
Each pool the smiles of every bathing beauty
Were proof of how Mick's staff performed their duty.

LXXXVI

After some months when little changed at all,
    Donny, still haunted sometimes by the spectre
Of Jeannie, whom he tried not to recall,
    Felt his efforts for the service sector
Of Perth's economy begin to pall.
    Unlike the bee, who never tires of nectar,
He found the lifestyle of this lotus-land,
Like its inhabitants, a tad too bland.

LXXXVII

Sydney beckoned. To himself he said, 'I
    Must see what lies on this land's other shore.
He bade the West adieu and caught the redeye,
    Flying into the great unknown once more
Like Captain Cook or some crusading Jedi,
    Although without the same *esprit de corps*.
Eager to learn what hedonism could teach,
He first of all set out for Bondi Beach

LXXXVIII

Where surf and sand and beauty were displayed.
    He found himself a flat. The rent was dear;
That's how it is in Sydney, I'm afraid.
    One evening he dropped in for a beer,
Into his local, where bands often played.
    He sat down with his drink in time to hear
The MC say, 'Let's big it up with feelin'
For our next act. It's Ken. He's from New Zealan'.'

***

The isles of Peace, the isles of Peace,
  Those nuclear-free though shaky isles
Where Beauty's in the snowy fleece
  Of ewes and their seductive smiles,
Where glacier'd mountain ranges rise
As massive as netballers' thighs:

Yes, Ao Tearoa, land
  Of flightless birds and malformed vowels
So difficult to understand,
  Where churnings of Earth's molten bowels
Can smash down cities, maim and kill,
Although I've left, I love her still.

And yet, sad as it is to say,
  Despite the joys of Marlborough plonk,
Of Pinot Noir and Chardonnay,
  Of Pinot Gris and Savvy Blanc,
I'm prey to fits, not of *grand mal*, d'ya
Know, but of the worst nostalgia.

For I'm stuck here across the ditch
  On the West Island (as it's known)
Scratching my nostalgic itch
  Until it bleeds. Why do I moan?
Because, as you may be aware,
There are no bloody jobs back there.

The geysers still perform their trick.
  Hot mud bubbles plop and burst
At Rotorua, but clever-dick
  Economists have done their worst.
The Bay of Plenty's now a bay
Of pretty close to sweet FA.

When Reagan, Thatcher and their sort
  With neo-liberal, *laissez-faire*
Advisors in the Eighties wrought
  Havoc on workers everywhere,
Before their mayhem had begun
They chose NZ for a dry run.

Earthquakes that cause the soil, once hard,
  To liquefy, dumped Aussie cheese,
French nuclear tests in her backyard,
  We will not think of themes like these.
New Zealand has withstood them all,
Even that sneaky underarm ball.

311

Though 'Rogernomics' was all bunk,
    It did what nothing else could do.
Much more than *Rainbow Warrior*'s sunk,
    The dollar's par with the razoo.
The Tasman's now a sea too far.
Dash down yon glass of Pinot Noir.

***

LXXXIX

Thus sang, or would, or could, or should have sung
    This Kiwi troubadour. DJ was gallant.
Nothing but words of praise came from his tongue,
    Although the merest modicum of talent
Was all Ken showed. He's surely not among
    (Besides, that accent is so damned repellant.)
The greatest that his homeland has let go,
Like Eric Beach, Ruth Park or Russell Crowe.

XC

Ken proved, however, friendly, so they shared
    A wine or two or three and got to chatting
On subjects ranging from the gigs they'd snared
    To politics and Stephen Fleming's batting.
No cricketer's good name was that night spared,
    Not even Hadlee's. Then Ken, thickly plaiting
His words and spilling his glass of Secret Stone,
Said, 'My dad owns a nightclub, *Chez Capone*.

XCI

'His regular DJ has got the clap
    Or some such untoward indisposition.
They need someone and you seem like a chap
    Who's heaven-sent to take on the position.
What say tomorrow night you fill the gap?
    I guarantee I'll get my dad's permission.'
They shook, swapped numbers, left and the next day
Ken rang to say his father'd said OK.

XCII

Chez Capone, it seems, was all the rage
    That month and might well be for weeks to come.
Fashions for clubs in our impatient age
    Rarely endure. Some go broke and some
Fall victim to the turn of fashion's page
    For no apparent reason. Well, the thumb
Of modish judgment howsoever earned
For *Chez Capone* was clearly upwards turned.

XCIII

Donny had heard of many a violent fight
    In Aussie nightclubs and in streets nearby.
But Ken assured him *Chez Capone*, despite
    Its name, was peaceful as a butterfly.
In fact, he said, the venue's a delight
    For punters who are very quiet and shy.
They're safe at *Chez Capone*. What really cheers 'em
Is its huge Maori bouncer, mean and fearsome.

XCIV

That night, 'round ten, Donny set out on foot
    Through Paddo and the Cross towards the city,
Observing as he went sights that would put
    To shame the sets of movies known as 'gritty'.
If morals were colours, Sydney'd be as soot,
    Although the Bridge is fine, the harbour pretty.
Quite soon, within a quarter-hour or less,
He'd reached what Ken had said was the address.

XCV

He thought himself the victim of some prank.
    This surely was no entertainment zone.
A building that once might have been a bank
    Back in the days when banks were made of stone,
Its windows blocked, its whole exterior blank,
    Was this the famous club, the *Chez Capone*?
Then he saw the neon, blinking blue,
And up a side lane an extensive queue.

XCVI

Donny proceeded to this long line's head
  And there, behind a length of velvet rope,
A giant, just as Kiwi Ken had said,
  Stood guard. There wouldn't be the slightest hope
Of getting past this model of NZ
  Musculature. You'd have to be a dope
To even try. Donny had never seen
So much muscle with a face so mean.

XCVII

Our hero, after one deep breath to quell
  His apprehension, made his business clear.
The bouncer spoke into his left lapel
  And looked back up with something very near
A smile, a look that would do just as well
  To frighten as to be a cause for cheer,
Jerking his thumb towards the interior's murk.
So Donny Johnny went in to start work.

XCVIII

Backstage he found a library of old vinyl,
  From '50s rockabilly to The Clash.
The kind of hoard that I wish had been mine, all
  Waiting to be mixed – hip-hop and thrash,
Ballads and bubblegum. He made his final
  Choice, including even Johnny Cash.
Then, as the punters filled the dim-lit space,
He socked it to 'em with more bass than grace.

XCIX

He mixed and scratched and spun from this weird list
  To a relentless beat. Zydeco, raga,
Tex-Mex and reggae, everything was grist
  To Donny's pounding mill. While Bundy, lager
And alcopops were flowing, all those pissed
  Young things shimmied to bits of Lady Gaga
Fused with the Stones and even the Big O
In DJ Donny Johnny's greatest show.

C

There was a break (Such things, I'm told, occur
　　From time to time in gatherings like this.)
From the sound's bewildering, rhythmic blur.
　　Even DJs need to take a piss
Occasionally, visit a masseur
　　Or change a sweaty outfit, though they miss
The adoration of the pulsing throng
And so they never leave the desk for long.

CI

While Donny Johnny took a welcome swig
　　Of water (well, there was no Chardonnay
Mentioned in his rider and the gig
　　Was causing him to sweat in the worst way.)
A female punter, eyes so very big,
　　Trim, tanned, blonde, cute and quite *décolletée*,
Came up and leaned across the desk and said,
'I'm Lara. Would you like to come to bed?

CII

'No man I've shagged has been known to complain.
　　Or come into the loo and snort a line?'
'Why, thank you, miss. I'll pass on the cocaine.
　　I've given up the powder, but for mine
The first option is one I'll entertain.
　　A blowjob in the toilet would be fine.'
Lara bridled. 'Hmmph. Blowjob my arse!
I'll have you know I am a girl with class.'

CIII

Donny apologised for his *faux pas*.
　　And Lara's anger seemed to be assuaged.
He spun a final set, his repertoire
　　Expanding as the drunken clubbers raged.
Finished at last, he headed for the bar
　　When Lara reappeared. Our hero gauged
From her demeanour that she was prepared
To let bygones... Then Donny stopped and stared.

315

CIV

Two chaps, not quite yet men, no longer boys,
    The kind who seem to have less brain than muscle,
Who, even sober, would be lacking poise,
    Shoved each other, fell, began a tussle,
Their bodies rolling on the floor, the noise
    Of fabric tearing heard above the hustle
Of last drink orders, girlish screams and clicking
Cameras, skin abraded, feet a-kicking.

CV

He realised that it was on for real
    When he saw a knife make ineffectual stabs.
If, in a brawl, I see a flash of steel
    I'm out of there quicker than Ali's jabs
It's straight to Macca's for a Happy Meal
    Or, better still, the Lebo's for kebabs.
Junk food is great to calm the frightened mind
And leave all thoughts of sudden death behind.

CVI

But Donny Johnny's made of sterner stuff
    And he had Lara hanging off his arm,
So where I'd do a bunk he came on tough
    And in a voice both menacing and calm
Said, 'OK you two. Now that's quite enough.
    I'll call the bouncer.' Panic and alarm
Suffused the faces of the brawling pair.
Testosterone dissolved into thin air.

CVII

Such was the Maori man-mountain's repute
    That no-one wanted him in the equation.
With peace, and Lara most impressed to boot,
    The time had come for her kind invitation
To be accepted. All that was in dispute
    Was that perennial question of location:
'Your place or mine?' Hers was closer by,
And so they stepped out under the dawning sky.

CVIII

A mere two city blocks, albeit across
　　Some pools of vomit, the odd prostrate form
Of weary reveller and assorted dross,
　　The night's detritus, very much the norm
These days when 'having a good time' means loss
　　Of consciousness, then, though a perfect storm
Of drugs and booze has finally prevailed,
You've neither been hospitalised nor gaoled,

CIX

And they were at the door of Lara's flat.
　　She fumbled with the key, he with the hook-
And-eye that held her tiny dress, whereat,
　　Having both succeeded, they both took
A tumble, tripping over the doormat
　　And her descending garment, then they shook
With laughter as they lay upon the floor
Entangled, each unwilling to withdraw.

CX

They helped each other stand, each body leaning
　　Into the other, for balance and from lust,
And then collapsed again, after careening
　　Towards her bed, on which they landed, just.
They next proceeded, if you get my meaning,
　　To parry like fencers, with less cut than thrust.
Modesty, as you've no doubt surmised,
Was not a virtue Lara greatly prized,

CXI

But you and I, dear reader, aren't like that.
　　And so we'll draw a modest veil athwart
The next half hour or so. Then, rat-a-tat!
　　There came a sudden knocking. Donny thought
The wreckers were demolishing the flat,
　　So loud it was. Lara, quite distraught,
Whispered, 'The wardrobe, quick !' There Donny sped,
Kicking his clothing underneath the bed.

CXII

Lara unlatched the door. He dared to peer
   Through a small crack to see who'd come to visit.
What met his eye caused him the greatest fear
   He'd ever known. With terror quite exquisite
He wished that he could somehow disappear
   Completely. Now it isn't common, is it,
To crouch, nude, in a lady's wardrobe, while
She entertains? At least it's not my style.

CXIII

But what made Donny's state the worst of all
   As he continued in that 'robe to skulk
Was that he recognised who'd come to call.
   Only one man had such impressive bulk.
It was the nightclub bouncer, eight feet tall
   And twice the width of the Incredible Hulk.
With direst panic DJ's heart was gripped
To see his muscles ripple as he stripped.

CXIV

Lara and her visitor, alack,
   retired to bed. Vain thought that she'd dismiss him.
As Donny watched them through that tiny crack
   He winced to note the heat with which she'd kiss him.
Then, as they made the 'beast with double back',
   He wondered if she'd staged the scene to piss him
Off as payback. Whether or not, 'It's clear,'
He thought. 'I really must get out of here.'

CXV

When finally, their sweet exertions ended,
   The pair were filling up that small apartment
With a duet of snores, why only then did
   Our hero, knowing what 'a pounding heart' meant,
With first one hesitant, light foot extended,
   Then his whole naked self, knew to depart meant
The risk of being caught, but that to stay
Meant he would never see another day.

CXVI

His clothes were irretrievable. To reach
  Beneath the lovers' bed where they were stashed
Would likely wake the giant. He kept each
  Slight movement minimal. An idea flashed
Into his mind (Dear reader, I beseech
  You not to judge him; he was quite abashed.
Morality dissolves when panic presses.)
He'd help himself to one of Lara's dresses.

CXVII

Thus clad he crept out to the city street,
  A busy one. The sun by now was high.
He'd left his phone behind, so could not tweet
  For help, but not one single passer-by
(This being Sydney) thought him ought but sweet
  (Lara always dressed to please the eye.)
He got back to his residence. No key,
No card, no cash, no clothes: a quandary.

CXVIII

Luckily, the landlord lived downstairs
  And was a pleasant fellow – a rare breed,
The pleasant landlord – so, thinking his cares
  (The worst of them, at least) were gone indeed,
He knocked and, muttering to himself some prayers
  For understanding in his hour of need,
Said, 'I've been in a closet. Now I'm free.'
The landlord looked him over. 'So I see.'

MIKE WILSON

i.m. R.E.W.

Part One

I

Lord Byron's Age was sweet and prelapsarian,
  all innocence, and having it away
with willing married women... Octogenarian
  affronted cuckold-husbands could not stay
his noble roving hand... The great Lotharian!
  The Honour'd Member rodding where it may...!
But Byron had refinement, none the less,
and surely it is anybody's guess

II

how he would judge the Morals of Today.
  For would he not bemoan the New Barbarian?
His Age of Innocence has given way
  to something sleazier, more post-millenarian,
and 'Manners Maketh Man' is well *passé*!
  The Age of the Un-penitent Vulgarian
is now upon us. What would Byron sneer
about, and mock, today – if he were here?

III

'I wouldn't say I have an axe to grind,
  I simply don't know where I stand on "gayness".
I hope I'm not insensitive or blind,
  or guilty of, like, shallowness, or feyness...
There was one thing that did – once – spring to mind:
  it must mean something... that it rhymes with anus...'
Don Johnny's in a TV studio,
impressing all, with all he doesn't know.

IV

The show is going well – or so he thinks...
  He's perched upon a pink and plastic sofa,
exchanging chat and flattery, on-screen drinks
  with a lovable celebrity-cum-loafer
who's in the news, accused of sky-high jinks,
  a shag-and-tell tale with the former chauffeur
of some B-Lister with a book to sell...
Getting paid for getting drunk. It's going well.

323

V

The hostess they're both talking to is called
   Candida – 'like the rash, but not such fun!'
she quips. She should be wrinkle-skinned, and bald,
   a Barbara Cartland left out in the sun,
except she's been completely overhauled
   (though her Botox-beauty's somewhat overdone:
it's left her looking like a stretched reptile
that cannot frown, or swallow, sulk or smile.

VI

She cannot feel her face or fingertips,
   or turn her head...) And yet... And yet... The sheen
of wealth has bought her Youth. She has the hips
   and bosom of a girl of seventeen;
and when she does that wink, and licks those lips,
   she knows that she's delightfully obscene...
She likes to quiz her guests about fellatio
(which always boosts the advertisers' ratio...).

VII

That shows like hers are deemed a great success,
   (and therefore worth appearing on) is due
to a culture-wide acceptance that Excess
   is always worth it – so it must be True.
Which means there's nothing, really, to repress
   these days. So, who we did or didn't screw,
and all the deepest secrets of the Id,
are now exposed, which once we would have hid.

VIII

The audience can't get enough of this
   post-Freudian confessional wet-dream.
They come to line the Shrine (or take the piss...?
   It could be either... both...) Their heroes seem
like ogres limping from some grim abyss,
   an effortless and seeming-endless stream:
asthenic starlets, plastic anorexics,
unfunny boors, and bombasts and dyslexics

IX

and flop-haired fops, and bimbo-blonde bleached whales,
   and former porn-stars, luckless Lottery punters...
the ruined rich, so many sad-luck tales...
   attention seekers, mad and ugly munters,
mis-fortunates with bitten fingernails
   and broken hearts... the faded star-light hunters
who prove that, when it comes to cashing cheques,
true Misery sells just as well as Sex.

X

(Or almost just as well... It sounds uncouth,
   but Ignorance sells pretty well, as well!
And best of all – that sad and simple truth –
   the main thing that can make the market swell
is the promise of the miracle of – Youth,
   the one thing that we'll always buy and sell...).
The sleazy strap-lines of this show reveal
what gives it such a prurient appeal:

XI

'My girlfriend topped herself, because I chucked her.'
   'He spent my alimony getting high.'
'My mam ran off with my pole-dance instructor.'
   'I punched somebody in the public eye.'
'A True Romance: a girl and her abductor.'
   'The Voices said the puppies had to die.'
These shows are ads for Social Work, and Care...
So why is Donny Johnny sitting there,

XII

with a smile that would eclipse the Dalai Lama's,
   as happy as a pregnant pig in shit,
amid the freak-show *flâneurs* in pyjamas,
   the hopeless wanna-bes, who think they're it?
Why isn't he somewhere in the Bahamas?
   Has his career just reached its deepest pit?
Don Johnny shrugs. It's nothing weird or funny:
it's just the need to be where there is... money.

XIII

And – as his agents, Lol and Con, would say –
   there's no such thing as bad publicity.
It's sad, but true: this featureless DJ,
   though somewhat lacking eccentricity,
begins to look quite interesting, *outré*,
   exuding charm and electricity
beside all those sham hams, and has-been hags...
The show's called *Wagging Tongues* (or *Tonguing WAGs*

XIV

depending on how cynical you are...).
   It's famed – or infamous – for dishing dirt,
it's won awards for lowering the bar.
   Why's Donny here? 'Cos he's a murderous flirt:
whomever he can lure into a car,
   they just have to be human, in a skirt...
He's looking for someone to save his life...
Or, failing that, a celebrity ex-wife,

XV

who's not as tall as him, and not as old,
   not cleverer than him (that wouldn't do!).
She has her own career, or family gold,
   she's best friends with billionaire or two...
Her looks are simply something to behold,
   and she would know exactly what to do
between the sheets (they'd never get up early!).
Think Kate Moss with the poshness of Liz Hurley,

XVI

Naomi Campbell's style, Madonna's cash...
   Is Donny's aim a bit... pie in the sky,
for a man whose looks are really nothing flash?
   But then – he's here, on TV, riding high,
his fawning fans are round him like a rash
   while Fame and Fortune stroke his inner thigh...
A bit of background might be useful here –
the Stock-take at the start of his career:

XVII

At seventeen poor Donny had no talents.
  His thoughts, and words, were ponderously slow.
His clothes, and hair, hung like his mother's valance.
  He had the perfect face for Radio.
He couldn't hold his beer, or keep his balance.
  There was so much he simply didn't know...
But he had grim ambition, laced with greed,
and he knew, deep down, that's all you really need.

XVIII

So – being devoid of charm, charisma, wit,
  and lacking acumen, and skills, and choice
did not deter Don Johnny – not one bit.
  His one distinctive feature was his Voice,
and he resolved to make the best of it.
  And it got him work, and laid, and a Rolls Royce!
For when he spoke, it sent the senses swimmin',
it touched the Souls of men (but mainly women).

XIX

Don Johnny's voice was silver, gold, and honey.
  A mellow magic breathed into your ear,
it made you think of hope, or bed, or sunny
  or wintry days, whatever time of year
you love... It made you think of Love, or money...
  Or Cantona, or Clooney, or Shakespeare...
It made you want to lie back and relax
(pure Wogan with a dash of Andrew Sachs...).

XX

It made you want to go and buy big stuff
  you knew, deep down, you couldn't quite afford.
It made you think you hadn't got enough
  new shoes... Perhaps you wouldn't be so bored,
your life so meaningless, and times so tough,
  if only you had... make-up, or... a sword,
or a pink laptop (the pink might bring you luck...).
Pure Brad Pitt, with a hint of... Daffy Duck.

XXI

Pure Gielgud with a hint... I could go on...
　　His whole career, this single, silken skill:
his voice sells anything, to anyone.
　　Three words (sweet chloroform!) and your free will,
along with half your bank account, was gone!
　　He found that, when he moved in for the kill,
he could sell a load of toxic bonds to bankers,
he could sell used condoms to a bunch of wankers.

XXII

For people did whatever he would tell 'em:
　　They'd give him jobs whenever he applied.
His whispered words (he never has to yell 'em)
　　would open doors, and soon he'd be inside
their wallets, or their clothes... He'd even sell 'em
　　(and he did this with a salesman's cut-throat pride)
the very things they did, in fact, possess:
the Railways, British Gas, the NHS...

XXIII

He started working for the BBC,
　　a lowly gopher, local radio.
He made a million milky cups of tea...
　　until one day he got the chance to go
behind the mike himself... and Destiny
　　made him the DJ on the *Morning Show*.
It was the perfect home for Donny's vanity:
that honeyed voice with all that bland inanity.

XXIV

From there he joined a more commercial station,
　　the sort that plays the pop-charts all day long.
He gained a rather raffish reputation
　　for spinning cheesy saccharine in song,
while his sleazy PR schemes (pure exploitation,
　　a sceptic might have said...) soon brought a throng
of ardent fans to worship at his altar.
(He bought a flat, and a holiday in Malta.)

XXV

One time, he called a minor luvvy-sleb
   (who'd been in *Upstairs Downstairs* years ago)
pretending he was from the World Wide Web,
   and asked the ageing actor: 'Did you know –
your sex-drive being clearly on the ebb –
   your wife has started dating So-and-So?'
With wit that raw, risqué, that tongue-in-cheek,
his fame and fortune blossomed by the week.

XXVI

And then there was the famous competition
   the station held, that caused such a furore:
the failure-fest they called *The Misery Mission*.
   The person who could tell the saddest story
would win ten thousand pounds. They would audition,
   parading fairground freaks in search of glory.
The station aimed to titillate and shock
so the pitiful and poor queued round the block,

XXVII

each with a personal tragedy to tell:
   the missing limb; the dad who didn't care;
the homeless, loan-less, loveless; the unwell –
   the cancer scare that wasn't just a scare...
Each window into someone's living hell,
   each trying to prise some hope from deep despair,
to turn their lives from tragedy to... fame.
(The station made its money just the same.)

XXVIII

From there, it was a short step up the ladder
   to working in TV. He had a go
as compère of a quiz called: *Yes, I've Had 'er!*
   and Shopping Channel's *Lowest of the Low*.
And Donny Johnny just kept getting madder,
   and badder, and more dangerous to know...
But richer too – and that was all that mattered,
since all he wanted was... his ego flattered.

XXIX

He did voice-overs: first, a Shock-umentary –
    'It's day nine thousand in the Fritzl house...'
then a Wild-Survival-Docu-Alimentary,
    where all there is for dinner is a mouse
's testicle; then, for the middle-gentry,
    The Sex-Life of the Younger Johann Strauss;
then *Who D'You Think You Are – You're Not My Mother*;
then a full-on porno-version of *Big Brother*...

XXX

Then – stellar popularity and fame –
    he fronted a campaign that left no doubt.
Adopt a Soldier – Keep Alive the Flame:
    'Our brave boys shouldn't have to do without...
You send us money, we'll send you a name...
    It's what true Patriotism's all about!
Donations help to keep your soldier warm.
(Remember: write your blood-type on the form,

XXXI

so we connect you with your perfect match.
    We'll only use your blood on your named squaddie,
and no-one else... And should we need to patch
    him up a teeny bit, one day (pray God he
won't need it) we will expertly detach
    your arm, your leg, or other bit of body...).'
It was the perfect home for Donny's suavity:
that honeyed voice with all that rank depravity.

XXXII

Now, let's back-track – before Candida's show:
    The Green Room is awash with alco-pops
and baklava bedecked with sturgeon roe.
    Don Johnny drinks too much, and sprawls and flops,
and tries to guess how much they earn, and owe,
    these sequinned starlets in revealing tops...
(We're envious of one another's fame,
and that is how the Green Room got its name.)

XXXIII

Then – there she is – a little late and flustered:
  a frown across her sulky baby face –
but only for a moment... Then she's mustered,
  from deep within, a smile that lights the space...
She seems to concentrate the light... it's clustered,
  it gathers in her gauche and childlike grace.
She, ever the professional, scans the room
to see who might be useful... Through the gloom,

XXXIV

she's soon dismissed the wedge-haired, chinless boys
  and fixed her sultry gaze on... Donny Johnny.
She does her cat-walk sashay through the noise
  of drunken young degenerates, all those bonny
young sex-workers the Pop Machine employs,
  and comes and kneels before him... Whereupon he
sits up a bit and tries to look more sober,
and as if he wasn't hoping to disrobe her.

XXXV

She rests her elbows on his knees. Behind her,
  the room goes dark, and stilled. And Donny's smitten.
This close, she's... lovely; but there's the reminder
  of something hungry, something pinched and bitten,
as if both Light and Darkness strive to bind her...
  She's a cross between a Porn Queen and a kitten:
there's all the firm-fleshed freshness of a child
with, underneath, the hint of something wild.

XXXVI

She fixes him with level, grey-green eyes.
  'I'm Luxie. Luxie Turner. How d'you do?'
Don Johnny stares at her in mute surprise
  as she goes on: 'I want... Someone like you.
At least, I think I might...' And then she sighs.
  '...especially after all that I've been through
these last few weeks... So... Now, I've got this plan:
My agent says I need an older man...'

XXXVII

She starts a monologue. Somewhere above him
  are angel choirs. At first he's all attention.
He wonders: if he listens, will she love him?
  He's like a happy schoolboy in detention.
Imagination gets the better of him:
  he's found his One True Love! Oh, did I mention
that Donny's this incurable romantic
with a PhD in being sycophantic?

XXXVIII

And so he settles back, content to listen.
  His new-found friend is nestled in his lap
and there is an expression close to bliss on
  his flabby face... He doesn't see the trap
until... his stifled yawn; his eyelids glisten
  with tears... He tells himself: 'She's talking crap!'
And on she goes: at coma-causing length:
the allergies that sap her inner strength,

XIL

the price of fame, her upbringing in Slough...
  That thing she said that caused a Twitter-riot...
Her new-found love for tantric sex and Tao...
  Kabbala... Her new Sperm-and-Seaweed diet...
Her brush with Crack (but that's all over now)...
  The lying gutter press who won't be quiet...
The footballer who teased her legs apart
on YouTube... then he went and broke her heart!

XL

How spiritual she is... Stiletto heels...
  Creative 'flow' when she is 'in the Zone'...
Then, as her new biography reveals,
  the dramas of a life lived on the phone...
How no-one understands the way she feels,
  and how she sometimes cries when she's alone...
He sat transfixed, unblinking and aghast,
'til finally she paused for breath at last,

XLI

and turned to him (it took an hour or two:
  he'd just begun to doubt that he'd live through it)
and asked: 'So what are *you* allergic to?'
  He wanted to say 'you', but somehow knew it
was prob'ly not the wisest thing to do:
  a flip remark like that, would, he'd intuit,
remove all hope of getting her in bed.
He assumed a solemn countenance, instead,

XLII

and sighed, and gave a rueful little smile:
  'I guess I'd have to say – a broken heart!'
and gave a rueful little chuckle, while
  he watched her pool-deep eyes begin to start
to grow a little wider... Crocodile-
  like tears welled up in his eyes too... Mozart
himself, who knew a bit about amour,
could not have penned a more romantic score.

XLIII

In half an hour, on camera, with their host,
  already they're an item, in their prime,
and all the other guests have been out-grossed.
  The gossip mags start working overtime.
This is the part Don Johnny loves the most,
  where everything he touches seems sublime.
That's why the blissed-out smile is on his face –
you'd probably do likewise in his place!

XLIV

For Lux, insouciant, sits on the couch,
  (and butter wouldn't melt, et cetera...)
leans forward in a semi-feline crouch
  (her ample implants bulging from her bra),
a languid hand on Donny's scrotal pouch
  inside the zip she's deftly teased ajar.
She chats and never looks in his direction
whilst fondling his balls and half-erection.

XLV

Candida is delighted with her scoop.
   'How long have you two love-birds been an item?'
'Three-quarters of an hour!' Candida's whoop –
   surprise and joy – goes on *ad infinitum*.
Like some bald eagle just about to swoop,
   she looks like she might lean across and bite 'em.
The loved-up couple, bashful and inane,
sit grinning while the whole world goes insane.

XLVI

And nevermore will they know true obscurity;
   and nevermore will they be truly poor.
Their souls approach the sort of crystal purity
   that Religion and Celebrity are for.
They're whisked away the moment that Security
   can beat the true believers from the door.
Lux mouths: 'I love you' then, and only then.
Their lives will never be the same again.

XLVII

And after all those years *sans* sex-appeal;
   the pleading, and the begging someone's pardon
for skipping foreplay, lunging for a feel;
   the waking drunk in someone else's garden,
his car keys in his mouth, after a meal;
   and all those times he couldn't really harden...
Don's heart's now lanced by Love's remorseless skewers!
(All this in front of several million viewers!)

XLIII

'Did you just say "I love you" – meaning me?'
   Don Johnny asks. They're settled in a Bentley,
their driver calmly cruising through a sea
   of weeping fans. Then Luxie, smiling gently,
repeats the words, so only he can see
   (as fifteen paparazzi lope intently
alongside, flashing cameras, and then
peel off to catch the start of *News at Ten*).

XLIX

'I love you too,' he whispers to his diva.
   And her response? She glances at her watch.
He promises that he will never leave her
   (she raids the bar and helps herself to Scotch).
In Love, and War, he couldn't be naïver.
   She lets the paparazzi glimpse her crotch
as she clambers from the car in Ladbroke Grove;
he only sees a true-love treasure trove.

L

'I'll see you later,' Luxie tells DJ.
   'My team will be in touch. Thanks for the ride!'
He feels as though he might be in the way
   but doesn't want to show his shattered pride...
and so he smiles a smile; and says okay...
   and watches as she disappears inside.
Now he can't wait until he's underneath her.
But that won't happen 'til they hit Ibiza...

***

Part Two

I

The soothing voice drones on: 'Please hold... Please hold...
    Your call's important to us... Please continue
to hold...' Don Johnny shivers. He's not cold,
    but a shaking seems to strain his every sinew.
He asks himself how often he's been told
    (how often have they tried to drum it in you?):
don't fall in love with someone half your years;
it never lasts, it always ends in tears.

II

DJ's at home. He's sitting on the bed.
    That voice intones so warm and calmingly,
yet thoughts of suicide run round his head.
    It's been a month or so since Lux and he
had started their relationship. Instead
    of sailing on a calm, sun-spangled sea
our star-crossed lovers crashed upon the rocks!
They'd had the chance to spend the equinox

III

in St Tropez, among the rich and fecund
    (a photo-shoot, a rag called *Jugs on Sundy*).
When, at the airport, Luxie'd waved and beckoned
    to a plastic slapper known as Gloria Mundy,
poor Donny didn't dream, not for a second,
    she'd be about as pleasant as Ted Bundy.
How ruthlessly she'd break his fragile heart
and tear his new relationship apart!

IV

For Gloria and Lux became a pair,
    inseparable for more or less the whole
duration of the trip. They didn't care
    about Don Johnny, poor neglected soul!
They bonded over products for their hair
    (a new conditioner made from shredded vole),
they traded tips on how to tone your labia,
and how to deal with death-threats from Arabia.

V

They showed their nipples to the paparazzi
  and kissed each other in a swimming pool;
had dinner with a millionaire ex-Nazi
  (that Nazi-lesbian look, these days, is cool).
And all the while their gooseberry, their patsy,
  Don Johnny waited, smiled, and felt a fool.
In short, they lived the high life on the Med
among the drop-dead gorgeous living dead

VI

where every car's a Mitsubishi Shogun,
  and every girl's Vanessa Paradis,
and every man's Tom Cruise (or Terry Wogan)
  and every yacht is pointing from the sea;
and every T-shirt bears the latest slogan:
  Is nappy-rash the latest STD?
Don Johnny scoffs, but Luxie says: 'My dear,
Youth Culture's getting younger every year!'

VII

'The latest thing,' says Gloria, quite straight-faced,
  (although, she stresses, it can cost kerzillions)
'you have your teeth removed and then replaced
  by children's teeth, imported in their millions.
Without recycling, they'd just go to waste!
  Apparently the best ones are Brazilians'...'
She turns to him and parts her lips and smiles;
he counts the milk teeth of those juveniles,

VIII

all gleaming there, and swiftly does his sums:
  a fortune. And the kids whose youth she bought,
who used to run around São Paolo slums,
  will never know their smiles have all been caught
on camera, in her young and healthy gums.
  The photo-shoot goes well. And so they thought
they all deserved to stay a week or so,
to paint the town... with old DJ in tow.

IX

In skimpy tops, and wearing nothing else,
　　they sauntered through the streets of St Tropez
displaying to the world vajazzled pelts.
　　Don thought he ought to look the other way,
so closed his eyes and thought: *Vanessa Feltz!*
　　It did no good – he's flesh and blood, not clay.
He stole a stealthy look and slipped on shades,
lust gliding through his veins on flame-tipped blades.

X

It came to nothing. All that lonely night
　　he wonders what his Luxie might be doing
beneath the fickle moon. Is she all right?
　　Is she with Gloria Mundy? Are they screwing?
If she comes back, he doesn't want a fight
　　(there's still so much he might be misconstruing).
Forgive, forget. An understanding shoulder.
There are advantages to being older...

XI

But in the midnight hours – a creeping doubt
　　(the ticking clock a mocking metronome),
an existential scream starts leaking out.
　　His vision blurs in murky monochrome...
He dials a phone-line someone spoke about:
　　'Continue please to hold...' There's no-one home.
He goes to bed and, trying not to weep,
he rocks himself into a sort of sleep.

XII

The plane banks through night-clouds. DJ and Luxie
　　are on their way back home from St Tropez.
It's safe to say they're in a state of flux. He
　　just feels, somehow, the magic's slipped away...
and as they haven't managed any fucks, he
　　's beginning to admit naïveté
has been the only winner in this fight.
Sometimes a wrong's so wrong, it won't come right...

XIII

[You have to understand – their points of view
   are incompatible: he's chalk, she's cheddar.
There's things she'll never bring herself to do;
   – she'd rather die than let him even bed her
not even for good money! Sad but true,
   but all he ever dreams of is to wed her.
For him, she represents sweet juvenilia;
for her, he's tantamount to necrophilia.]

XIV

As Luxie nestles in her panda furs,
   DJ's resentful, staring at the sea:
'Although my love is much more real than hers
   you spent more time with Gloria than me!'
He brightens, slyly, as a thought occurs:
   'Unless you two are hoping for a three...'
'No way!' she says. 'Don't even think about it!
Well, Gloria might... On second thoughts, I doubt it.'

XV

'Continue, please, to hold...' the voice repeats,
   'your mental illness is...' And far below,
like scattered diamond-necklaces, the streets
   of London lie in wait. The ebb and flow
of city life, the hopes and the defeats
   come flooding back. 'And can we really know,'
Don Johnny asks himself, 'a cure for fear?
Or... should I just get on with my career?'

XVI

Ah yes! His curse, his only consolation!
   Celebrity! That trivial pursuit
that manages somehow to grip the nation!
   You're in the limelight – 'til the next recruit
takes centre stage, and cash, and adulation...
   They let you keep a little of the loot,
but there's only so much grinning you can do
when everyone has stopped adoring you...

XVII

[I sometimes think we need these D-list 'slebs'
    like Ancient Greeks once needed minor deities:
they're more than just the opium of the plebs,
    they teach us how to live. Though some would say it is
'how *not* to live'... And oh, the tangled webs
    we weave, to prove that spontaneities
are really running things; and superstition
is just as valid as our own volition;

XVIII

and Science is... Progress, meaning faster cars,
    and smaller gadgetry, with more precision;
and cleaner, more efficient abattoirs...
    But when it comes to making a decision
you can't rely on Science! Ask the stars:
    they're in the tabloids, on the television...
Forgive them, for they know not what they're doin'.
They haven't read their Warhol and McLuhan!]

XIX

Soon 'Lux 'n' Glo' have touched the nation's hearts.
    They feature in a BBC production,
then host a DVD that tops the charts:
    Pole Dancing and the Art of True Seduction;
two books: *I Owe It All to Topless Darts*
    and *The Anorexics' Guide to Weight Reduction.*
They pose together in some skimpy gym-slips
at the opening of the twenty-twelve Olympics.

XX

Then Luxie hosts a game-show competition
    (celebrities in leotards all trying
to master some athletic sex-position,
    a show called simply *One of Us Is Lying*).
But Gloria, with more naked, raw ambition
    (with bigger breasts her prospects will be flying!)
becomes size 38, and double-G,
an Adviser to the Silicone industry.

XXI

She then presents a series on TV,
   while Luxie's starring in some West End drama.
Soon Lux receives an honorary degree,
   and Gloria starts dating Simon Schama.
When Luxie shags a prominent MP,
   Miss Mundy lunches with Michelle Obama...
She gets Rebekah Brooks' old job at *Sky*;
while Luxie gets to chair the CBI.

XXII

But then their friendly rivalry turns serious.
   Their marketing departments thought it through:
for reasons that are not at all mysterious,
   bad news sells more than good (you know it's true).
And in that way that clichés tend to weary us,
   (like happy endings, or a dose of 'flu),
they'll have a massive fall-out in September
and best of friends again by mid-November.

XXIII

It's in October, DJ gets the call:
   poor Luxie's lonely. 'Couldn't you come round?
I'm in a dark place, heading for a fall.'
   Her little baby voice, the sweetest sound...
and Donny melts. His heart's a sudden squall,
   he's like a teddy in the Lost and Found.
He feels his breathing stop, the loss of power.
'I'll be there in a quarter of an hour!'

XXIV

But once he gets there, what does Donny find?
   She won't shut up about that bloody Gloria!
He's quite convinced that Luxie's going to wind
   herself into a state of near-euphoria:
and now it seems that what she's got in mind
   are murder scenes that couldn't get much gorier!
He tries to calm her (how he longs to kiss her!)
then Lux breaks down: 'The problem is... I miss her!'

XXV

Before too long, she's sobbing in his arms
   and Donny's holding on for all he's worth.
He salivates, immune to all alarms:
   her tears, her body pressed against his girth...
He is, he knows, while relishing her charms,
   the luckiest celebrity on earth.
'I'm glad you're here,' she murmurs, and he's floating.
DJ permits himself a gentle gloating,

XXVI

which, later, back at home, he half-remembers.
   He sits back on his bed and thinks it over.
'Oh babe,' he moans. His half-tumescent member's
   lubricious, with a slick of musk and clover.
His heart starts thrumming (like so many djembes).
   Inside, he knows he's still a Casanova!
And, like so many forty-something men,
he fumbles, and feels seventeen again.

XXVII

Yet... everything about her seems... rehearsed.
   And all those camera crews... can drive you mental...
But then she looks at him... He's blessed... And cursed.
   She'd been a nurse of some sort (was it dental?).
His fantasy is to be cared for, nursed...
   He knows a Costume-place where they do rental...
And all his thoughts go squidgy, soft and warm
at the thought of Luxie in her uniform.

XXVIII

There's simply something wonderful about her
   (the thought of Luxie on her hands and knees...).
He hasn't got the inner strength to doubt her,
   and though he knows full well they're chalk and cheese,
he realises he can't live without her.
   'Your madness is important to us... Please...'
He's holding... And it slowly starts to dawn...
As he sits there... He almost could have sworn

XXIX

he's heard this pleasant, soothing voice before:
    familiar... and rather reassuring,
attractive, even... some old paramour?
    No: male, and so not sexually alluring...
Someone he used to know, perhaps? A bore
    he'd managed to get rid of? Was it during...?
And then it hits – as cold as mammoth bone:
the voice on the recording is... his own.

XXX

It must have been his first, full-paying gig:
    A fifty-quidder for some unknown charity,
before he got so famous, and so 'Big',
    so... *happy*... and... *un*-happy... The disparity
(between him, then, and now) he doesn't twig...
    For suddenly, outside, there's noise (hilarity?),
a cry of 'God is Good!', a wild commotion...
a flash of light – the force of an explosion,

XXXI

a deep, sub-sonic 'whump'. The door then flies
    across the room. A man comes striding in,
a medieval farmer, in disguise
    as modern terrorist: the bearded chin,
the look of calm indifference in his eyes;
    the certainty – he'll die, so he can win.
He sees DJ and, giving thanks to God,
he signals to the others in his squad:

XXXII

'All Praise His Name! His Justice Will Prevail!
    The Target is located. He's in here!'
And nine Kalashnikovs poke through the veil
    of dust and smoke. The stench of primal fear
pervades the room, as they begin to wail
    their incantations... DJ needs a beer,
his mouth's as dry as sand upon a beach.
Their Leader glowers at him and makes this speech:

XXXIII

'D'you think there is no Consequence to Sin?
  Your Sins have tracked you down! They are your Dread
and your Despair, the Secret Fears within
  the Empty Chasms of your Soul. Your Bed
of Stones. Your long-lost Evil Twin,
  your Nemesis. Your black and bitter Bread.
You cannot hide, or plead, so save your breath.
Your Sins have sentenced you to Righteous Death.'

XXXIV

Don Johnny tries to reason (big mistake):
  'But some of my best friends support Islam...'
The terrorists all do a double-take.
  'ISLAM?!' the Leader roars, 'My Good God-Damn!
I ain't no Ay-rab Moose-lum oil-rich Sheikh!
  Those meedy-evil Shi-ites are a sham!
My friend, we're Christian, just as White as you:
the Militant Amish Deathsquad – comin' through!'

XXXV

They all stand to attention, and it clicks
  in Donny Johnny's over-racing brain.
He realises that he's in a fix
  more terrible and deadly and insane
than anything he's known... And all the chicks,
  the booze, the dodgy mates, all that cocaine,
now flash before his eyes (as some will say
can happen when we face our Judgement Day).

XXXVI

The Amish man goes on: 'Your Sin is strong.
  We're makin' an example out o' you.
Now, we don't want the world to make a song
  and dance... no outraged-liberal ballyhoo...
no martyrs here... Hell, that would be all wrong!
  I promise we'll be quick: it wouldn't do
to make you wait... And there's some consolation,
being killed by someone from a Caring Nation...'

344

XXXVII

He strokes his beard. The muzzle of his gun
   is pointing right at Donny Johnny's head.
If only he had had a bit more fun –
   in half a dozen seconds he'll be dead!
He tries to think of countryside and sun,
   and not his flesh and bone being lanced by lead.
He tries to think of Buddha, or of Zen,
'accepting' ways to live... And die... And then...

XXXVIII

It seems our hero's stranded, in a spot.
   It's hard to think just how he can pull through.
And whether you would want me to or not
   I'll now digress a stanza, page, or two:
a huge, Byronic detour from the plot.
   (It's what he would have wanted me to do.)
Subversive and ironic; need I mention
it's also pretty good for building tension?

XXXIX

It's customary (though you'll maybe hate us)
   to do as Byron did, in this position:
impose on you, dear readers, this hiatus,
   this monologue, this random disquisition
(debate, but with no answering debaters)
   this discourse (rather prone to repetition).
A rant, in short, on some prevailing topic
which proves me cynical and misanthropic.

XL

The trouble is I have no mighty thoughts,
   as Byron did, on Pope, and Castlereagh,
and Wellington... And I'm not in reports,
   and in disgrace, as he was in his day,
I have less need to prove myself in courts...
   So we might as well get back to Donny J.
We left him at the mercy of those men.
Where had we got to? Ah! That's right: *'And then...'*

XLI

A second bomb-blast, louder than the first.
  The SAS come storming through the wall.
Don Johnny hears a loud staccato burst
  of rifle fire. He sees the Amish fall,
and soon the situation is reversed.
  The Green Berets come striding down the hall
and close behind, in fetching combat gear,
strides lovely Luxie, bringing up the rear.

XLII

A camera flashes, and she's kneeling down
  (despite the tightness of that khaki skirt).
She looks at Donny with a mannered frown
  and murmurs 'Oh my darling, are you hurt?
I couldn't let that dreadful Amish clown
  be horrible!' Her half-unbuttoned shirt
can scarce contain the swell of heavy breasts,
and this is where a grateful Donny rests

XLIII

his face a while... Until a voice says: 'Cut!'
  and Luxie drops him like a hot potato,
and scissors from the room, her sexy strut
  admired by Amish and the boys from NATO.
Appreciatively, someone mutters *'Slut!'*.
  Don Johnny, philosophical as Plato,
and sitting like that statue by Rodin,
observes the Amish, actors to a man,

XLIV

stand up, shake off the dust, light cigarettes
  and stroll off, chatting, sharing thespian jokes.
Don Johnny's left in ruins and regrets.
  How come he knows the sort of bastard blokes
who'd do such things? They probably torture pets
  in their spare time. Or never see their folks.
And still DJ is sitting on his bed
and thoughts of suicide run round his head.

XLV

He's gripping, still, the handset of the phone,
   from which his own voice speaks to him: 'Hold on.
Your madness is important...' How alone
   can one man feel, he thinks, when Hope is gone.
The voice a soothing, reassuring drone:
   'Our experts make you feel you're Number One!
You're Number Ninety-Seven in the queue...'
(Another hour or two, he might get through.)

XLVI

And that's when Luxie Turner reappears.
   She tiptoes in, and (with a camera crew)
she says 'My darling, dry your bitter tears.
   I can't just wait around all day for you
to make a move – we'll be here bloody years!
   We're getting married in a month or two
(and in a while, when True Love's run its course,
I'll screw someone and give you a divorce...).

XLVII

'It's all decided: all I'm going to wear
   's a see-through thong (no time for self-deception!).
To officiate, I've asked the London Mayor.
   I've booked Balmoral for the main Reception
(and my first extra-marital affair)
   and Elton John's place for our first conception.
For better or for worse, for good or ill, you
had better bloody be there, or I'll kill you!'

XLVIII

She takes him by the plump and fetid hand
   and gets him down upon his bended knee.
'And now, my sweet, am I to understand
   there's something you would like to say to me?
The answer's yes – your wish is my command!'
   Permits him – once – to kiss his bride-to-be,
a chaste kiss, with no tongues and with closed lips
and coyly interlocking fingertips.

XLIX

Don Johnny sleeps a happy man that night:
　　he's only had to wait, to hold his nerve,
and everything's turned out to be all right.
　　And Luxie Turner, queen of body-swerve,
has just had sex with him – without a fight!
　　He smiles. At last, they've got what they deserve.
He's confident, as he turns out the lamp,
that Time will heal – and dry that patch of damp.

L

But in his captive sleep, a glimpse of Truth:
　　Old Age is just nostalgia and *ennui*.
We'll never know those sweet-shops of our youth
　　again. And you don't really need to be
a Sherlock Holmes, or any other sleuth,
　　to realise what's there for all to see:
the young are all our Hope, and our Despair
(and they don't even know, or even care).

LI

Now Donny sleeps with Lux, his faithless wife;
　　marshmallow bosoms cushion his bad dreams.
One day, he might acknowledge that his life
　　is every bit as empty as it seems;
but he won't let mere existential strife
　　impede his Fame-and-Fortune-chasing schemes.
He'll quote you (he thinks this one might be Milton):
'We are such Dreams as Avarice is built on…'

LII

This work of Art is beautiful and true
　　(it's worthy of the Venice *Biennale*!)
but the ending of our tale's long overdue;
　　the curtain gently falls on our finale.
Our players sleep. We bid them both *adieu*.
　　And, as I often say to my son Charlie:
Sweet daggered Night creeps in, with stealth and fawning.
Pray God we'll all still be here in the morning!

THE CONTRIBUTORS

Ben Borek was born in London in 1980. His work has appeared in various anthologies including *London – a History in Verse, City State, Dear World & Everyone in it*. He is the author of a verse-novel *Donjong Heights*. He currently lives in Warsaw.

Andy Croft's books of poetry include *Comrade Laughter, Ghost Writer, Sticky, Three Men on the Metro* (with W.N. Herbert and Paul Summers) and *Nineteen Forty-eight* (with Martin Rowson). He writes a regular poetry column for the *Morning Star* and runs Smokestack Books. He lives in Yorkshire.

Claudia Daventry studied French and Spanish at Oxford and has worked in a number of European cities as a writer and translator. Her work has been widely published in magazines and has won various awards, including the Bridport Prize in 2012. She is currently working on a PhD about poetic version and translation at the University of St Andrews.

Ian Duhig has written six books of poetry, including *The Lammas Hireling, The Speed of Dark* and *Pandorama*. In 1987 he won the National Poetry Competition. His books have been shortlisted for the Forward, Whitbread, TS Eliot and Costa prizes. He lives in Leeds.

Rachel Hadas is Board of Governors Professor of English at the Newark campus of Rutgers University and the author of many books of poetry, essays, and translations. Her most recent books are *Strange Relation: A Memoir of Marriage, Dementia, and Poetry* and *The Golden Road: Poems*.

W.N. Herbert is Professor of Poetry and Creative Writing at Newcastle University. He has published eight collections of poetry and six pamphlets, including *Forked Tongue, Cabaret McGonagall, The Big Bumper Book of Troy, Bad Shaman Blues* and *Omnesia*. He has edited, with Yang Lian, the Chinese anthologies *Jade Ladder* and *The Third Shore*. In 2013 Herbert was appointed Dundee's first *makar*.

George Jowett recently retired after thirty-nine years in social work. A previous winner of the Littlewood/Arc Northern Poetry Competition, his poems have appeared in many magazines. He has published two pamphlets of poetry, *The Old Campaigners* and *Blow by Blow*. He lives in Richmond, North Yorkshire.

John Lucas is Professor Emeritus at the Universities of Loughborough and Nottingham Trent. His many books include studies of Dickens, Clare, Bennett and Gurney. His most recent books are *Next Year Will Be Better, Second World War Poetry in English* and *A Brief History of Whistling*. His books of poetry include *Studying Grosz on the Bus, One for the Piano, A World Perhaps, Flute Music* and *Things to Say*. He runs Shoestring Press.

Amit Majmudar is a novelist, poet, essayist and diagnostic nuclear radiologist. He has published two books of poetry, *0',0'* and *Heaven and Earth,* and two novels, *Partitions* and *The Abundance*. He lives in Dublin, Ohio.

Sinéad Morrissey is the author of five collections of poetry. Her most recent collection, *Parallax*, was awarded the 2013 TS Eliot Prize. Her previous awards include a Lannan Literary Fellowship, First Prize in the UK National Poetry Competition and the *Irish Times* Poetry Prize. She is Reader in Creative Writing at the Seamus Heaney Centre for Poetry, Queen's University, Belfast.

A.E. Stallings was born in 1968. She studied classics at the universities of Georgia and Oxford. She has published three books of poetry, *Archaic Smile, Hapax,* and *Olives*, as well as *The Nature of Things*, a verse translation of Lucretius' *De Rerum Natura*. She lives in Athens, where she is poetry director of the Athens Centre.

George Szirtes was born in Budapest in 1948 and came to the UK as a refugee in 1956. His most recent books of poetry are *Reel, New and Collected Poems, The Burning of the Books* and *Bad Machine*. *Reel* was awarded the TS Eliot Prize for 2004. He teaches Creative Writing at the University of East Anglia.

N.S. Thompson is co-editor of *A Modern Don Juan*. His *Letter to Auden* was published by Smokestack in 2010 and his work appears in *Able Muse* (USA), *New Walk, The Spectator* and *Stand*. He is currently translating a major Italian crime trilogy for Quercus Books and his translations of Italian poetry have appeared in *The Penguin Montale* and *The Faber Book of 20th-Century Italian Poems*.

Tim Thorne lives in Launceston, Tasmania. He has published thirteen books of poetry, including *A Letter to Egon Kisch* and *Yeah No*. He is a former Director of the Tasmanian Poetry Festival and was the Managing Editor of Cornford Press. He is Tasmanian convener of the political lobby group, Now We the People.

Mike Wilson is a writer and musician. His musical credits include a one-man Jack Thackray show and the Eisler-Weill show *Teeth Like Razors*. He has written over eighty fiction and non-fiction books for beginner-readers. His poetry publications include *Desperanto* and *Redeemer*. He lives in Nottingham.

A Modern Don Juan was made possible
by the support of the following subscribers

Kathleen Bell
Jane Bluett
Florence Boos
Charles Boyle
 (CB Editions)
Bromley House Library
Nadine Brummer
Allan Chatburn
Jane Commane
 (Nine Arches Press)
Alex Coxen
Michael Crowley
Jonathan Davidson
Alan Dent
Sue Dymoke & David Belbin
Mr and Mrs P.A. Elliston
Ruth Fainlight
Jacqueline Gabbitas
Sheelagh Gallagher
Cathy Galvin
John Goodridge
Pippa Hennessy
David Jackson
Bob Joly
Angela Kirkby
Maxine Linnell

Marilyn Longstaff
Sean Matthews
Rita Meek
Bob Morland
Peter Mortimer
 (Iron Press)
Nicholas Murray
Rosemary Norman
John Payne
Penrallt Gallery and
 Bookshop
Barbara Preston
Judith Rodriguez
Saison Poetry Library
Gerda Stevenson
Jenny Swann
 (Candlestick Press)
James Walker
Matthew Welton
Dennis Wemyss
Andrew Whitehead
Gregory Woods
Ken Worpole
Marion & Dave Wright
Lynne Wycherley